ONE LOAF, ONE CUP

ECUMENICAL STUDIES OF 1 COR 11 AND OTHER EUCHARISTIC TEXTS

Because there is one loaf,
we, though many, are one body;
for all of us share in the one loaf.

1 Corinthians 10:17

NEW GOSPEL STUDIES 6

ONE LOAF, ONE CUP

ECUMENICAL STUDIES OF 1 COR 11 AND OTHER EUCHARISTIC TEXTS

The Cambridge Conference on the Eucharist
August 1988

---

studies by

Otto Knoch	Ben F. Meyer
William R. Farmer	Hans-Josef Klauck
Otfried Hofius	Alkiviadis C. Calivas

edited and with an introduction by
Ben F. Meyer

PEETERS   MERCER

ISBN 0-86554-398-4   MUP/H324

One Loaf, One Cup.
Ecumenical Studies of 1 Cor 11
and Other Eucharistic Texts
Copyright ©1993
Mercer University Press, Macon, Georgia 31207 USA
All rights reserved
Printed in the United States of America

Library of Congress Cataloging-in-Publication Data

Cambridge Conference on the Eucharist (1988 : University of Cambridge)
One loaf, one cup : the Cambridge Conference on the Eucharist. August 1988
/ studies by Otto Knoch . . . [et al.]
: edited and with an introduction by Ben F. Meyer.
xiii+152pp. 6x9" (15x23cm.)—(New Gospel Studies : 6)
Includes bibliographical references.
ISBN 0-86554-398-4 (alk. paper).
1. Bible, N.T., Corinthians, 1st, xi, 23-26—Criticism, interpretation, etc.—
Congresses. 2. Lord's Supper—Biblical teaching—Congresses. I. Knoch, Otto.
II. Meyer, Ben F., 1927– . III. Title. IV. Series.
BS2675.6.L67C36   1988
234'.163—dc20   91-32868

                                                        CIP

Table of Contents

In Memoriam

Gustaf Dalman (1855–1941)
necnon
Joachim Jeremias (1900–1979)
quorum operibus patet via in veritatem
textuum Novi Testamenti eucharisticorum
rectior latior certior

Acknowledgments

The Cambridge Conference on the Eucharist took place at St. Edmund's College, Cambridge, 5–8 August 1988, under the auspices of the International Institute for the Renewal of Gospel Studies.

The following data relate to publications elsewhere of papers presented at Cambridge. Hans-Josef Klauck, "Präsenz im Herrenmahl. 1 Kor 11,23-26 im Kontexthellenistischer Religionsgeschichte," in Klauck, *Gemeinde—Amt—Sakrament. Neutestamentliche Perspektiven,* 313-30 (Würzburg: Echter, 1989). Otfried Hofius, "Herrenmahl und Herrenmahlsparadosis. Erwägungen zu 1 Kor 11, 23b-25," *Zeitschrift für Theologie und Kirche* (1988–1989): 371-408; reprinted in Hofius, *Paulusstudien,* 204-40 (Tübingen: Mohr-Siebeck, 1989). William R. Farmer, "Peter and Paul, and the Tradition Concerning 'the Lord's Supper' in 1 Cor 11:23-26," in *Criswell Theological Review* 2 (1987): 119-40; the version presented here is revised. Otto Knoch, " 'Tut das zu meinem Gedächtnis' (Lk 22,20; 1 Kor 11,24f). Die Feier der Eucharistie in den urchristlichen Gemeinden" in *Freude am Gottesdienst. Aspekte ursprünglicher Liturgie,* Festschrift J. G. Plöger, ed. Josef Schreiner, 31-42 (Stuttgart: Katholisches Bibelwerk, 1983); this essay, too, has been lightly adapted and updated. B. F. Meyer, "The Expiation Motif in the Eucharistic Words: A Key to the History of Jesus?" *Gregorianum* 69 (1988): 461-87; the version presented here is lightly revised.

The biblical texts cited here conform to no one English version of the Bible, although the Revised Standard Version is better represented than any other. This is true even of those texts translated into English (the essays of Professors Knoch, Klauck, and Hofius), where the translations reflect the German text, but cohere with the RSV where possible. The translator of Otto Knoch's essay is Sylvia Keesmaat, now studying at Oxford; the translator of the essays of Hans-Josef Klauck and Otfried Hofius is Barry D. Smith of Atlantic Baptist College, in Moncton, New Brunswick.

Introduction

July of 1984: a private conversation in Basel—Markus Barth telling some friends who had gathered for a meeting of the SNTS (*Studiorum Novi Testamenti Societas*) of his delight at Xavier Léon-Dufour's recent monograph on the Eucharist—was the initial stimulus to the discussions that have now culminated, seven years later and on another continent, in the publication of this book. Among Barth's conversation partners on that occasion was W. R. (Bill) Farmer of the Perkins School of Theology at SMU and a founding member of the International Institute for the Renewal of Gospel Studies, headquartered in London and Dallas. Within a week Markus Barth, Bill Farmer, and Bernard Orchard (a Benedictine from London and another founding member of the IIRGS) were scouting the countryside near Basel for a locale at which a conference on the themes of Léon-Dufour's book might be held in a year's time.

In midsummer 1985 an international group of a dozen or so New Testament scholars, Protestant and Catholic, met in Switzerland, at Leuenberg lodge, near Basel, for two days of informal converstions both on the Léon-Dufour book and on the eucharistic texts in their own right. The book that prompted this response was titled *Sharing the Eucharistic Bread: Le partage du pain eucharistique selon le Nouveau Testament* (Paris: Seuil, 1982).[1] What had fired the intensely sympathetic reaction of Markus Barth, who at the time had begun work on his own monograph on the Eucharist (which would appear in 1987),[2] was the whole series of points at which Léon-Dufour, dean of French Catholic New Testament scholars, was clearly and eloquently close to, and indeed in parts at one with, Barth's own thinking on such themes as faith, symbolism, and community.

The Leuenberg discussions ranged over practically all New Testament texts that bore on the theme of the Eucharist. To be sure, not all participants were favorable in every detail to *Le partage du pain,* nor did the will to ecumenical convergence succeed in resolving the contentious issues inherited from diverse confessional traditions. But, at the end of two days' discussion and in accord with the

---

[1]E.T. *Sharing the Eucharistic Bread: The Witness of the New Testament* (New York: Paulist, 1987).

[2]Marcus Barth, *Das Mahl des Herrn* (Neukirchen-Vluyn: Neukirchener Verlag, 1987).

suggestions especially of Xavier Léon-Dufour (Paris), Otto Knoch (Passau), and Otto Betz (Tübingen), the group proposed to meet again, if possible, and more formally; to concentrate on the text of 1 Corinthians 10 and 11; and to make sure that the meeting would include representatives of Eastern Orthodoxy and patristics. In the persons of Bernard Orchard and Bill Farmer, the Institute for the Renewal of Gospel Studies pledged to consider whether it would be possible to pay for the organizational and per diem expenses of such a conference. A few weeks later the fellows of the Institute gathered in Norway agreed to do so, and the present writer received a letter deputing him to organize the meeting, with the help of Dom Bernard.

First scheduled for Trier, but changed finally to Cambridge so as to coincide in location with the meeting of SNTS, the conference on the Eucharist (accenting 1 Cor 10 and 11) took place at St Edmund's College, Cambridge, in early August 1988. Despite the much regretted absence of Père Léon-Dufour and of Professor Barth, both of whom had other commitments, the Leuenberg group was largely reunited, with the addition of an Orthodox participant, Dean Alkiviadis Calivas of Holy Cross Greek Orthodox School of Theology in Brookline, Massachusetts; a patristic scholar, Willy Rordorf of Neuchâtel; and a systematician, Roch Kereszty, of the Cistercian Abbey in Irving, Texas and the University of Dallas.

Those who agreed to prepare papers were Otto Knoch (Passau), on the whole range of New Testament texts; W. R. Farmer (Dallas), on Peter, Paul, and the historicity of the eucharistic words; Otfried Hofius (Tübingen), on 1 Cor 10 and 11 from the standpoint of Judaic backgrounds; Hans-Josef Klauck (Würzburg), on 1 Cor 10 and 11 from the standpoint of Hellenistic parallels; Willy Rordorf (Neuchâtel), on a new view of the Roman Canon in the light of some patristic texts; and Alkiviadis Calivas (Brookline), on the leading traits of the Greek Orthodox theology of the Eucharist.

Commentators included Otto Betz (Tübingen) on Farmer's paper; James D. G. Dunn (Durham) on Hofius's paper; David L. Dungan (University of Tennessee), on Klauck's paper; the present writer (McMaster University, Canada) on Rordorf's paper; and Roch Kereszty (Dallas) on Calivas's paper.

Up to now I have been reporting on the background to the present volume— mostly dealing with matters of objectively ascertainable fact—of at least (I hope) mild interest to the reader. From here on, however, I intend to offer a personal and necessarily impressionistic account of the Cambridge meeting on the Eucharist.

Ecumenical discussion groups do not always jell. We would certainly be better able to plan and prepare them, if only we knew what the secret reasons were that explain why one group is able and another unable to enter at least briefly into that "flow" that athletes speak of, when a team, for a few usually decisive minutes, enters a state of natural grace in which everything goes right. But no one I have discussed this with has ever claimed to know with any assurance how or why it happens.

It happened, I would say, in Cambridge, on the third day of the meeting and beginning with the discussion that followed Willy Rordorf's paper. We were dealing with an issue that is mysterious in itself, on which the earliest patristic documentation is ambiguous and puzzling, and which since the Reformation has been quite painfully contentious: whether the eucharistic service is a sacrifice. There came a moment at which all present found themselves genuinely puzzled, collectively at a loss, and this was followed in the discussion by a convergence of partial insights: that the paschal mysteries of Christ's expiatory self-offering, his death, and his Resurrection perdure in the risen Christ, part of him; that the participation that is communion is no mere passive act, but a becoming one with Christ, limbs of his "body," and so drawn to conformity with his self-offering to the Father; and that the uniqueness of Christ's self-offering need not be conceived as endangered by the Eucharist as sacrifice.

Not all shared all these views; without really or wholly resolving our differences, we were nonetheless caught up in a sudden recognition that, somehow at bottom and despite all our divisions, *we share one faith,* and that through it we are in touch with a vital and profound mystery that transcends us all. Though we had, and still have, no clear plans to meet again, this shared experience made most of those present reluctant to lose touch with one another as a group.

Our efforts to prepare a consensus statement on the theme of the Eucharist came to naught. The efforts began on the first day of the conference and in response to a statement drawn up by Otto Knoch. There was, in fact, a considerable area of agreement respecting all the issues that Prof. Knoch outlined: the historicity of the texts, the normativity of the canon, the context in which to appropriate our eucharistic heritage, how to convert diverse interpretations into heuristic principles that might carry us further, how to treat ecumenical documents, many of which crystallize already existing agreements among the diverse churches on such topics as baptism, Eucharist, office, and the imperative, grounded in the will of Christ as attested in the New Testament, of corporate Christian unity.

But a statement has to be articulated in particular words, and we were not able to settle, in full peace of mind, on the particular words, beginning with how to speak of the historicity of the Last Supper texts. The problem, ironically, was not the usual one among New Testament scholars—namely, the impossibility of winning any meaningful agreement on historicity issues from practitioners of radical criticism. Just the opposite: some of us thought the statements on the reliability of the texts as coming from Jesus were too weak! And this irresolvable initial disagreement took the punch out of further efforts to come up with a common statement. (Perhaps three days are in any case too short a time in which to work out a set of satisfactory consensus statements.)

What the individual participants carried away from Cambridge is only partly reproduced in the pages of this book, for the discussions introduced by the formal responses were the principal fruit of the meeting. But it did seem to us that the major papers, though representing differences of genre, were very much worth making available to a larger public.

From the outset Willy Rordorf had let us know that the paper he agreed to prepare would simply make available for the consideration of the participants some work done in recent years by others—especially H.-J. Schulz and Robert Trottmann—and so would be brief and provisional, not a full-dress treatment appropriate for publication. So be it; though, like all Rordorf's work, the paper itself was of the highest quality. To fill the gap I agreed to include a paper the substance of which I had prepared for and presented at the Leuenberg conference; it was published in *Gregorianum* in 1988 (just in time to make offprints available to members of the Cambridge meeting) and is reprinted here with permission.

As we expected, certain major themes turned out to be recurrent in the papers printed here: the theme of *presence* (prominent in the Léon-Dufour monograph, and in these pages most explicitly treated by Hans-Josef Klauck); the fully conscious and formalized *processes of tradition,* which have clearly impinged on the issues of genre, historicity, early Church liturgical practice, etc. (in most of the papers); *the relation of liturgical practice to the Last Supper* (Knoch, Farmer, others); the effort to *reconstruct the liturgical practice in Corinth* (Klauck and Hofius).

Again there are some particular emphases here: the ecumenical aspects of the Eucharist (e.g. Farmer on Paul and Peter); the relation backwards in time from the eucharistic words to the life of Jesus (Meyer) and forward in time from the eucharistic words to the life of the ancient church (Calivas); the absolute centrality of the "for you" (Hofius); parallels to the eucharistic words in the Greek (Klauck) and Judaic (Hofius and others) worlds.

The subtitle of the present volume calls these "ecumenical studies," and the ending of Otto Knoch's essay quite deftly epitomizes the purposes, intentions, goal of all participants: the "unity of all Christians at the table of the Lord."

> B. F. Meyer
> Les Verrieres, Switzerland

Abbreviations

BZ	*Biblische Zeitschrift*
EKKNT	Evangelisch-katholische Kommentar zum Neuen Testament
ET	English Translation
EvT	*Evangelische Theologie*
EWNT	*Exegetisches Wörterbuch zum Neuen Testament*
GOTR	*Greek Orthodox Theological Review*
KD	*Kerygma und Dogma*
KEK	Kritisch-exegetischer Kommentar über das Neue Testament
KNT	Kommentar zum Neuen Testament
LTK	*Lexikon für Theologie und Kirche*
NTS	*New Testament Studies*
SBL	Society of Biblical Literature
ScEccl	*Sciences ecclésiastiques*
SUNT	Studien zur Umwelt des Neuen Testaments
TLZ	*Theologische Literaturzeitung*
TRE	*Theologische Realenzyklopädie*
WUNT	Wissenschaftliche Untersuchungen zum Neuen Testament
ZNW	*Zeitschrift für die neutestamentliche Wissenschaft*
ZTK	*Zeitschrift für Theologie und Kirche*

"Do This in Memory of Me!"
(Luke 22:20; 1 Corinthians 11:24ff.)

The Celebration of the Eucharist
in the Primitive Christian Communities

Otto Knoch

Among the traits that from the outset distinguished the community of Jesus' followers from the Jews—in addition to the confession of Jesus as Messiah and Lord and to the effort to make life accord both with his words and with baptism unto him—there was *the celebration of a table-fellowship* traced back to Jesus' last meal with his disciples.[1]

Drawing on the authority of New Testament testimony, we propose here to inquire into the distinctiveness and importance of this meal in the life of the primitive Church and to search out its meaning, with a view to finding leads to the proper celebration of the Eucharist today.

1. The Celebration of the Lord's Supper:
a Datum from Earliest Christianity

There are numerous New Testament references to the first Christians' cultic celebration of a meal in their communities within the Roman Empire.[2] Besides the

---

[1] On early Christianity, cf. Leonhard Goppelt, *Christentum und Judentum im I. und 2. Jahrhundert* (Gutersloh: Bertelsmann, 1954). Jürgen Becker et al., *Die Anfänge des Christentums,* 4th ed. (Gütersloh: Mohn, 1976); Hans Conzelmann, *Geschichte des Urchristentums,* 5th ed. (Göttingen: Vandenhoeck & Ruprecht, 1983); Wilhelm Schneemelcher, *Das Urchristentum* (Stuttgart: Kohlhammer, 1981); Georg Kretschmar, "Das Abendmahlsverständnis in der Geschichte der christlichen Kirchen," in *TRE* 1:58-89.

[2] On the state of research, see Heinz Schürmann, "Abendmahl, letztes," in *LTK* 2:26-31; Hans Lessig, "Die Abendmahlsprobleme im Lichte der neutestamentlichen Forschung seit 1900" (diss. Bonn, 1954); Helmut Feld, *Das Verständnis des Abendmahls* (Darmstadt: Wissenschaftliche Buchgesellschaft, 1976); Günther Bornkamm, "Herrenmahl und Kirch

Last Supper accounts (Mark 14:17-25; Matt 26:20-29; Luke 22:14-23; cf. John 13:21-26), we should also refer to 1 Cor 11:23-25; 10:1-22; Luke 24:30-32; Acts 2:42; 20:7-12; John 6:51-59; Heb 6:2-5; 13:1-4; 1 Pet 2:2; Jude 12; Rev 3:20.

1.1 Celebrating "the Breaking of the Bread"

In Acts 2:42, 46 Luke narrates:

> They [those newly baptized on Pentecost, together with the Apostles and other followers of Jesus] devoted themselves to the Apostles' teaching and to the fellowship, to the breaking of bread (κλάσις τοῦ ἄρτου) and to the prayers. . . . And day by day, attending the temple together and breaking bread in their homes, they partook of food in joy and simplicity of heart.

According to this statement, itself based on old traditions, the original Jewish Christians of Jerusalem constituted, alongside the cultic community of Judaism, a distinctively patterned community of prayer and worship within their own households. In Luke "the breaking of the bread" refers to the earliest Christian eucharistic worship service, as shown by the account of Paul's Sunday worship service in Troas (Acts 20:7-12). This service takes place during the night between the Sabbath and the first day of the Jewish week; the whole is called "the breaking

---

bei Paulus," *ZTK* 53 (1956): 312-49; Gerhard Delling, "Das Abendmahlsgeschehen nach Paulus," *KD* 10 (1964): 61-77; Rupert Feneberg, *Christliche Passafeier und Abendmahl* (Munich: Kösel, 1971); Ferdinand Hahn, "Die alttestamentlichen Motive der urchristlichen Abendmahlsüberlieferung," *EvT* 27 (1967): 337-74; idem, "Zum Stand der Erforschung des urchristlichen Herrenmahls," *EvT* 35 (1975): 553-63; C. M. Haufe, "Ergebnisse heutiger exegetischer Bemühungen um das heilige Abendmahl," in *Lehrgespräch über das heilige Abendmahl,* ed. Gottfried Niemeyer, 54-59 (Gütersloh: Mohn, 1961); Joachim Jeremias, *Die Abendmahlsworte Jesu,* 4th ed. (Göttingen: Vandenhoeck & Ruprecht, 1967): ET *The Eucharistic Words of Jesus* (Philadelphia: Fortress, 1966); Hans Kessler, *Die theologische Bedeutung des Todes Jesu,* 2nd ed. (Düsseldorf: Patmos, 1971); Helmut Merklein, "Erwägungen zur Überlieferungsgeschichte der neutestamentlichen Abendmahlstraditionen," *BZ* 21 (1977): 88-101, 235-44; Paul Neuenzeit, *Das Herrenmahl* (Munich: Kösel, 1960); Hermann Patsch, *Abendmahl und historischer Jesus* (Stuttgart: Calwer, 1972); Eugen Ruckstuhl, *Die Chronologie des letzten Mahles und des Leidens Jesu* (Einsiedeln: Benziger, 1963); Adrien Schneker, *Das Abendmahl als Brennpunkt des Alten Testament* (Einsiedeln: Benziger, 1977); Heinz Schürmann, *Das Paschamahlbericht Lk 22,* 2nd ed. (Münster: Aschendorff, 1968); idem, *Jesu Abschiedsrede Lk 22, 21-38* (Münster: Aschendorff, 1957); idem, "Einsetzungsberichte," in *LTK* 3:762-65; idem, *Jesu ureigener Tod* (Freiburg: Herder, ;s11975, ;s21977); Eduard Schweizer, "Das Abendmahl im Neuen Testament: Forschungsbericht," *TLZ* 79 (1954):577-92; Rudolf Pesch, *Das Abendmahl und Jesu Todesverständnis* (Freiburg: Herder, 1977); Adolf Kolping, *Fundamentaltheologie* 2:14a: "Das letzte Mahl Jesu" (Münster: Aschendorff, 1974) 574-619; Gerhard Delling, "Abendmahl. Urchristliches Mahlverständnis," in *TRE* 1:47-58.

of the bread." It consists of two parts: the address (by the Apostle) and "the breaking of the bread" in a narrower sense (v. 11).

In his gospel Luke traces this custom, first, back to Jesus' Last Supper (Luke 22:19: "he took bread and, when he had given thanks [εὐχαριστήσας], he broke it [ἔκλασεν], and gave it to them, saying, 'This is my body. . . . Do this in remembrance of me.' "); second, back to when the risen Jesus, appearing to the disciples on the road to Emmaus, again directs attention to this "breaking of bread" (Luke 24:28-30: "he took bread, gave thanks [εὐλόγησεν], and breaking it [κλάσας], gave it to them"). Scholars take the Jewish custom of beginning every meal, after prayer, with the head of the household's ritual breaking of bread to have sponsored the coining of the early Christian technical expression "the breaking of the bread" for the celebration of the Eucharist.[3]

1.2 Celebrating the Lord's Supper

The oldest reference to the primitive Christian eucharistic service is found in Paul's first letter to the Corinthians, written ca. A.D. 54/55. This service took place in conjunction with a community meal and formed its conclusion. Paul called this type of worship service "the Lord's Supper" (κυριακὸν δεῖπνον). This should be understood as a statement about the origin of the rite as well as about the presence of the risen Lord at its performance. "I received from the Lord (κύριος) what I also delivered to you: Jesus, the Lord, on the night he was betrayed, took bread, and when he had given thanks (εὐχαριστήσας), broke it and said, 'This is my body, for you; do this in remembrance of me.' In the same way, after supper, he took the cup and said, 'This cup is the New Covenant in my blood; do this, whenever you drink of it, in remembrance of me!' " (1 Cor 11:23-25).

At this cultic meal, which Paul, at the founding of the community (ca. A.D. 51/52), introduced as sacred Apostolic tradition, the risen Lord himself becomes efficaciously present in the gifts of the meal, bread and wine (cf. 1 Cor 11:26-30). The meal is accordingly sacramental in character. Paul does not say how often this meal took place. It appears to have been frequent (cf. 1 Cor 11:17-22). Alongside the eucharistic service there are also services of the word properly so called (1 Cor

---

[3]Cf. Johannes Behm, κλάω, κλάσις, κλάσμα, TDNT 3:726-43; Josef Gewiess, "Brotbrechen, biblisch," *LTK* 2:706ff.; on this see Paul Neuenzeit, *Herrenmahl,* passim; Gerhard Schneider, *Die Apostelgeschichte* (Freiburg: Herder, 1980) 283-87. On celebration in house-churches, see H.-J. Klauck, *Hausgemeinde und Hauskirche im frühen Christentum* (Stuttgart; Katholisches Bibelwerk, 1981), and Peter Stuhlmacher, "Exkurs: Urchristliche Hausgemeinden," in idem, *Der Brief an Philemon,* 2nd ed. (Zurich: Benziger, and Neukirchen-Vluyn: Neukirchener Verlag, 1981) 70-75, at 74: "These house-church communities were accordingly places where out of a common celebration of the Lord's Supper there grew together a pluriform body of Christ, a community of the reconciled."

12; 14). Cultic meal celebrations were doubtless led by community authorities, the "administrators" (κυβερνήσεις, 1 Cor 12:28; 16:15-18) of the community. We may also take it that "the Lord's Supper" was always celebrated on "the Lord's Day" (Rev 1:10).

1.3 The Witness of the Last Supper Accounts of the Gospels

The so-called Last Supper accounts in the synoptic gospels, like the tradition recounting the words, acts, and fate of Jesus (Passion and Resurrection narratives), do not have a primarily historical function. Rather, they are intended to support Christian faith and, by reference to Jesus, to ground and undergird the life of the church. This particularly holds for the risen Lord's mandate to baptize (cf. Luke 24:45-47; Matt 28:19-20) and to celebrate the Eucharist (Luke 22:19; cf. Matt 26:26-27). The divergent words of institution in Mark and Matthew on the one hand (Mark 14:22-24; Matt 26:26-29: "my covenant-blood," without the explicit mandate to celebrate the Eucharist), and in Luke on the other (Luke 22:14-22), "the New Covenant in my blood," with the mandate to celebrate accompanying the word on the bread; cf. 1 Cor 11:23-25), thus already represent different liturgical eucharistic traditions.[4]

1.4 Further Testimonies in the New Testament

The fourth gospel expresses the meaning of Jesus' Last Supper with his disciples before his death (John 13:1-12) through the symbol of Jesus' washing of feet. His death, represented in the meal, is an expression of complete self-giving to mankind and especially to the disciples. The discourse on the Bread of Life (chapter 6), a "mystery catechesis," allows the fourth evangelist to interpret theologically, from the vantage point of the Resurrection, the ecclesial practice that he has presupposed: that of "eating the flesh of the Son of man and drinking his blood." "My flesh is food indeed and my blood is drink indeed. Whoever eats my flesh and drinks my blood abides in me and I in him. . . . Whoever eats my flesh and drinks my blood has eternal life . . . " (John 6:51-55). The eucharistic meal is traced back to Jesus, already typologically prefigured in his miraculous multiplication of the loaves, itself sacramentally interpreted.[5]

Paul, similarly, sees the eucharistic meal of the church prefigured in the gift of manna and in the Covenant—God's wondrous gift of water to his people journeying in the wilderness (1 Cor 10:1-7). According to Paul the broken

---

[4]On this see esp. the works of Jeremias, Schürmann, Patsch, and Pesch (n. 2, above).
[5]Cf. Rudolf Schnackenburg, *Das Johannesevangelium* (Freiburg: Herder, 1971) 82-102.

eucharistic bread and the eucharistic drink from a single cup give the Christian a real share in the body and blood of Christ (1 Cor 10:15-23), and so are sacramental in character. The common meal, together with one baptism, constitutes the communion of the church as the body of Christ (cf. 1 Cor 10:17; Gal 3:26-29; also Eph 4:4).[6]

The letter to the Hebrews also presupposes a sacrificial food offering of Christians, analogous to the sacrificial food offerings of the Jews when the temple still stood (cf. 13:10). This letter also points to baptism and the Eucharist, along with faith, as the foundations of Christian existence (6:1-5: taste the "heavenly gift," γεύεσθαι).[7]

Perhaps 1 Pet 2:1 ("spiritual milk")[8]and Rev 3:20 ("we shall sup together")[9]should also be understood as references to the eucharistic meal of the early church.

Jude 12 speaks of the defiling participation of false teachers and sinners in the love feasts of the community.[10]

Most of the above-mentioned passages refer to the regular celebration of a cultic meal, the Eucharist, in the early church, whereby the elements of bread and wine realize, symbolically, the pneumatic reality of the crucified Christ raised from the dead, and impart a share in the life of the risen Lord.

2. The Premise: the Farewell Meal of the Risen Jesus

Both the Apostle Paul (1 Cor 11:23) and the gospel tradition of the Last Supper trace the eucharistic celebrations of the post-Easter church back to Jesus' Last Supper with his disciples before his death. Several questions arise in this context.

---

[6]Supporting evidence in Neuenzeit, *Herrenmahl.*

[7]In virtue of the correspondence of repentance, baptism, the laying-on of hands (Heb 6:2) with (once-and-for-all) enlightenment, the taste of the heavenly gift, and participation in the Holy Spirit (Heb 6:4), enlightenment is here referred to baptism, the taste of the heavenly gift to the Eucharist (cf. 1 Clem 36:2). On the last text, see Otto Michel, *Der Brief an die Hebräer,* 8th ed. (Göttingen: Vandenhoeck & Ruprecht, 1949) 148; Otto Knoch, "Eigenart und Bedeutung der Eschatologie im 1. Clemensbrief," *Theoph* 17 (1964): 330-32.

[8]See K. H. Schelkle, *Die Petrusbriefe, Der Judasbrief* (Freiburg: Herder, 1961) 540-57.

[9]Johannes Behm, δεῖπνον, δειπνέω, TDNT 2:34-35

[10]Cf. Schelkle (see above, n. 8) 161-62.

2.1 Was the Last Supper of Jesus a Passover Meal?

According to the synoptic gospels, the Last Supper was a Passover meal. Jesus and his disciples constituted a table-fellowship gathered to eat the Passover lamb (Mark 14:12, 14, 16; Matt 26:17-30; Luke 22:7-9, 11-22). Paul's notice, "after supper" (1 Cor 11:25), likewise suggests that between the breaking of the bread at the start of the main meal and the drinking of the third cup, the Paschal lamb was eaten.

According to John the meal took place on the day before Passover, the so-called Day of Preparation. Thus, Jesus would have celebrated a meal without a Paschal lamb, for these lambs were slaughtered in the temple court before the evening of Passover. He would have died on the cross ("as the true Paschal lamb!") at the very hour at which the Paschal lambs were slaughtered in the temple (John 13:1; 18:28).

To this day the above difference has not been satisfactorily resolved.[11] But it is not of any great importance for the early Christian celebration of the Eucharist, since the synoptic tradition as well as 1 Cor 5:7-13. show that the first Christians interpreted Jesus' death as the beginning of the promised New Covenant and so understood the Last Supper associated with this death as the founding of the New Covenant: "For Christ, our Paschal lamb, has been sacrificed. Let us, therefore, celebrate the festival, not with the old leaven . . . " (1 Cor 5:7b-8).

It is a novelty that, in contrast to the Jewish Passover, the Eucharist, as the commemoration of the death of Jesus, was celebrated not just once a year but on the night before the first day of each week (the day of Jesus' Resurrection) or, indeed, even daily. This shows that the tie with the Jewish Passover was not constitutive for this celebration. New Testament tradition in all its testimony respecting the Last Supper presupposes that the Passover meal did not function as a constituent part of the celebration of the Eucharist.[12]

2.2. What Were the Words of Jesus on the Bread and the Wine at the Last Supper?

The New Testament offers two forms of the words of institution: the Markan-Matthean form, "Take (eat), this is my body. . . . This is my blood, the blood of the covenant, which will be poured out for many (for the forgiveness of sins)" (Mark

---

[11]For full discussion, see above all the works of Lessig, Feld, Schweizer, and Kolping (see n. 2).

[12]See esp. Heinz Schürmann, *Jesu ureigener Tod,* 2nd ed. (Freiburg: Herder, 1977) 78-96, which shows how the coalescent interpretative actions of Jesus are constitutive for the Eucharist.

14:22, 24; Matt 26:26, 28). This form lacks the mandate of commemorative celebration. The Pauline-Lukan form reads, "This is my body (which is) for you; do this in remembrance of me. . . . This cup is the New Covenant in my blood; do this, as often as you drink of it, (in remembrance of me!)" (1 Cor 11:24-25; Luke 22:19), with the allusion to the New Covenant and the mandate of remembrance. Here Mark is more original than Matthew, and Paul more original than Luke. Paul derived his liturgical libretto for the Eucharist either from Syria/Antioch, or from Jerusalem. In view of the agreement with Luke and of several Hellenistic elements, Antioch is to be preferred as the place of origin for the Greek formula. The text of Mark, which is susceptible of complete retroversion into Hebrew (and into Aramaic), might—though more recent in terms of literary text—have originated earlier than that of Paul, and might well go back to an original Palestinian form.

Paul's introductory formulation—"I received from the Lord (ἀπὸ τοῦ κυρίου) what I passed on to you"—reflects rabbinic transmission formulas (παρέλαβον–παρέδωκα) and attests the Eucharistic *ordo* as of primitive Apostolic institution. We must accordingly understand the text as cultic aetiology, as liturgical rite, namely, as a binding liturgical *ordo* of primitive Apostolic institution. In contradistinction thereto, Mark's text is in essence a historically reliable tradition, older than Paul's liturgically developed double formula, with its Hellenistic cast. To be sure, it has not thus far been possible to determine unmistakably what original form stood behind the two streams of tradition.[13]

2.3 Did Jesus Wish to Establish a Commemorative Celebration?

According to trustworthy synoptic tradition, Jesus at the Last Supper pledged the celebration of a new meal with his disciples at the consummation of God's reign (Mark 14:25; Matt 26:29; Luke 22:18-30; cf. 1 Cor 11:26). Jesus' Last Supper concluded with this eschatological prospect. He expected, then, that despite his violent death, the kingdom of God would come. Since Jesus had this kingdom in imminent prospect, it is scarcely probable that he understood his farewell meal as the model for commemorative meals of his messianic community in a temporally expanding interim between now and the arrival of the kingdom of God. But since Jesus left the future of his work entirely in the hands of his Father, he also entrusted to the wisdom of God the ongoing impact of the particular cast of his Last Supper

---

[13]In the debate over the most ancient tradition, we incline to the view of Markan priority emphatically represented by Rudolf Pesch, *Das Markusevangelium,* HTKNT, vol. 2 (Freiburg: Herder, 1977) 340-77, with the excursus on the Last Supper tradition and the synopsis of New Testament eucharistic texts. The designation of 1 Cor 11:23-25(26) as a cultic aetiology derives from Pesch. See his efforts to determine the oldest form of the words of institution.

(cf. Mark 14:36: "Abba, Father, everything is possible for you. . . . May your will be done!" Mark 13:32: "But of that day or that hour no one knows . . . not even the Son, but only the Father").[14]

2.4 Did Jesus Give a Soteriological Meaning to the Last Supper?

Because the soteriological formulas of interpretation at the Last Supper are not identical and because they underwent development in the course of transmission (Mark/Matthew: words of interpretation over the cup: "blood, poured out for many"; Paul/Luke: words both over the bread and over the cup), it is still debated whether Jesus ascribed an atoning efficacy to his death and whether at the Last Supper he anticipated, symbolically, the realization of his death. But inasmuch as Jesus ascribed absolute salvific meaning to his own person (cf. Luke 12:8 par.), took account of his own death beginning at a particular point in time (Mark 9:31), and, to interpret it (Mark 10:45), seized on the Song of the Suffering Servant (Isa 52:13–53:12), we have good grounds for affirming that Jesus at the Last Supper consciously specified the sense of this death through the spirit of self-sacrifice for others. This he did by focussing attention, with an interpretative word of his own, on the ritual breaking of the bread at the beginning of the main meal, and by focussing on the third cup, the cup of blessing, following the main meal, likewise with an interpretative word of his own. Interpreting the bread by reference to his body, that is, his person, and interpreting the contents of the cup by reference to the shedding of his blood, that is, his death, while meantime abstaining from eating and drinking with the others, so impressed his supper partners that after his death these two elements alone were held fast and fused into a new symbolic whole; and this, even though the memory of the original sequence persisted (cf. "after supper," 1 Cor 11:25; Luke 22:20).

Together with Jesus' eschatological confidence, these interpretative words and gestures became the nucleus and vector of the disciples' post-Easter proclamation of the death of Jesus in the light of his Resurrection. The fact that shortly after his death the original participants in the Last Supper established and contoured this rite of representation is our gurarantee that their celebration of the Lord's Supper aptly expressed and realized, in the perspective of Easter, the original purposes of Jesus. It should be further observed that the thesis of an originally unsoteriological celebration of the Eucharist (as pure commemorative meal) has to this day remained mere hypothesis. In the post-Easter reality of the church God has displayed the work of Jesus, including his suffering and dying, and made it

---

[14]On the so-called eschatological prospect, see Patsch (above, n. 2) 106-51. Patsch affirms that despite his expectation of imminent consummation, "Jesus, even on the last evening, left intact the sovereign reservation of God."

effective. This holds, too, for the eucharistic celebration as representation, in the form of the Lord's Supper, of the death of Jesus.[15]

3. The Meaning of the Eucharistic Celebration for the Primitive Church

God accepted the death of Jesus as an act of atonement for "the many" and showed this by raising the crucified one from the dead. The death of Jesus brought to completion the saving significance of his advent and activity. Through proclamation in his name, through baptism, and through the celebration of the Eucharist, the primitive church enacted in history the saving power of the death of Jesus. Like baptism, the celebration of the Eucharist became bearer and mediator of the saving significance of the Risen Lord.[16]

3.1 "You Proclaim the Death of the Lord Until He Comes"
(1 Cor 11:26)

In the celebration of the Eucharist the church pledges itself to the risen Lord and participates in the atoning power of his death. It thus becomes the messianic community, the communion of the church wherein the saving power and saving grace of Christ are present and operative.

3.2 "At Table in My Kingdom" (Luke 22:30)

In celebrating the Lord's Supper the church by anticipation shares in full communion with its Lord in the splendor of the kingdom of God. It recognizes itself as already belonging to the kingdom. Luke's exposition of the Last Supper brings this to expression: "And now I vest in you the kingdom . . . so that you may eat and drink at my table in my kingdom" (Luke 22:29-30). In the celebrations of the Lord's Supper the faith-conviction of belonging at the final banquet in the kingdom of God found living expression (cf. Jesus' promise of joyous supper-fellowship in the reign of God: Matt 22:1-14; Luke 14:16-24; also Matt 8:12; 25:1-13, 14-30).

---

[15]On the whole issue, see Patsch, 151-230; Jürgen Roloff, "Anfänge der soteriologischen Deutung des Todes Jesu (Mk 10,45 und Lk 22,27)," NTS 19 (1972/1973): 38-120; Heinz Schürmann, "Jesu ureigenes Todesverständnis," in *Begegnung mit dem Wort,* H. Zimmermann Festschrift, ed. Josef Zmijewksi and Ernst Nellessen, 273-309 (Bonn: Hanstein, 1980).

[16]Cf. Karl Kertelge (ed.) *Der Tod Jesu: Deutungen im Neuen Testament* (Freiburg: Herder, 1976). On εὐλογεῖν and εὐχαριστεῖν and in eucharistic context in the New Testament, see Hermann Patsch, "Abendmahlsterminologie ausserhalb der Einsetzungsberichte," *ZNW* 62 (1971): 210-31.

This is why the cry of longing, μαράνα θά (1 Cor 16:22) concluded the worship service of the primitive community.

3.3. "He Abides in Me and I in Him" (John 6:56)

In the fellowship of the eucharistic meal the early Christian communities experienced, in the midst of affliction, the sustaining, heartening union with the risen Lord. This appears above all in the designation of the alimentary elements as the body/flesh and blood of Christ (cf. John 6:51-58; 1 Cor 11:26-30). John speaks of the eucharistic food and drink as bestowing eternal life on its partakers (John 6:51, 53, 57, 58). Paul goes so far as to say that the health and wellbeing of Christians depends on worthy participation in the eucharistic meal (1 Cor 11:26-30). The growing tendency to outfit the accounts of the multiplication of loaves with eucharistic traits (see the use of the verbs εὐλογεῖν, εὐχαριστεῖν, and the introductory motif of the ritual breaking of bread) stands in the service of this assertion (cf. Mark 6:30-44 par.; 8:1-10 par.; John 6:1-13).

3.4 The New Community: Internal Relations

At the Lord's table the first Christians, regardless of all divisions and differences, experienced their belonging to one another. This is why Paul fought passionately to make the table fellowship of Jews and Gentiles possible. The so-called Apostolic Council opened the way to this (cf. Gal 2:1-12; Acts 15:1-13). At the table of the Lord, accordingly, the love and goodness of Christ had to be the all-commanding highest rule and inner law (cf. 1 Cor 11:17-22). Indicative of the character of this new community are the address "brother" and "sister," and the "holy kiss" that was exchanged in the eucharistic part of the primitive Christian worship service (cf. Rom 16:16; 1 Cor 16:20; 2 Cor 13:12).[17]

4. Prospect

In the light of these ascertainments the principal tasks of the church should be, above all: recovery of the eschatological orientation and of the communion and unity of all Christians at the table of the Lord.

---

[17]On how the eucharistic reception of the body of Christ and Body-of-Christ communion belong together, see Neuenzeit, *Herrenmahl,* 201-19.

The Expiation Motif
in the Eucharistic Words:
A Key to the History of Jesus?

Ben F. Meyer

Literary criticism, in the sense of reconstructing the original wording of a text, poses problems enough, but the literary criticism of the eucharistic words intensifies certain common difficulties and adds others peculiar to the eucharistic words. The combination has ordinarily been defeating.

By way of comparison and contrast, consider the Our Father. The generally accepted effort of literary criticism to recover the probably original wording of the Our Father has proceeded in accord with a hypothesis: Where the Matthean version offered lines not found in Luke, these lines were not an omission by Lukan tradition or by Luke, but an addition by Matthean tradition or by Matthew. The rule of thumb: Liturgical texts expand.

What happens when this procedure is applied to the eucharistic words? First, the words of application on the bread τὸ ὑπὲρ ὑμῶν ("[which is] for you") in 1 Cor 11:24 and τὸ ὑπὲρ ὑμῶν διδόμενον ("[which is] given for you") in Luke 22:19 drop, for they are not found in the Markan and Matthean parallels. The words of application on the cup τὸ ἐκχυννόμεν ὑπὲρ πολλῶν ("[which is to be] poured out for many") in Mark 14:24; τὸ περὶ πολλῶν ἐκχυννόμενον εἰς ἄφεσιν ἀμαρτιῶν ("[which is to be] poured out for many for the remission of sins") in Matt 26:28; and τὸ ὑπὲρ ὑμῶν ἐκχυννόμενον ("[which is] poured out for you") in Luke 20:20 drop, for they are not found in the Pauline parallel. Second, the invitation λάβετε ("take") in Mark 14:22 or λάβετε φάγετε ("take, eat") in Matt 26:26 drops, since it is lacking in Luke and Paul. Third, the anamnesis motif in Luke 22:19 and 1 Cor 11:24-25 drops, for it is not found in Mark or Matthew. Such is critique by simple subtraction.

Gerhard Friedrich: Exposition and Critique

Something very like it seems to have been assumed in Gerhard Friedrich's 1982 book, *Die Verkündigung des Todes Jesu im Neuen Testament.*[1] At the Last Supper Jesus said simply "This is my Body," that is, "I am that" (*Das bin ich*).[2] The bread symbolized the person. And "This is my Blood," that is, "I must die."

Granted that the circumstance of Jesus' meeting with the circle of his closest disciples in a situation of danger for him must have invested "I am that" and "I must die" with no little pathos and solemnity, still one cannot help wondering at the extraordinary development from these bare utterances to the joyous celebration of the breaking of the bread in the earliest community, to say nothing of the Lord's Supper as Paul understood it (1 Cor 10:14-17; 11:20-30). Friedrich reconstructs the sequence as follows. (a) The earliest community joyously celebrated the breaking of the bread. The death of Jesus, then, must have had a present meaning (*Gegenwartsbedeutung*) for them. (b) "Consequently, the death of Jesus began to be interpreted, and there came into being the formulations: 'poured out for many' (Mark 14:24), 'poured out for many for the forgiveness of sins' (Matt 26:28), 'poured out for you' (Luke 22:20)."[3]

What remains unexplained in this reconstruction is how cultic celebration could have had present meaning prior to and independent of an interpretation of Jesus' death that went beyond "This is my body" ("I am that") and "This is my blood" ("I must die"). Even for a sympathetic reader, the historic sequence proposed by Friedrich is scarcely intelligible. By putting present meaning before interpretation of the death of Jesus, it leaves "present meaning" altogether unaccounted for. Even the sometimes artificial recourse to "the Easter experience of the disciples" is left in abeyance. Friedrich offers literally nothing to make sense of his alleged preinterpretative, present meaning of Jesus' death and of the eucharistic celebration of it.

Behind Friedrich's views of a Last Supper stripped, on the one hand, of the motifs of sacrifice and expiation, and on the other hand, of historical intelligibility as the source of the Lord's Supper in earliest Christianity, stand Friedrich's own unresolved problems respecting the relevance to God's saving act in Christ of themes such as sacrifice and expiation. It is perfectly conceivable that one might find these important New Testament themes to be themselves luminously intelligible, and still, on other grounds, deny that they belonged to the original deposit of eucharistic tradition. This, however, is not the case with Friedrich's

---

[1] G. Friedrich, *Die Verkündigung des Todes Jesu im Neuen Testament* (Neukirchen-Vluyn: Neukirchener Verlag, 1982).
[2] *Verkündigung*, 13.
[3] *Verkündigung*, 35.

monograph. Negatively, the thrust of his entire treatment of Christ's saving death is to reduce the motifs of sacrifice and expiation and indeed all cultic images and meanings to negligible dimensions. Positively, it is to define alternative, life-affirming, soteriological meanings of Christ's death, to insist on their independence of cultic notions (which in our time, he observes,[4] have become enigmatic and unacceptable), and to maximize the presence of these positive motifs elsewhere in the New Testament. A result of the negative effort, however, is so resolutely to overlook or misvalue basic aspects of New Testament and especially Pauline texts as to shake the reader's confidence in the whole enterprise. It is no surprise, in retrospect, that Friedrich's reconstruction of the eucharistic words and of the historical process by which they came to be expanded collapses almost immediately upon examination and reflection. The writer has an axe to grind—not so much a positive thesis as a recoil and flight from unwanted meaning.

In anticipation of the objection that this recoil from themes of sacrifice is an anti-Catholic reflex, Friedrich points out that it is represented among Catholic scholars, too.[5] He cites only Paul Neuenzeit, but, so far as the eucharistic words in particular are concerned, he could easily have extended the list to include half a dozen more.[6]

Xavier Léon-Dufour: Exposition and Critique

Simultaneously with the publication of Friedrich's book on the death of Jesus there appeared Xavier Léon-Dufour's *Le partage du pain eucharistique selon le Nouveau Testament.*[7] A monograph devoting leisurely care to the totality of New Testament texts on the Eucharist, it includes a review of eucharistic practice as recoverable from Acts and from Paul (23-59); a synchronic reading of the four texts transmitting the eucharistic acts and words (60-91); a first division of the texts on the Last Supper into two traditions, the liturgical or cultic tradition of the synoptists and Paul, and the testamental tradition of the farewell meal in John 13-17 (95-114); a second division of the cultic tradition into two orientations, that of the Antiochene tradition (Paul and Luke) toward a noncultic covenantal theology and that of the Markan tradition (Mark and Matt) toward liturgical libretto (115-21).

---

[4]*Verkündigung*, 145.

[5]*Verkündigung*, 77.

[6]P. Neuenzeit, *Das Herrenmahl* (Munich: Kösel, 1960). Among others listed by Rudolf Pesch, *Das Abendmahl und Jesu Todesverständnis* (Freiburg: Herder, 1978) 14-16 and 20, are Anton Vögtle, Peter Fiedler, Joachim Gnilke, Peter Wolf, Hans Kessler, and Helmut Merklein.

[7]Xavier Léon-Dufour, *Le partage du pain eucharistique selon le Nouveau Testament* (Paris: Seuil, 1982). E.T. *Sharing the Eucharistic Bread: The Witness of the New Testament* (New York: Paulist, 1987).

There follows an effort to reconstruct Jesus' eucharistic acts and words. The conclusion is essentially an affirmation of the historic priority of the Lukan text, though minus the word on the cup, minus the anamnesis command, and with postplacement of "the eschatological perspective" (Luke 22:18; Mark 14:25; Matt 26:29; cf. 1 Cor 11:26) as in Mark and Matthew. We shall return presently to the detail of this lengthy section (95-209).

The book concludes with a consideration of Mark in redactional context (216-35), of Paul in literary and historical context (236-65), of the Lukan presentation of the "testament" of Jesus (266-84), and of the eucharistic theme in John (285-317). An epilogue, titled "Ouverture," reflects on the duality of cultic and testamental tradition, and invites the reader's entry into the universe of religious symbol, which includes a positive consideration of sacrifice (321-43). Two brief appendixes deal with solemn Jewish meals (345-47) and with a recapitulation and contradiction of several elements of Joachim Jeremias's argument for the Last Supper as a Jewish Passover meal (348-51).

Our principal interest in this wide-ranging study bears on the critique that recovers eucharistic words of Jesus stripped, as in Gerhard Friedrich's analysis, of the motifs of sacrifice in general, expiation in particular. Unlike Friedrich, Léon-Dufour holds no dogmatic brief against sacrifice, representative atonement, ransom, and so forth as *unsachgemäss*[8] respecting the death of Jesus. Nevertheless, there are a few telltale passages indicating clearly enough the basis of Léon-Dufour's resolute effort to reduce to the minimum the expiation motif in the New Testament. For example,

> the cultic-sacrificial interpretation of the death of Jesus proposed by Paul is only one among others in his letters, and the least frequent, finding expression only in rare texts which it is not always easy to understand.[9]

It seems fair to say, on the other hand, that this minimizing tendency in the assessment of the expiation motif in Pauline soteriology is currently losing ground, partly under pressure of Old Testament scholarship's rediscovery of the sense of expiation and expiatory sacrifice[10] and partly under pressure of a direct result of this rediscovery, namely, a more exact Pauline exegesis. Hence the striking convergence—precisely with reference to the theme of expiation and its keystone role in the edifice of Pauline soteriology—of the works of Stanislas Lyonnet with more

---

[8]*Verkündigung,* 145.

[9]*Le partage du pain,* 145.

[10]See Luigi Moraldi, *Espiazione sacrificale e riti espiatori nell'Antico Testamento* (Rome: Biblical Institute Press, 1956). Klaus Koch, "Sühne und Sündenvergebung um die Wende von der exilischen zur nachexilischen Zeit," *EvT* 26 (1966): 217-39. Hartmut Gese, "Die Sühne," in *Zur biblischen Theologie* (Munich: Kaiser, 1977) 86-106. Bernd Janowski, *Sühne als Heilsgeschehen* (Neukirchen-Vluyn: Neukirchener Verlag, 1982)

recent studies by Peter Stuhlmacher, Karl Kertelge, Ulrich Wilckens, and Otfried Hofius, among others.[11] So far from being a Pauline peculiarity, the expiation theme is solidly grounded in pre-Pauline faith formulas that in all probability derive as well from those whom Acts calls ἑβραῖοι (e.g., Rom 4:25; 1 Cor 15:3-5) as from those whom Acts calls ἑλληνισταί (e.g., Rom 3:25-26). So far from being rare in Paul, the theme is frequent (cf. 1 Cor 11:24; 15:3; 2 Cor 5:21; Gal 1:4; Rom 3:25; 4:25; 8:3). So far from being marginal in Paul, it belongs to the conditions of the possibility of the Pauline themes of reconciliation[12] and righteousness,[13] and it is better represented in Paul's last great letter than anywhere else in his correspondence.

The question is whether this substantial datum of the earliest Christian faith finds its historic point of departure in the Jesus tradition. Léon-Dufour's negative answer hinges on a certain exegetical strategy. To concentrate on the eucharistic texts, one notices, first, that in the symbolic reading of John urged by Léon-Dufour (which, to be sure, has the merit of enhancing the tie between faith and the Eucharist) the superficially buried parallelism between John 6:51c and the eucharistic words, rather than being uncovered and highlighted, is further buried and its contour lost.

Second, the "cultic tradition" which is contrasted with John undergoes a reduction by the supposed orientation of the Antiochene tradition (Paul and Luke) toward a noncultic covenantal theology. That leaves Mark and Matthew. But, third, the Markan text is systematically shorn of reference or allusion to the category of expiatory offering, since ἐκχυννόμενον ὑπὲρ πολλῶν ("[to be] poured out for many") need not relate to it (173). Fourth and last, that leaves Matthew, to whose version of the eucharistic words, since it specifies the phrase "to be poured out for many" by the further phrase "for the remission of sins," Léon-Dufour at last

[11]Stanislas Lyonnet and Léopold Sabourin, *Sin, Redemption, and Sacrifice* (Rome: Biblical Institute Press, 1970). Peter Stuhlmacher, *Reconciliation, Law, and Righteousness: Essays in Biblical Theology,* trans. Everett R. Kalin (Philadelphia: Fortress, 1986) esp. 78-81, 85-87, 103-105, 156-58. Karl Kertelge, *"Rechtfertigung" bei Paulus,* 2nd ed. (Münster: Aschendorff, 1967) esp. 104-105, 211, 216-17, 248. Ulrich Wilckens, Der Brief an die Römer, *EKKNT,* 3 vols. (Zurich: Benziger and Neukirchen-Vluyn: Neukirchener Verlag, 1978-1982) esp. 1:201-202, 232-33, 233-43. Otfried Hofius, "Erwägungen zur Gestalt und Herkunft des paulinischen Versöhnungsgedankens," *ZTK* 77 (1980): 186-99; " 'Gott hat unter uns aufgerichtet das Wort von der Versöhnung' (2 Kor. 5,19)," *ZNW* 71 (1980): 3-20. In my book, *The Early Christians: Their World Mission and Self-Discovery* (Wilmington: Glazier, 1986) 150-58, I made the effort to correlate the work of Lyonnet, Kertelge, Stuhlmacher, and Wilckens on expiation themes, as well as to take account (123-27) of Hofius's work on the same theme.
[12]See esp. P. Stuhlmacher, "The Gospel of Reconciliation in Christ—Basic Features and Issues of a Biblical Theology of the New Testament," *HBT* 1 (1979): 161-90.
[13]Stuhlmacher, *Reconciliation,* 78-81, 173-77.

attributes an expiatory sense, congratulating Matthew in a single paragraph (in this book Matthew is the forgotten man) on having thought to give expression to this otherwise unexpressed dimension of the mystery of Christ's death.

So, we began with a contrast between John and cultic tradition, there being four texts in the cultic tradition. We end with one text in the cultic tradition, that of Matthew, whose supposed originality in this particular is given a treatment reduced to the absolute minimum.

Just as Gerhard Friedrich felt no need to offer a credible account of how and why the expiatory motif entered post factum into the tradition of Jesus' words, so Léon-Dufour is silent on the matter; but the two cases differ. Friedrich cleanly cut the Gordian knot from the start by reducing the eucharistic words to "this is my body" and "this is my blood." He consequently felt no need to remove the reference to expiation exegetically, as Léon-Dufour has done, from τὸ ὑπὲρ ὑμῶν ("[which is] given for you," 1 Cor 11:24), from τὸ ὑπὲρ ὑμῶν δεδόμενον ("[which is] given for you," Luke 22:19), from τὸ ὑπὲρ ὑμῶν ἐκχυννόμενον ("[which is] poured out for you," Luke 22:20), and from τὸ ἐκχυννόμενον ὑπὲρ πολλῶν ("[which is to be] poured out for many," Mark 14:24. Friedrich's was a clean, if arbitrary, solution. Having relativized the cultic and expiatory dimension of the texts by attributing their origin to the post-Easter community, he lost interest in further analysis, leaving open, for example, the respective contributions of the Aramaic-speaking and of the Greek-speaking Christian communities. Whether Léon-Dufour's solution is more plausible, it is certainly more laborious. At least three aspects of his procedure call for some comment.

The first relates to the criteria for (better, indexes to) historicity.[14] These are reduced to *différence* (or "discontinuity") and *cohérence*. This clear and simple reduction of indexes thus bypasses both the necessity and the possibility of dealing concretely with Jesus' language either in the sense of mother tongue or in the sense of irreducibly personal idiom. Indexes other than *différence* and *cohérence* are taken to be indecisive and the matter is left at that. Nothing is said of how indexes indecisive of themselves might by accumulation and convergence generate a positive probability. But in concrete historical work it is precisely the latter case that is recurrent and crucial. Without resources with which to address it, the historian is bound to produce a truncated and implausible presentation of the Jesus of history both in general and in detail.

Léon-Dufour's inattention to the peculiar nature of a cumulative and convergent argument is nowhere more clearly exposed than in the appendix on the

---

[14]On these numerous indexes, see B. F. Meyer, *The Aims of Jesus* (London: SCM, 1979) 81-87. See also Meyer, "Objectivity and Subjectivity in Historical Criticism of the Gospels," in *Critical Realism and the New Testament* (Allison Park: Pickwick, 1989) 129-45.

question of whether the Last Supper followed the rite of a Passover meal. Here Léon-Dufour considers his case against Jeremias to be made in simple and straightforward fashion: First, five of Jeremias's observations are dismissed without discussion as irrelevant; then, the remaining nine observations are dismissed in turn as not independently cogent. Now, inasmuch as Jeremias did not present his fourteen observations as independently cogent, what is gained by making the point that they are not independently cogent? What emerges most clearly is the critic's insensitivity to the peculiar character of a cumulative and convergent argument. This is of a piece with reduction of the indexes to the historicity of data to *différence* and *cohérence*. The exercise, moreover, concludes with a mistaken inference. From Jeremias's circumspection vis-à-vis any flat, definitive denial of the Johannine chronology of the passion, Léon-Dufour infers that Jeremias himself found the reciprocally reinforcing elements of his patiently assembled argument in favor of the Last Supper as a Passover meal finally unconvincing. Once again what this betrays is the same misvaluation of historical reconstruction and of the probability, not certainty, that is normally attendant on it, that had earlier dogged Léon-Dufour's efforts to recover Jesus' eucharistic acts and words.

The second item calling for comment is the question of whether Léon-Dufour is right in rejecting Riesenfeld's interpretation of ὑπέρ + gen. (when it designates the beneficial quality of someone's death) as intelligible "only against the background of the sacrificial concepts of the O.T."[15] Riesenfeld, following Jeremias, argued that the Semitic expression behind ὑπὲρ πολλῶν ("for many") in Jesus' word on the cup (Mark 14:24) was the matrix of further liturgical and catechetical uses. Léon-Dufour does not consider the Markan ὑπὲρ πολλῶν to be original; he rejects the generalization of the sense of ὑπέρ as expiatory; finally, he points out that there are numerous Pauline uses of ὑπέρ in the service of such wider categories as love and reconciliation.

Disagreement on what texts have the best claim to antiquity and historicity is obviously inevitable if one critic accepts linguistic indexes to antiquity and historicity and the other rejects them. But is there any way of illuminating and resolving the second and third points, which bear on the uses of ὑπέρ? Something perhaps may be gained by evoking, with Léon-Dufour, the categories of love and reconciliation and in posing the further question of whether they imply or suppose expiation. What has emerged from recent developments in Pauline exegesis is that Paul has placed the expiatory death of Christ at the root of salvation in all its modalities: as redemption and justification (note the role of ἱλαστήριον in Rom

---

[15]Harald Riesenfeld, ὑπέρ, TDNT 8:507-16, see 511. By oversight or misprint, Riesenfeld referred on 510-11 to "ὑπὲρ ὑμῶν [rather than ὑπὲρ πολλῶν] in the cup saying in Mk."

3:21-26[16] and the allusion to Isa 53:5 in the faith formula that crowns the text of Rom 4:22-25); as reconciliation (= release from "enmity" and rescue from "wrath," Rom 5:6-11;[17] note the chiasmus binding the reconciliatory deed of God and the reconciliatory message of his servants in 2 Cor 5:19-21[18]); and as the transition to "life" (the the lifting of condemnation, the gift of the Spirit, freedom from sin and death and the flesh, in Rom 8:1-4).[19] Now, the use of ὑπέρ in cultic and catechetical formulas may reflect a comparable state of affairs. The word belongs to a fixed schema following words of sacrifice or dedication and is used to specify their beneficiaries. To be sure, it is not limited to this schema, but in formulaic usages and in usages that are nonformulaic but influenced by formulas, complete abstraction from the sphere of the expiatory is perhaps the exception rather than the rule.

This appears to find support in a survey of the thirty-odd texts on the death of Jesus that use ὑπέρ + gen. to signify the beneficiaries of the death.[20] A certain number of these ὑπέρ texts co-signify the expiatory character of the benefit. Five sets of texts in particular deserve attention, for they attest the expiation motif by allusion to Isa 53.

First, in eucharistic texts such as the word on the cup in Mark 14:24, τὸ αἷμά μου . . . τὸ ἐκχυννόμενον ὑπὲρ πολλῶν (see also Luke 22:20, τὸ ὑπὲρ ὑμῶν ἐκχυννόμενον; cf. Matt 26:28, τὸ περὶ πολλῶν ἐκχυννόμενον), the combination

---

[16]See the full discussion in Peter Stuhlmacher, "Recent Exegesis on Romans 3:24-26," in *Reconciliation, Law, and Righteousness* (see above, n.11) 94-109. Others, of course (notably S. Lyonnet), earlier urged the same view.

[17]Rom 5:1-11 sketches a קל וחמר argument: if, while we were still enemies of God, we have been reconciled to him by the death of his Son (ch. 1–4), then now that we have been made righteous, we shall the more surely be saved by sharing in his risen life (ch. 5–8). Since the if-clause is a reprise especially of Rom 3:21-26, the reference to being made righteous "by his blood" in 5:9 and to being "reconciled" in 5:10 resume the expiation theme in Rom 3:25.

[18]See Otfied Hofius, "Gott hat unter uns aufgerichtet," 3-9.

[19]What "the Law was unable to do" (Rom 8:3) was to *defeat* sin. Judgment as victory evokes משפט and משפטם in the Psalms and Prophets, where by metonymy God's "judgment" signifies his victory and reign in the restoration of Israel; see John Gray, *The Biblical Doctrine of the Reign of God* (Edinburgh: Clark, 1979) 66-71 and passim thereafter. This victory, according to Rom 8:3c, was achieved by God's sending of his Son περὶ ἁμαρτίας, as a sin offering (cf. LXX Lev 14:19, etc.) to win for all mankind the forgiveness of sins. Paul thus places expiation at the root of divine acquittal (Rom 8:1), liberation from "the law of sin and death" (Rom 8:2), and the fulfillment of the Law under the impulse given by the Spirit (Rom 8:4) to a life of love (cf. Rom 13:8-9).

[20]Mark 14:24; Luke 22:19,20; John 6:51; 10:11,15; 11:51,52; 15:13; 17:19; 18:14; Rom 5:6,8; 8:32; 14:15; 1 Cor 1:13; 11:24; 15:3; 2 Cor 5:14-15, 21; Gal 1:4; 2:20; 3:13; Eph 5:2, 25; 1 Thess 5:10 (v.l.); 1 Tim 2:6; Titus 2:14; Heb 2:9; 7:27; 10:12; 1 Pet 2:21; 3:18; 4:1 (v.l.); 1 John 3:16.

of "pour out" with the inclusive sense of "many"[21] clinches the reference to Isa 53:11-12. Ἐκχυννόμενον alludes to Isa 53:12 (הערה) and πολλοί to Isa 53:11-12 (רבים).[22] Likewise, John 6:51 ἡ σάρξ μού ἐστιν ὑπὲρ τῆς τοῦ κόσμου ζωῆς reflects the eucharistic words and, through them, Isa 53:12.[23]

Second, in the kerygmatic and confessional formula of 1 Cor 15:3-5, ὑπὲρ τῶν ἁμαρτιῶν ἡμῶν in v.3 evokes Isa 53:5 in the Hebrew text or the Targum (cf. Rom 4:25, where the allusion to Isa 53:5 is equally certain, but where διά + acc. is used rather than ὑπέρ + gen.).

Third, formulas connecting παραδιδόναι ἑαυτόν with ὑπέρ + gen. (Gal 2:20; Eph 5:2,25; cf. Rom 8:32; 4:25) reflect Targ Isa 53:5,12 or LXX Isa 53:6. The closely related formula διδόναι ἑαυτόν (or τὴν ψυχὴν αὐτοῦ) with ὑπέρ + gen. (Gal 1:4, 1 Tim 2:6; Titus 2:14, cf. Mark 10:45; Matt 20:28) evokes Isa 53:10 (שים נפשו).

Fourth, several texts with ἀποθανεῖν or παθεῖν and ὑπέρ + gen. reflect various verses in Isa 53 (Rom 5:6,8; 2 Cor 5:14-15; 1 Pet 2:21; 3:18).[24]

Fifth, reference to LXX Isa 53:10 (περὶ ἁμαρτίας) is found in Rom 8:3 and 2 Cor 5:21, of which the latter text exhibits the ὑπέρ formula.

---

[21]See below.

[22]The Hebrew text is presupposed, for though ערה in the niphal, piel, and hiphil = pour out/be poured out, the LXX never translates it by ἐκχεῖν/ἐκχύννεσθαι (cf. Gen 24:20; 2 Chron 24:11; Ps 141:8; Isa 32:15; 53:12).

[23]The correspondence of John 6:51 with Isa 53:11-12 has been mediated by the application motif in the eucharistic words inspired by the Isaian text. Originally attached to the word on the cup, as in Mark 14:24, this motif was soon transferred also to the word on the bread (see Luke 22:19), and in 1 Cor 11:24 is attested only for the word on the bread.

LUKE 22:19	1 COR 11:24	JOHN 6:51	MARK 14:24 (MATT 26:28)	ISA 53:10-12
τοῦτο	τοῦτο	ὁ ἄρτος δὲ ὃν ἐγὼ δώσω		
ἐστιν το	μού ἐστιν	ἡ σάρξ		
σῶμά μου	τὸ σῶμα	μού ἐστιν		
τὸ ὑπὲρ ὑμῶν	τὸ ὑπὲρ	ὑπὲρ τῆς τοῦ	ὑπὲρ πολλῶν	אשם . . .
δεδόμενον	ὑμῶν	κόσμου ζωῆς	(περὶ πολλῶ)	לרבים . . .
				חטאי־רבים

[24]On Rom 5:6,8: v.6 reflects the motif of the many as the undeserving wicked (Isa 53:5-6, 10-12); vv. 6 and 8 both reflect Isa 53:10 (שים נפשו). That Isa 53 has registered a decisive influence on Rom 5:6-11 is clear from the analysis of Hofius, "Erwägungen zur Gestalt," esp. 192-94 on Rom 5:10-11. On 2 Cor 5:14-15, see Hofius, "Erwägungen zur Gestalt," 196. Context urges that 1 Pet 2:21 be understood to derive from LXX Isa 53: the following verse, 1 Pet 2:22, cites Isa 53:9, and shortly thereafter 1 Pet 2:24 cites Isa 53:12. Again in 1 Pet 3:18 περὶ ἁμαρτιῶν reflects LXX Isa 53:10 (περὶ ἁμαρτίας) and δίκαιος ὑπὲρ ἀδίκων reflects LXX Isa 53:11-12 (δικαιῶσαι δίκαιον . . . πολλοῖς . . . ἁμαρτίας πολλῶν ἀνήνεγκεν).

There are accordingly fifteen texts or passages (Mark 14:24; Luke 22:20,[25] John 6:51; 1 Cor 15:3; Gal 2:20; Eph 5:2,25; Gal 1:4; 1 Tim 2:6; Titus 2:14; Rom 5:6-8; 2 Cor 5:14-15; 1 Pet 2:21; 3:18; 2 Cor 5:21), many of them liturgical or catechetical formulas or reflective of such formulas, independent of one another in terms of their immediate transmission history, in which ὑπέρ + gen. carries a sense defined by reference to Isa 53 as expiatory. Inasmuch as Isa 53 exploits and transforms the theme of the אשם offering, it would seem that Riesenfeld's thesis stands on solid ground.

The third and last item in Léon-Dufour's procedure that calls for comment is his treatment of words in relation to the meaning of symbolic acts. The eucharistic acts of Jesus are the culmination of a series of symbolic acts that began with his baptism in response to the call of the Baptist and continued through the whole of his career (choice and establishment of "the twelve"; sending out of the twelve; cures and exorcisms; dining with sinners; entry into Jerusalem and cleansing of the temple). One of the reasons why the acts involved in the cleansing of the temple have so baffled efforts of historical reconstruction is that the words accompanying them (Mark 11:17 keeps the Isaian reference to "a house of prayer for all nations"; in Matt 21:13 and Luke 19:46 the reference to the nations is dropped; in John 2:16 the word of Jesus is modified and no scriptural text is cited) seem to be open to the most diverse construals. But the intended role of Jesus' words, whether in the cleansing of the temple or at the Last Supper, is clear enough. They specify the meaning of the acts.

Now, Léon-Dufour has insisted on the unambiguous and compelling meaning of the eucharistic acts. Jesus provides for a new mode of presence among his followers. He gives himself to them as food and drink. The symbolism of the act—*le partage du pain eucharistique*—is virtually self-interpreting; hence, it is in function of this act that one is to understand the accompanying words.

> . . . the symbolism of food first of all suggests another interpretation [than that of the "one" victim for "all"]. The word immediately signifies: "I give you myself as food that you may have life": such, then, is the sense of "on your behalf," for if one eats, it is to live.

---

[25]I am taking the view that the eucharistic words in Luke 22 are not a rewriting of Mark 14:22-25, but an independent branch of tradition (but I leave open its relationship to 1 Cor 11). Cf. Joachim Jeremias, *Die Abendmahlsworte Jesu*, 3rd ed. (Göttingen: Vandenhoeck & Ruprecht, 1960) 149-50, 153-65 (ET *The Eucharistic Words of Jesus* [London: SCM, 1966] 156, 160-73).

A consequence should be specified. By this word Jesus does not announce that he is going to his death as a saving "means." . . .[26]

What follows from this reversal of roles, according to which the prima facie sense of the acts limits the possible sense of the words? It follows that the symbolic act of giving oneself as food to eat and drink practically rules out the foreign concept of expiation. True, Jesus' blood is "poured out"; but to pour out, argues Léon-Dufour, is not "cultic." Moreover, if the eucharistic words were to have a clearly cultic sense, the appropriate command would be, not to take and drink, but to take and sprinkle.

> The disciples are not invited to use the cup in order to sprinkle each other with the blood of Jesus, but simply to drink it. Hence, in place of the purification that sacrifices of expiation obtain through the sprinkling of blood, we truly have to do here with drink and vital growth.[27]

This fanciful line of reflection (to be met, oddly enough, in Friedrich's monograph also, though in somewhat different form)[28] hinges on an oversight, a failure to grasp the role of the eucharistic words as specifying the meaning both of the elements (the broken bread, the cup of wine) and of the acts of giving them to the disciples to eat and drink. Once this role is acknowledged, however, the crucial questions become (1) What were the original words? (2) How did they interpret the elements? (3) How accordingly did they interpret the distributing to eat and drink?

Supposing for a moment[29] that the Markan text approximates the original words more closely than any other, we may answer the second and third questions as follows. A first word related the bread to the body of Jesus soon to be put to death; a second word related the wine to the blood of Jesus soon to be shed, in fulfillment of two sacrificial "types": the sacrifice that seals the covenant and the expiatory death of the Servant of God for the sins of the world.[30] To give the disciples this bread to eat and this cup to drink was accordingly to give them a share in the eschatological covenant now defined by the imminent death of Jesus for the forgiveness of sins. As Jeremias put it, Jesus interpreted the bread and wine to signify his death for the "many."

> If, immediately following his words on the bread and immediately following his words on the wine, Jesus gives the same bread and the same wine to his

---

[26]Léon-Dufour, *Le partage du pain* (see above, n. 7) 146.

[27]Léon-Dufour, *Le partage du pain*, 169.

[28]Friedrich, *Verkündigung*, 55.

[29]See the treatment of Rudolf Pesch, presented below.

[30]In the saying on the cup, the word "blood" evokes Exod 24:8; "to be poured out" alludes to Isa 53:12 (הערה); cf. LXX Exod 24:6. On the universal reference of the Servant's suffering, see below.

disciples, this act signifies his giving them a share, by their eating and drinking, in the atoning power of his death.[31]

Jesus' symbolic words and acts contributed in complementary fashion to the actualizing of symbolic meaning. The words charged the acts of distributing and of eating and drinking with a precise significance, whereas the actual distributing of the bread and distributing of the wine and the actual eating and drinking thereof *enacted* the symbolic intention of the words. To eat and drink the eucharistic bread and wine was, indeed, as Léon-Dufour urged, to "live." But by evoking the motifs of covenant and expiation the eucharistic words specified "life" as a new fellowship or communion in purification from sin. It was a dispensation of forgiveness, the lifting of liability to condemnation—a change of destiny destined to be a wellspring of celebration for all time to follow.

Rudolf Pesch: Exposition and Critique

In 1978—so, four years earlier than the monographs of Friedrich and Léon-Dufour—Rudolf Pesch had already offered a sharply contrasting alternative to their views.[32] Taking his own stand in the tradition of exegetical and historical study of the eucharistic words inaugurated by Dalman and advanced by Jeremias,[33] Pesch clarified the analysis of two sets of texts (Mark-Matt and 1 Cor-Luke) by defining, more persuasively than had ever been done before, their literary genre. The genre of the Markan tradition, as well as of the Matthean tradition dependent on Mark, was historical narrative, originally conceived as part of the passion story. The genre of the tradition in 1 Cor 11:23-25 was cultic aetiology. Pesch took Luke's text (the long text) to be a mixed genre, dependent on Mark 14 and 1 Cor 11.

In support of the difference of genre between the Markan and Pauline versions, let the following selective summary of Pesch's points suffice. The Markan text (14:22-25) is embedded in the situation of the Passover meal of Jesus with his disciples (Mark 14:17-21,26). The addressees of the words on the bread and on the wine are the twelve. Narrative traits (introductory καί; narrative καὶ ἔδωκεν; the invitation λάβετε; narrative καὶ ἔπιον ἐξ αὐτοῦ πάντες, etc.) abound, whereas liturgical traits such as the anamnesis command (1 Cor 11:24c,25c) are absent. The Pauline text, on the other hand, is an independent literary unit. Reference to the original group of the disciples has been dropped, yielding to the "you" of the celebrating comminity. Narrative traits are lacking, whereas the aetiological

---

[31]Joachim Jeremias, *Abendmahlsworte*, 224-235 (ET *Eucharistic Words,* 233). The translation above is my own.

[32]See above, n. 6.

[33]Gustaf Dalman, *Jesus-Jeshua: Studies in the Gospels* (London: SPCK, 1929) 86-184. Jeremias, *Abendmahlsworte/Eucharistic Words.*

anamnesis is accented. The text is introduced asyndetically with a solemn liturgical notice (1 Cor 11:23). The so-called eschatological perspective, which in Mark 14:25 connects the meal situation with the imminent death of Jesus, is missing in Paul (though 1 Cor 11:26 makes the past event of Jesus' death a ground of intercession envisaging its complementary counterpart, the parousia).[34]

Mark presents a concrete setting (the last Passover meal of Jesus and his disciples) with its concrete dramatis personae. Paul rehearses a tradition that in part, at least, has left the concrete setting and its original figures behind, so functioning all the better as a model for liturgical celebration. Anchored in the original scene depicted, the elements of the Markan text as a whole (vv.22-24) are clearly narrative (26 narrative words, 17 spoken words for a ratio of 1.5 to 1). The Pauline text by contrast (23 narrative words, 34 spoken words for a ratio of .67 to 1) is a community-oriented liturgical libretto.[35] There is one imperative in Mark, λάβετε, belonging to the historic situation in which Jesus specifically invites the disciples (in contradistinction to himself) to "take" (i.e., and eat, cf. Matt 26:26). Two imperatives in Paul (ποιεῖτε . . . ποιεῖτε) envisage the celebrating community. Correspondingly, the following ὁσάκις γὰρ ἐάν ("as often as") (1 Cor 11:26) evokes the Lord's Supper as repeatable event. Once it is pointed out, this set of contrasts is obviously relevant to and, in fact, reflects and clinches the diversity of genre.

We have already given some intimation of how these generically distinct texts were genetically related; detailed comparison indicates the secondary origin of the cult-aetiology. For, here the more likely of the alternatives is that the Markan words of application on the cup (τὸ ἐκχυννόμενον ὑπὲρ πολλῶν) have been added to the word on the bread and made to refer immediately to those present (τὸ ὑπὲρ ὑμῶν, 1 Cor 11:24). Again, the covenant has become explicitly "the new covenant" (ἡ καινὴ διαθήκη) and it is no longer tied to the situation of Jesus' impending death, as in Mark 14:24. As we have already observed above, the word of Jesus prophesying his death (Mark 14:25) is now referred to the repeatable (ὁσάκις γὰρ ἐάν . . .) Lord's Supper, transposed into a memorial of his death and an anticipation of his parousia (1 Cor 11:26).

Pesch follows this analysis with separate treatments of the Pauline eucharistic tradition (originating, he conjectures, in translation for the Jerusalem ἑλληνισταί of the primitive Aramaic-speaking Jerusalem community's own liturgy) and of the Markan narrative text (taken to be the basis for inquiry into Jesus' own understanding of his death).[36]

---

[34]Pesch, *Das Abendmahl*, 34-51.
[35]*Das Abendmahl*, 35-36.
[36]*Das Abendmahl*, 54-55 on the likely origin of the aetiological text; 69-102 on Mark as point of departure for historical reconstruction.

This historical inquiry (pp. 69-102) results in confirmation of the purely narrative, non-aetiological genre of the Markan text and of its determining theme: Jesus' interpretation of his imminent death (see especially vv. 24-25 on the cup and on the prophecy of death). The elements of the immediate context all have this theme in view: see v. 8 on Jesus' coming burial; vv. 17-21 on the imminent betrayal; vv. 26-31 on imminent abandonment by the disciples, on the imminent denial of Peter, on the imminent fulfillment of the prophecy of the shepherd stricken and the sheep scattered in Zech 13:7; the amen-words of vv. 9, 18, 25, 30 and Son-of-man prophecies in vv. 21 and 41.

It is tempting to pause over the detailed treatment relating the eucharistic words in Mark to the Last Supper of the historical Jesus with his disciples and especially to the retrieval of Jesus' interpretation of his imminent death. Our present interest, however, centers even more on the ramifications of this treatment for historical-Jesus research in general.

Pesch's response to those who find Last Supper themes historically incompatible with Jesus' proclamation of God's unconditional mercy, "the reign of God," is most rewarding. He begins with John the Baptist and with Jesus' new, post-Johannite proclamation of news of salvation even for notorious sinners. Jesus' offer was free, but he did not conceive a positive response to it to be purely optional for Israel. On the contrary, the gracious proclamation was simultaneously a radical demand. On it hinged the status of Israel. Refusal would accordingly create an anomaly: The good news risked turning into a condemnation. Was the mediator of eschatological salvation to become, then, the mediator of eschatological ruin for Israel?[37]

Pesch sees Jesus' understanding of this conflict epitomized in the parable of the wicked husbandmen (Mark 12:1-9). What was to be the fate of those who would reject (even kill!) the last messenger of God? The question calls to mind the so-called "unpardonable sin," i.e., the refusal of pardon. What could be done for the refuser in this situation of refusal? Pesch locates the resolution of this issue in Jesus' act of intending his death as expiatory for Israel.[38]

So far from competing with the good news of the reign of God, this intention maintained and enhanced it—against the grim consequences otherwise entailed by Israel's refusal. Conceived biblically, expiation was not a "demand" incompatible with "grace"; it was pure grace. Moreover, the intention of Jesus respecting his death generated a new consequence of its own: the institution of the new covenant.

This summarizes Pesch's retrieval of the controlling perspective of Jesus, his final response to refusal. There follow three historical corollaries, all bearing on the role of the expiation motif in accounting historically for post-Paschal develop-

---

[37]*Das Abendmahl,* 103-105.
[38]*Das Abendmahl,* 105-109.

ments: (a) the renewal of the mission to Israel; (b) the adoption of the baptismal rite now conceived as baptism εἰς τὸ ὄνομα 'Ιησοῦ = יֵשׁוּעַ לְשֵׁם = with reference to Jesus; (c) the universal saving efficacy of Jesus' death.

Following their "Easter experience," the disciples did not, like the Qumran covenanters, settle down in expectation of the condemnation soon to overtake Israel at large. Rather, they launched a new mission to Israel. What gave them the impulse and authority to place this act? The apostolic kerygma provides a key: "Christ died for our sins according to the scriptures" (1 Cor 15:3). It belonged to early Christian faith that in the death of Christ God had made expiation on behalf of Israel for the rejection of its Messiah. Israel could benefit from this act only by accepting it. The faith of the Easter community (1 Cor 15:3) led its leaders to offer Israel a new chance of conversion.[39] But no grounding of this faith is plausible other than Jesus' own intention, expressed at the last Passover meal with his disciples. Thus, Jesus' interpretation of his death is something like a "missing link" in the historical explanation of the renewed mission of the disciples to Israel.

Similarly, the expiatory intention of Jesus throws new light on the historical riddle of the post-Paschal Christian adoption of baptism. It is evident that the mission to gather the true Israel before the impending day of judgment was a "constant" or invariable in the life of the Easter community. In this situation, so like the situation which the Baptist understood himself to address, the community of Jesus' disciples seized on baptism as the proper instrument for the ingathering of Israel. But now baptism was reconceived in the light of the expiatory death of Jesus and his Resurrection from the dead. By being baptized Israel would find a share in the atoning and saving power of the Paschal mysteries. Once again, early Christian consciousness of Jesus' intentions respecting his own death illuminates a historically puzzling primitive Christian policy.[40]

The book ends with an all too brief and sketchy effort to correlate the expiatory death of Jesus with its universal efficacy. Pesch's embarrassment at this point derives, no doubt, from his having chosen to understand the phrase in Mark 14:24 ὑπὲρ πολλῶν (cf. Matt 26:28) in the sense of "on behalf of all Israel." He has argued that in the tradition of Jewish interpretation generally, "the many" in Isa 53:11-12 were understood as "all Israel." Three factors, however, seem to me to tell against the conclusion that this settles Jesus' own interpretation and usage.

The first is not a compelling factor, but it is an essential one, for it has to do with whether סַגִּיאִין ("many, the many") in the Aramaic of Jesus' day was an expression easily intelligible in the inclusive sense of "all (human beings)." The answer is yes, for it is beyond doubt that the "many" of Matt 8:11 (cf. Luke 13:29)

---

[39]*Das Abendmahl,* 112-13.
[40]*Das Abendmahl,* 115-22.

are the peoples of the whole Gentile world.[41]

The second factor is that in the original text of Isaiah and probably in Enoch as well (cf. 1 Enoch 46:4-5; 48:8; 55:4; 62:1-9; 63:1-11), "the many" of Isa 52:14-15 are the Gentile peoples and their kings; but, unless the text is entirely lacking in structural cohesion, the many of Isa 52:14-15 and the many of Isa 53:11-12 are identical.

The third and decisive factor is that where the formula of Mark 14:24 par. (cf. Mark 10:45 par.) is rendered in equivalent terms elsewhere in the New Testament, "the many" are all mankind. Thus, John 6:51 renders the tradition by the phrase "for the life of the world."[42] 1 Tim 2:6 is of exceptional importance here, for it offers so clearly a word-for-word transposition of the saying in Mark 10:45 ("to give his life as a ransom for many") as follows: "who gave himself as a ransom for all."[43] Nowhere in the New Testament do we find any hint that the many in Isa 52-53 and Mark 10:45 par./14:24 par. refers only to Israel.

Apart from this disagreement over "the many," there are inevitably many details in Pesch's reconstruction that remain open to question. The main thrust of his work nevertheless seems to me to remain intact. Whether the Markan version is itself the primitive form of the eucharistic words, this nonaetiological text presents itself in any case as the earliest available evidence of the Last Supper. Pesch's genre-analysis is a cardinal forward step. He has added to the probability of the historicity of the eucharistic words. He has shown how they represented Jesus' last word on his imminent repudiation (ἀποδοκιμασθῆναι) by the chief priests and elders and scribes. He has vindicated the compatibility of the eucharistic words with the public proclamation and public acts of Jesus. He has illustrated the historical productiveness of the expiation motif in the eucharistic words by showing how it illuminated such post-Paschal developments as the renewed mission to Israel, the adoption of baptism, the radical openness to the Gentiles.

This, moreover, seems to me to be only the beginniing of the historical light to be thrown on the gospels by this climactic esoteric tradition. As climactic, it clarifies the entire esoteric tradition beginning with Mark 8:31-33 parr. as well as the continuous symbolic acts of entry into Jerusalem and the cleansing of the temple.

---

[41]*Das Abendmahl*, 115-22.

[42]See Joachim Jeremias, *Jesus' Promise to the Nations* (London: SCM, 1958) 55-56. Jacques Dupont, " 'Beaucoup viendront du levant et du couchant . . . ' (Matthieu 8,11-12; Luc 13.28-29)." *ScEccl* 9 (1967): 153-67.

[43]See Jeremias, *Abenmahlsworte*, 173-74 (ET *Eucharistic Words*, 181-82). (Obviously, Israel is preeminently included among the "all.")

Carrying Pesch's Work Forward
by Reflecting Backward on Jesus' Career

Let the nature and direction of the argument be clear: If Pesch's ascertainments on the Last Supper are correct, new light is cast on other thematically charged traditions, especially the esoteric traditions that lead up to it, but not only them. The thematic motifs principally in question are the identity/eschatological destiny of Jesus and the divine scenario in which he is the central, eschatological figure. Both of these themes were fundamental to the eucharistic words.

If, on the model of the Isaian Servant (Isa 53), Jesus at the Last Supper understood his imminent death to be expiatory for Israel and the world, and if he understood the new covenant evoked by the prophets (Jer 31) and longed for the pious (Bar 2:35) to be about to be sealed by his own death, then we must infer that whatever the further determining particulars of his self-understanding, they included this fundamental feature: He was the climactic and definitive fulfiller of the hopes of Israel.

Again, if Jesus understood that the expiatory and covenantal sacrifice of his life would be followed by the eschatological banquet at which he would drink the new wine of salvation with his disciples, then whatever the further determining particulars of the divine scenario for the eschaton, it exhibited this basic pattern: woe followed by weal, the woe of Israel's savior slain, the weal of his restoration with the coming of the reign of God.

The thematic clasps defining the so-called "central section" in Mark and its parallels and the originally unified sequence of the entry into Jerusalem, the cleansing of the temple, and the subsequent clash with the authorities over the authority of Jesus are now seen to add "further determining particulars" to the Last Supper traditions. These particulars are significant. They include (still under the headings of Jesus' self-understanding and of the eschatological scenario) the motifs (a) Jesus the Messiah; (b) [the Son of man] who would suffer and be glorified; (c) the temple in God's holy intention versus the temple in man's sinful practice; the temple (Luke 21:5) or temple buildings (οἰκοδομαί, Mark 13:1-2; par. Matt 24:1) destined for ruin; and the sanctuary to be destroyed versus the sanctuary to be built in (or after) three days.

Mark's central section (Mark 8:27–10:45 [52]; par. Matt 16:13–20:20 [34]; cf. Luke 9:18-50) derives its thematic coherence from its beginning, from its repetitions of Jesus' predictions of death and vindication, and from its end. It opens with Simon's confession of Jesus as Messiah; this is followed by Jesus' prophecy of imminent repudiation, suffering, death, and glorification "after three days" (with variant expressions in Matthew and Luke). The theme of Jesus' imminent repudiation and suffering generates related motifs. The first is a new call to discipleship[44] (Mark 8:34; par. Matt 16:24; Luke 9:23), an invitation to Jesus' disciples—now, equivalently, the messianic עֲנָוִים (poor/lowly)—to enter into the frightening mystery of his destiny. There follows a baffling issue expressed in riddle (Mark 8:35; parr. Matt 16:25; Luke 9:24) and question (Mark 8:36; parr. Matt 16:26; Luke 9:25): What can a man give in return for his life? The classic answer was "nothing" (Ps 49:8). But the end of the central section yielded a new answer. No one can buy life. But he, Jesus, can give life, ransoming the world by his death (Mark 10:45; par. Matt 20:28).

In the light of the eucharistic words the theme of Jesus' messiahship appears as no more than a particular and appropriate specification of the status and role of Jesus. Furthermore, recent American research has shown that in late second-temple Judaism the theme of messiahship served as a rallying point for the Palestinian peasantry.[45] The result has been to recover the context in which a gospel tradition such as that of the Galilean crowd following Jesus that intended "to make him king" (John 6:15) is both intelligible and plausible. This same recovery of context assures us of the historical intelligibility of Jesus' act of entry into Jerusalem in a manner charged with biblical symbolism. Again, Marinus de Jonge's reconsideration of Markan materials and structure and of the use of "anointed" in contemporary Jewish sources has shown that the activity recounted in Mark 1-8 could very well have grounded the conclusion and confession of Simon.[46]

If the historicity and meaning of the eucharistic words lend a certain radical intelligibility to Jesus' self-understanding as Messiah, that messianic consciousness, in turn, bears positively on the Last Supper through the mass of ancient traditions that connected Passover not only with the Exodus but with the advent of messianic redemption. Dalman made these traditions an inalienable part of scholarship on the Last Supper[47] and, of course, much has been done since Dalman.[48]

---

[44]This supposes that the confession of Simon was the hidden turning point in Jesus' career and that the revelation of his destiny to his disciples immediately followed it. Pointing in the same direction is the deft translation of this verse offered by Paul Joüon, *L'évangile de Notre-Seigneur Jésus-Christ,* 3rd ed. (Paris: Beauchesne, 1930) 107: "Les deux verbes ἐλθεῖν ὀπίσω et ἀκολουθεῖν ont exactement le même sens 'suivre.' . . . Le sens est donc 'Si quelqu'un veut me *suivre,* qu'il se renonce lui-même, qu'il prenne sa croix et qu'(ainsi) il me suive."

[45]See R. A. Horsley and J. S. Hanson, *Bandits, Prophets, and Messiahs* (Minneapolis: Winston, 1985).

[46]M. De Jonge, "The Earliest Christian Use of *Christos.* Some Suggestions," *NTS* 32 (1986): 321-43.

[47]G. Dalman, *Jesus-Jeshua* (London: SPCK, 1929) 86-184.

[48]Matthew Black, *An Aramaic Approach to the Gospels and Acts,* 3rd ed. (Oxford: Clarendon, 1967) 236-38. Earlier: (Hermann L. Strack and) Paul Billerbeck, *Kommentar zum NT aus Talmud und Midrasch,* 6 vols. (Munich: Beck, 1922–1928) 4/1:41-76, esp. 54-76. Also, Markus Barth, *Das Mahl des Herrn* (Neukirchen-Vluyn: Neukirchener

As for the Son-of-man theme, there is little point here in going over the current state of the question on the title, but it is worth remarking that, quite apart from the use of בר אנשא ("Son of man") with reference to Jesus' destiny of suffering (and glorification),[49] the eucharistic words make previous communication by Jesus to the disciples on his coming destiny intelligible, appropriate, and plausible. The same should be said of the new call to discipleship and of the ransom-word, for the historicity of which Peter Stuhlmacher has presented a new and persuasive argument.[50]

The most overlooked feature of the complex of traditions on the cleansing of the temple has been that the accounts have left unmistakable traces in the tradition of having been a dangerous memory resolutely toned down by the evangelists. For over fifty years, from Maurice Goguel in 1928 to the present, e.g., A. E. Harvey (in 1982) and E. P. Sanders (in 1985)[51] the exactly opposite hypothesis has been repeatedly urged. To Goguel the historical matrix of the narratives on the cleansing of the temple may have been "some words of protest that, in the gospel narratives, have been transposed into acts."[52] Harvey was unable to make historical sense of any of the words attributed to Jesus in explanation of the cleaning.[53] He suggested that for his symbolic purposes Jesus "need have attacked only one or two stalls."[54] Like Harvey, Sanders adopted the common view that the cleansing (so-called) was a symbolic act, but he made the distinctive point that it was a purely symbolic act, i.e., that it had no purpose on a pragmatic level, and so was not a cleansing at all.[55] But, like Harvey, Sanders was puzzled by particulars in the texts and, where they did not fit his theory of pure symbolism, e.g. the detail that Jesus "would not allow anyone to carry anything through the temple" (Mark 11:16), he let them drop from consideration.[56]

Verlag, 1987) 20-51.

[49]It is nonetheless worth considering the hypothesis of Joachim Jeremias on the reconstructed original and deliberately ambiguous text behind Mark 9:31; parr. Matt 17:22; Luke 9:44, namely, מתמסר בר אנשא לידי בני אנשא: "Man/the Man is [about to be] delivered [by God] into the hands of men." See Jeremias, *New Testament Theology.* Part 1. *The Proclamation of Jesus,* trans. John Bowden, NTL (London: SCM; New York: Scribner's, 1971) 282.

[50]Stuhlmacher, "Vicariously Giving His Life for Many, Mark 10:45 (Matt 20:28)," in his *Reconciliation, Law, and Righteousness* (n. 11 above), 16-29.

[51]M. Goguel, "La Parole de Jésus sur la destruction et la reconstruction du Temple," in *Congres d'histoire du christianisme,* vol. 1, ed. P. L. Couchoud (Paris: Rieder; Amsterdam: Van Holkema & Warendorf's, 1928) 117-36; A. E. Harvey, *Jesus and the Constraints of History* (Philadelphia: Westminster, 1982); E. P. Sanders, *Jesus and Judaism* (London: SCM; Philadelphia: Fortress, 1985).

[52]Goguel, "La Parole de Jésus," 123.

[53]Harvey, *Jesus and the Constraints,* 132-33.

[54]*Jesus and the Constraints,* 131.

[55]Sanders, *Jesus and Judaism,* 61-69.

[56]*Jesus and Judaism,* 363-64n1.

Pragmatic purpose, however, is not to be denied. John's account makes explicit what all the accounts imply: Passionate protest powered the event (John 2:17). To determine the precise object of this protest we might begin by observing that Jesus stood well outside the world of scribal halaka. He allowed what the scribes forbade (e.g., on food and Sabbath regulations) and forbade what they allowed. Unlike the scribes, Jesus did not acquiesce in any of life's routine disorders—the routine use of oaths (Matt 5:34-37), routine verbal abuse (Matt 5:22), what one might call routine concupiscence (Matt 5:28). He fiercely protested against halakic appeal meant to circumvent obligations, e.g., the spuriously pious refusal to help parents in need (Mark 7:10-12; par. Matt 15:3-6) or the taken-for-granted concessions to human frailty like divorce and remarriage (Mark 10:2-12; par. Matt 19:3-12). He warned that the heedlessly slanderous word would be remembered at the judgment (Matt 12:36-37) and that sins of speech were the epitome of uncleanness (Mark 7:15; par. Matt 15:11). In brief, he censured the shifts and dodges of *l'homme moyen sensuel,* which Israel like the world at large simply accepted as part of the human condition.

There is a pragmatic observation not infrequently met in discussions of the cleansing of the temple, namely, that money changers were needed to provide Tyrian coinage in accord with temple policy and that, if the temple was to have a sacrificial system at all, it was essential that birds and animals for sacrifice be ready to hand. The observation is helpful in a way not always suspected: It retrieves the tolerant mentality of the temple practices against which Jesus passionately protested. The object of the protest was routine irreverence pragmatically sanctioned by authority. Authorities and populace alike tolerated the installation of tables and stalls on the temple pavilion itself. At the same time, the Mishnah calls for reverence touching the entire holy precinct of the temple; hence the protest, like that of Jesus, against commercial or any other use of the temple court as a shortcut between Ophel and the eastern suburbs (m. Ber.9:5). This secures the context for the detail of Mark 11:16, and so clinches the "protest" and "cleansing" character of the event. The word of Jesus contrasting the temple in God's holy intention ("a house of prayer," and indeed "a house of prayer [destined] for all peoples," Isa 56:7) with the temple in man's sinful history ("a den of robbers," not, of course, in the proper sense of these words, but in the hyperbolic sense that roughly corresponds to that of Jer 7:11: "Has this house, which is called by my name, become a den of robbers in your eyes?") makes perfectly good sense in view of Jesus' well-attested stance on routine sinfulness.

That we have to do, in the cleansing of the temple, with symbolic action is beyond reasonable doubt. According to a fixed, age-old Near-Eastern structure of symbols, royal acclamation is followed by the new king's establishment or restoration of cult.[57] The acclamation belonged to the entry narrative. Form critically, the entry narrative is a legend. Stylistically, it is marked by folkloric (Mark 11:1-6; parr. Matt 21:1-6; Luke 19:28-32) and midrashic (Mark 11:9a; parr. Matt 21:9a; John 12:13)[58] motifs. The probability of historicity is nevertheless supported by the semantic bond referred to above. This bond could be severed, as the gospel of John shows, but it is clear from the synoptic tradition that the two events—entry and cleansing—derive from one matrix and were originally elements of a single symbolic structure.

The entry motifs were inescapably royal and calculated to evoke biblical traditions, particularly that of the king celebrated in Zech 9:9, "lowly and riding upon an ass." Though the cleansing scene itself featured no established messianic motif, there are reasons for relating it to messianism. In Israel, as Roland de Vaux has shown, temple-building and the tasks of establishing, maintaining, and restoring the cult were reserved to the king, as in Mesopotamia.[59] The combination of the entry and the cleansing symbolically evoked a climactic renewal. The epiphany of the royal son of David signalled the advent of the age to come. This symbolism, to be sure, exhibited an open, unfinished structure, for it did not specify the character or content of eschatological cult. This open structure would not find its concrete fulfillment until the Last Supper, for it was to be at that Last Supper that a central correlate of the reign of God, namely, the new covenant, would be defined, and the central ritual act of the new covenant be given form.

The cleansing of the temple, then, has been widely misjudged for three reasons. First, the evangelists themselves have very sharply reduced its dimensions with a view to forestalling the interpretation of Jesus as a revolutionary. This is true of Mark, who represents Jesus as acting alone, despite the fact that his disciples' collaboration was doubtless entailed by the prohibition expressed in Mark 11:16. Matthew and Luke have further reduced the event, each giving a two-verse account and neither acknowledging the causal nexus of the event to the conspiracy against and arrest of Jesus (contrast Mark 11:18). Finally, John has altogether removed the cleansing of the temple from the prologue to the passion story.

---

[57]See Joachim Jeremias, *Jesus als Weltvollender* (Gütersloh: Bertelsmann, 1930) 35-42, on Marduk and the Babylonian new year; enthronement and cult renewal among the biblical kings; eschatological myth in 1 Enoch and 4 Ezra 9 and 10; application to the gospel texts on entry and cleansing; interpretation of the sanctuary riddle in terms of (a) the eschatological ordeal and (b) the playing off the destruction of the sanctuary (of the Jerusalem temple) against the parousia and its attendant revelation of the transfigured community.

[58]Jeremias, *Eucharistic Words*, 256-60, on the midrash on Ps. 118.

[59]Roland De Vaux, *Ancient Israel*. Vol. 1, *Social Institutions*; vol. 2, *Religious Institutions* (New York: McGraw-Hill, 1961) 1:113-14; 2:320-29.

Second, many interpreters, insofar as they have been in basic accord not with the sensibility of recoil from routine irreverence but with precisely that all-too-human pragmatic mentality that Jesus censured, have been unable to lay hold of the event at the level of pragmatic purpose, i.e., as a "cleansing." Again, they have created needless difficulties for themselves respecting the explanatory words, essentially quite intelligible, with which Jesus accompanied his actions.

Third, whereas all Jerusalem could feel and register something of the symbolic thrust of the event—the Messiah had entered onto the scene and his task necessarily included the eschatological restoration of cult—the fulfilling complement that would finally lay bare the cult appropriate to eschatologically restored Israel was not spelled out in the public forum. It would be revealed to Jesus' intimate disciples on the night he was betrayed.

In the synoptic tradition, the entry into Jerusalem and the cleansing of the temple are followed by the question about Jesus' authority (Mark 11:27-33; parr. Matt 21:23-27; Luke 20:1-8). It is remarkable, however, that none of the synoptists connects it immediately with the cleansing. Moreover, as it stands, the question about authority portrays a peculiarly undramatic, halakic tone. By contrast, John presents the cleansing as immediately followed by the demand of "the Jews" for a sign that would vindicate Jesus' intolerable pretention to authority. That John has retained the original context of the riddle on the sanctuary, though hardly provable, is not at all improbable.

The original wording of the riddle is perhaps irrecoverable. The subtraction of Markan redactional touches (Mark 14:58) would yield

I will destroy this sanctuary
and in three days I will build another.

The main problem felt by Mark and Matthew as well as by modern readers has had to do with the words "I will destroy" (ἐγὼ καταλύσω = אֲנָא סתר). Matthew offers "I am able to destroy" (δύναμαι καταλῦσαι, which need not suppose any different Aramaic substratum). In John's version Jesus says: "Destroy this sanctuary and . . . , " in which the imperative has conditional force,[60] and this may reflect the actual words of Jesus. Jesus had told his closest circle of disciples that not one stone of the temple buildings would be left upon another, but he had by no means attributed this aspect of the imminent eschatological ordeal to his own agency.

The second line of the riddle presents fewer difficulties. Behind it stood the oracle of Nathan, the classic source of royal messianism (2 Sam 7:13-14), making the building of the sanctuary the task of David's son. A Qumran text (4QFlor 1-13) offers a messianic reading of the oracle, though without specifically thematizing a

---

[60]K. Beyer, *Semitische Syntax im Neuen Testament I. Satzlehre, Teil I,* SUNT 1 (Göttingen: Vandenhoeck & Ruprecht, 1962) 1/1:252.

messianic building of the sanctuary. The riddle of Jesus in any case brings together (a) the eschatological ordeal epitomized in the destruction of the sanctuary, (b) the short time, "three days," between the outbreak of the ordeal and its resolution,[61] and (c) the resolution, epitomized in Jesus' fulfillment of the messianic function (cf. Zech 6:12-13) of building the new sanctuary. In one sense the swiftly sketched scenario adds little to that already settled by the eucharistic words. On the other hand, the specificity of the motif of the new sanctuary, which seamlessly correlates with that of the new covenant, significantly strikes the messianic note. Further, the three-days motif adds a certain specificity to the many parallel data in the gospels which suppose the imminent saving consummation of history.[62]

What is the moral of this story of correlations between the eucharistic words and gospel texts on Jesus from Caesarea Philippi on? It seems to be this: If one establishes the meaning and historicity of the eucharistic words in the manner described above, the gospel accounts including the confession near Caesarea Philippi, the predictions of the passion, the entry into Jerusalem, the cleansing of the temple, the riddle on the new sanctuary and other temple texts are endued with enhanced coherence and historical probability. This enhancement depends on our having ascertained something of Jesus' intentions respecting his death. He incorporated his death into his mission by intending it as covenant sacrifice and expiatory offering. The first (Jer 31:31-34) implied as the goal of his mission the eschatological restoration of the people of God, correlative to the advance presence of the reign of God. The second (Isa 53) took the Isaian Servant as a "type" to be realized: expiation on behalf of Israel and the peoples. This second dimension penetrated, broadened, and deepened the first. In life and in death Jesus was bent on a mission of reconciliation "for the life of the world" (John 6:51d).[63]

---

[61]The "three-days" motif denotes a short time but does not necessarily put the main accent on this shortness. See J. Jeremias, "Die Drei-Tage-Worte der Evangelien," in *Tradition und Glaube: Das frühe Christentum in seiner Umwelt. Festgabe für Karl Georg Kuhn zum 65. Geburtstag,* ed. Gert Jeremias, H.-W. Kuhn, and H. Stegemann (Göttingen: Vandenhoeck & Ruprecht, 1971) 221-29.

[62]That the consummation was coming soon: (a) the "this generation" texts (Mark 13:30; parr. Matt 24:34; Luke 21:32; Matt. 23:36); (b) Mark 9:1; (c) Matt 10:23; (d) Matt 26:64 (ἀπ' ἄρτι = מעתה = soon, Luke 22:69); (e) the sign of the coming consummation is "this present moment" (Luke 12:56); (f) the present of Jesus' career was itself borrowed time (Luke 13:6-9); (g) heedless Israel stood in imminent danger, like a bird about to be snared (Luke 21:34). Precisely thematizing the divine abbreviation of the ordeal: Mark 13:20 par. Matt 24:22.

[63]See above, n. 23.

Peter and Paul, and the Tradition concerning "The Lord's Supper" in 1 Corinthians 11:23-26

William R. Farmer

Since World War I there has been a widespread tendency, especially in circles open to form criticism, to accept the judgment of Rudolf Bultmann that there is no longer any need to prove that a "cult legend" lies behind the synoptic tradition concerning the Lord's Supper. As astonishing as it may seem, Bultmann was able to defend this judgment without any reference to, let alone any discussion of, the crucial textual evidence preserved in 1 Cor 11:23-26. (Not so Joachim Jeremias, who always considered the relevant synoptic texts in close relationship to their parallel in 1 Cor 11:23-26.) The purpose of this essay is to demonstrate the critical wisdom of beginning a discussion of the authenticity of the eucharistic texts, by first undertaking a discussion of 1 Cor 11:23-26, where we can consider the question of authenticity in the context of the history of pre-Pauline tradition preserved in Paul's letters and with special attention to the historical and theological relationships between the apostles Peter and Paul.

With reference to the Lord's Supper Paul wrote as follows.

> The tradition which I handed on to you [concerning the Lord's Supper], originated with the Lord himself. That tradition is [I need not remind you] that, "The Lord Jesus, during the night in which he was delivered up, took bread. And after giving thanks, he broke it and said, 'This is my body, which is for you; do this in remembrance of me.' In the same way, after supper he took the cup, saying 'This cup is the new covenant in my blood. Do this, as often as you drink it, in remembrance of me. For as often as you eat this bread and drink the cup, you proclaim the death of the Lord, until he comes." (1 Cor 11:23-26)

The relationship between Peter and Paul is constitutive of the history of the primitive Christian community. In order to understand this relationship and its importance for understanding the origin and significance of 1 Cor 11:23-26, we can begin by asking, "By what authority does the Apostle to the Gentiles assure the

Corinthian church that the tradition concerning the Lord's Supper he had received and had in turn passed on to them, originated with Jesus himself?" Paul would never have claimed that he was an eyewitness to what happened during the night in which Jesus was delivered up. Nor can we understand him to be claiming that this is a tradition that had been revealed to him verbally by revelation from the risen Christ. All the technical terminology used by Paul indicates that this tradition like that concerning the Resurrection appearances he mentions later (15:3-7), has been handed on as a well formulated statement in the conventional manner of the time.[1]

It is most likely that, in the first instance, Paul received these vital traditions he passed on to his churches from the church he had persecuted before he became a Christian. But in matters as important as these, it is not unlikely that Paul took pains to be sure about what he was authorizing his churches to receive as tradition concerning the normative events of the Gospel.

In the case of the tradition concerning the Resurrection appearances, Paul had his own direct experience of the risen Christ to serve as a control by which to judge the tradition he had received. And it is clear that he knows, or at least firmly believes, that the appearance of the risen Lord to him is of the same order as that to the other apostles.

Paul tells the Corinthians that most of the over five hundred brethren to whom the Lord appeared on a single occasion were still alive at the time of writing (15:6). While it is possible, indeed probable, that Paul had the opportunity both preceding and following his conversion, to discuss the Resurrection of Jesus with some of these Christians, this would hardly have satisfied the unquestioned concern for truth regarding events of the past that were decisive for the pastoral and theological task of expediting the gospel, which we know motivated Paul (cf. Gal 1:20; 2:5, 14).

Since the tradition he had received concerning the Resurrection placed Peter and the twelve at the beginning of the series of Resurrection appearances, to have discussed these appearances with Peter would have been of importance to Paul. Did Paul have the opportunity to hear anything directly from Peter on these matters, or on matters bearing on Paul's belief that the Resurrection appearances to Peter and the other apostles were of the same order as his? The answer is, he certainly did.

Galatians

In his letter to the churches of Galatia, Paul informs his readers that three years after his conversion he went up (from Damascus) to Jerusalem to visit (or get to know) Peter. And he adds that he remained with Peter fifteen days (Gal 1:18).

---

[1]See Birger Gerhardsson, *The Origins of the Gospel Traditions* (Philadelphia: Fortress Press, 1978).

In order to begin to comprehend the far-reaching consequences of this meeting it is necessary to answer certain questions. Granted that Paul presumably wanted to make contact with church authorities in Jerusalem (he did see James, for example), why did he go to Peter? And why did he remain with Peter fifteen days? In this connection we need to ask what we can learn from a philological analysis of the text about the probable parameters of Paul's purpose or purposes in undertaking this history-making trip.

In answering these questions we face three main tasks: the first is to ascertain as best we can what Paul had been doing during the three year period between his return to Damascus mentioned in v. 17 and his visit to Peter referred to in v. 18; the second is to determine the most probable meaning in this context of the verb Paul used that is generally rendered in English by "to visit" or "to get to know"; and the third is to analyze the verbal phrase "and I remained with him" in relation to the temporal phrase "for fifteen days."

The first task presents no great difficulties. Paul tells us in v. 21 that after he had finished his business in Jerusalem he set out for the regions of Syria and Cilicia, and that at that time he was still unknown by face to the churches of Christ in Judea (v. 22). What these churches knew about him was only what they could learn from the reports they heard about him, and these reports were to the effect that "the one who formerly persecuted us, now preaches the faith he formerly ravished" (v. 23). To which Paul simply adds: "And they (i.e. those whom Paul formerly persecuted) glorified God in me" (v. 24). Where were these Christians who glorified God in Paul?

Beginning in v. 16 Paul tells his readers that (contrary to what they may have heard from others) following his conversion he did not immediately confer with flesh and blood, nor did he go up to Jerusalem to (make contact with) those who were apostles before him, but rather he went away into Arabia, and then (without specifying how long he remained in Arabia) he adds: "and I returned again to Damascus" (v. 17). This clearly implies that Paul had been in or near Damascus at the time of his conversion. Since the churches of Christ in Judea did not know Paul by face, but only by reports they heard from others, it is clear that Paul had been preaching the Gospel in some area outside Judea during the three-year interval in question, and it presents the least difficulty if we conclude that he had been doing this in and around Damascus, or perhaps more broadly in the general area of southern Syria. It had to be in some place outside Judea, some place where his earlier persecuting activity was still vividly remembered and could be existentially juxtaposed to his present activity.

Since in v. 21 Paul writes that upon leaving Jerusalem he went into the region of Syria and Cilicia, and then includes not one word about what he did for the next fourteen years before returning to Jerusalem for the apostolic conference of Gal 2:1-10, we are to conclude that the terse phrase "into the regions of Syria and

Cilicia" is directional and that Paul is opening up a new phase of his missionary career that at least in its initial stage was to see him through the Cilician gates. Paul would in any case most probably have come into Galatia from Cilicia. Once the Galatians came to know Paul they would have had reason to follow his career with interest. But where Paul had been before he came to Galatia from Syria and Cilicia would have been relatively vague to them. The one thing they did not know and needed to get straight was Paul's earliest contacts with the Jerusalem-based apostles. This explains Paul's relatively detailed account on this point. From this account we can infer a great deal more than he explicitly tells us.

From our analysis we conclude that during the three years in question, Paul had been preaching the gospel outside Judea in an area of his former persecuting activity, and that during this period of evangelization he had laid the groundwork for beginning a westward mission to the Gentiles. His going to Jerusalem of necessity must have proceeded from the reality of these three years of preaching and from his decision to embark on this far-reaching mission.

To Visit Cephas

In v. 18 Paul explains that he went up to Jerusalem to visit Peter. The verb used is ἱστορῆσαι which in this case can be best understood if we begin with its cognate noun form ἵστωρ. The ἵστωρ in ancient Greece functioned as examiner and arbiter in legal matters. He was learned in the law and skilled in examining witnesses. He knew how to ask the right questions of people who were being examined in order to ascertain the truth in matters of dispute. The truth he was after was not philosophical truth in some abstract metaphysical sense, but rather the kind of truth that can issue in practical wisdom. In the final analysis the ἵστωρ would be called upon to make a judgment. The ἵστωρ was a judge.

The first Greek historians were geographers who explored the great rivers that emptied into the known seas. Having penetrated inland as far as they could safely travel, they would then interrogate people who had come down these rivers from further inland to get from them eyewitness accounts about the unexplored sources of the great rivers running further back up into the unknown interiors of the continents. These same Greeks would question the priests living in the temples which were supported by these ancient river cultures, about records kept in the temples, about the genealogies of the local kings, and the customs of the local inhabitants. The reports of these geographers constituted the beginnings of what came to be called "history."

The verb ἱστορῆσαι can mean to inquire into or about a thing, or to inquire about a person. Or it can also mean to "examine" or to "observe." Such a questioner or observer would then become "one who is informed" about something, or "one who knows."

In the case at hand the verb is used with the accusative of person, so that it can mean to "inquire of" or "to ask." One can inquire of an oracle. Lexicographers are led to place our text in this context and cite Gal 1:18 as follows: *"visit a person for the purpose of inquiry,* Κηφᾶν." Such a meaning equivalent is contextually preferable to those one generally finds in English translations: RSV "visit"; NEB "get to know"; Goodspeed "become acquainted with"; or the *Amplified New Testament* "become (personally) acquainted with." Even the paraphrase "visit Cephas *for the purpose of inquiry*" is lexicographically limited in that it fails to suggest as strongly as it might the well-established usages "examine" and "observe," both of which are faithful to the function of the ἵστωρ and open up rich possibilities for understanding what Paul meant and how his readers would have understood his phrasing in this instance.

The linguistic evidence examined thus far by no means limits us to a view that Paul meant to suggest that he had simply made a courtesy call or that he went up to Jerusalem for an innocuous social visit with Peter. As we go deeper into the lexicographical evidence offered by Liddell and Scott, we are carried even farther away from such an understanding of the text.[2] The word of course, can mean simply "to visit." But should we so understand it in the context in which we find it?

The most complete study of ἱστορῆσαι as used by Paul has been made by G. D. Kilpatrick.[3] Kilpatrick takes into consideration the Latin, Coptic, and Syrian

---

[2]In other contexts this verb means "give an account of what one has learned," "record." As ἱστορῆσαι it is used in the sense of "inquiry"; it is so used in the title of a work by Theophrastus: Περὶ φυτῶν ἱστορία, "Systematic (or Scientific) Observation regarding Plants." In the absolute it is used of "science" generally, of "geometry," and in empirical medicine for "body of recorded cases." Ἱστορῆσαι is also used in the sense of "knowledge obtained through inquiry and observation," that is, "information." And finally we have the meaning of ἱστορῆσαι as a "written account of one's inquiries," "narrative," or "history." (*A Greek-English Lexicon,* comp. Henry George Liddell and Robert Scott, 9th ed. rev. and augmented by Henry Stuart Jones [London: Oxford, 1940] 1:842.) WUNT cites examples from Hellenistic Greek which mean simply "get to know," which meaning has been accepted by the translators of NEB. However, on the basis of context, "visit a person for the purpose of inquiry" is to be preferred.

[3]"Galatians 1:18 ΙΣΤΟΡΗΣΑΙ ΚΗΦΑΝ," in *New Testament Essays: Studies in Memory of Thomas Walter Manson,* ed. A. J. B. Higgins (Manchester: Manchester University Press, 1959) 144-49. Cf. James D. G. Dunn, "The Relationship between Paul and Jerusalem according to Galatians 1 and 2," *NTS* 28 (1982): 461-78; Otfried Hofius, "Gal 1:18: ἱστορῆσαι Κηφᾶν," *ZNW* 75 (1984): 73-85. Hofius is intent on a formal point: ἱστορῆσαι with the accusative means (a) to get to know personally; (b) to inquire about. The formal point leaves open the reasons why Paul wished to get to know Peter personally, or why he had inquiries about Peter. The object of the present paper is to deal with just those matters left open. Thus, Hofius, 84, thinks it *denkbar* that Paul was interested in testimony about Jesus. This paper is written in the conviction that it is not only *denkbar,* but highly probable.

versions, all of which understand ἱστορῆσαι in the sense of "to see." He notes, however, that later commentators were not content with this interpretation. Chrysostom perceived that ἱστορῆσαι must here mean more than "see." He makes a distinction between ἰδεῖν and ἱστορῆσαι and explicitly notes that Paul does not write ἰδεῖν Πέτρον, but ἱστορῆσαι Πέτρον. Kilpatrick discusses the views of other writers, Greek and Latin, and concludes that the oldest identifiable interpretation is that of the versions which treat ἱστορῆσαι as the equivalent of ἰδεῖν and dates it second century. Chrysostom's comment, which is shared by Latin commentators, he dates as earlier than the middle of the fourth century, and suggests that it perhaps belongs to the Antiochene tradition of exegesis.

On the basis of Liddell and Scott's article which Kilpatrick regards as probably the best guide we have, but also taking into account other lexicographical aids, he concludes that "ἱστορῆσαι Κηφᾶν at Gal 1:18 is to be taken as meaning 'to get information from Cephas' " (p. 149). In coming to this conclusion Kilpatrick notes that the reason that ancient commentators rejected this interpretation is that it appeared to them to be "inapplicable" in Paul's case. On the basis of Gal 1:11-12, where Paul says that he received "the Gospel" by revelation, "they argued that St. Paul had already received the requisite knowledge by revelation and so had no need to visit St. Peter for that purpose." Those who took this position and at the same time recognized that ἱστορῆσαι must mean more than ἰδεῖν, generally followed Chrysostom in making Paul visit Peter "to pay his respects." Kilpatrick notes that for Augustine the visit was merely a token of friendship. For Victorinus and Ambrosiaster the visit is an acknowledgement of "the primacy of Peter" (p. 146).

Kilpatrick has his own theory as to why Paul would have sought information from Peter. He notes that the interpretation suggested by Liddell and Scott "to visit a person for purpose of inquiry," i.e., "to get information," satisfied the conditions of the context, so long as the meaning of εὐαγγέλλιον does not mean "information about Jesus," and since Paul seeks information from Peter and not from James, with whom he also had some contact, Kilpatrick asks: "Is there any information that one had to give him that the other could not provide?" In answer he writes, "St. Peter had been an eye witness and disciple of Jesus. St. James could not claim to be a comparable informant about the teaching and the ministry." In conclusion Kilpatrick writes, "We know then of one kind of information for which St. Paul would go to St. Peter rather than St. James, information about Jesus' teaching and ministry."

Kilpatrick considers but rejects the first meaning that Liddell and Scott give, "that of inquiry into or about a person or thing" (p. 147). He cites Plutarch's *Moralia* 516 C, *De Curiositate* 2.3.314 in the last Teubner edition, for an example of the use of ἱστορῆσαι for "getting information" about both persons and things. "Aristippus is so excited by what he hears of Socrates that he is beside himself. . . . He found out about the man, his utterances and his philosophy." For some unaccountable reason, Kilpatrick dismisses the lexicographical implications of this text from a near contemporary of Paul by saying, "But we may exclude at once the explanation that ἱστορῆσαι κηφᾶν meant 'to inquire into, investigate, Cephas.' " In fact "to get information from Cephas" is not incompatible with "to inquire into, investigate Cephas." Because of the very close relationship of Peter to Jesus, and because Jesus first appeared to Peter, for Paul to go to Peter for information about Jesus' teaching and ministry, entails from the outset that Paul is involved in questioning Peter not only about Jesus, but in effect about Peter's memory of Jesus, his beliefs about the meaning of Jesus' death and Resurrection, and thus Peter as a witness is inextricably bound up together with that to which he is a witness. The two cannot be separated as simply as Kilpatrick suggests. We see no objection to combining Liddell and Scott's first meaning for ἱστορῆσαι with their suggested interpretation. To be sure, the focus of Paul's inquiry would be Jesus, but that can hardly have precluded serious attention by Paul to the question of Peter's credibility. Indeed, we may say that the apostolic witness preserved in the New Testament rests primarily upon Paul's conviction of Peter's credibility as a witness, as well as upon Peter's conviction of Paul's credibility as a witness. Their mutuality in finding one another to be credible witnesses is absolutely basic for understanding Christian origins.

At issue is how we are to understand certain phrases Paul uses in arguing for his independence of the authority of the Jerusalem apostles, or as he refers to them "those who were apostles before me" (Gal 1:17). The translators of the New English Bible have a firm grasp of the essential character of Paul's argument so we can best follow his thought by citing that translation. In his opening words Paul strikes this note of apostolic independence: "From Paul, an apostle, not by human appointment or human commission, but by commission from Jesus Christ and from God the Father who raised him from the dead" (Gal 1:1). To remind his readers that Jesus Christ has been raised from the dead by God the Father immediately places Paul who has seen the risen Jesus on an equal footing with all the other apostles and cuts the ground out from any argument that would proceed from some presumed advantage on the part of those apostles who had known Jesus before his death and Resurrection.

> I must make it clear to you, my friends, that the gospel you heard me preach is no human invention. I did not take it from any man [not from Peter or James for example]; no man taught it me; I received it through a revelation of Jesus Christ. (Gal 1:11-12)

Paul is not denying that he has ever taken over anything from anyone, least of all is he denying that he has ever been taught by anyone. The fact that in his first letter to the Corinthians he explicitly states that he is handing on a tradition that he had received—"That Christ died for our sins, in accordance with the scriptures

. . . "—makes it clear that there was tradition, including factual information concerning Jesus that Paul did receive. But for Paul facts themselves do not the Gospel make. No doubt Paul, as a Pharisee of the Pharisees, in his role as persecutor of the church, made himself acquainted with the essential content of the gospel as it was being preached and defended by those within the covenant community with whom he was contending. Indeed, it would not be out of character for this great theologian to have achieved an even more firm and comprehensive grasp of the essential content of this gospel than was in the head of many of the faithful who, under persecution from authorities like himself, were willing to die for it.

What was at issue for Paul was not the factual content of the gospel, but its truth, including of course the truth of its factual content. As he persecuted the church and ravished the faith, he was convinced that the gospel preached by the Christians was false. That is why he was willing to persecute them unto death if necessary. Everything hinges on the "truth of the gospel." Once it pleased God to reveal his Son to Paul, so that Paul could see Jesus as the Son of God, everything changed (see Gal 1:12, 15; 1 Cor 9:1; 15:8, and Phil 3:21). What had been perceived as false, was now recognized as true on the basis of Christ's appearance to Paul. That in essence is the nature of Paul's conversion. The factual basis of Christian faith did not change. For example, that Jesus had died, or even that he had been crucified, was never in dispute between the Christians and the pre-Christian Paul. But the belief that Jesus had died "for the sins" of others, "according to the scriptures"—that was a faith claim made by the church whose truth the pre-Christian Paul could never have accepted, but whose truth, on the basis of Christ's resurrection appearance to him, he was now prepared to embrace, pass on to his converts, and presumably himself proclaim. That there were factual details concerning these deep matters of faith that may have interested Paul should not cause alarm for those who wish, at all costs, to preserve his independence of those eyewitnesses upon whom he would have been dependent for finding adequate answers to some of his questions.

We take this position because the answers Paul received were always received within the context of a faith already firmly and irrevocably grounded in the decisive revelation that preceded and led to his questions. Most if not all of Paul's postconversion questions would have been of the nature of questions for the purpose of clarification in detail. Paul would hardly have asked Peter "Did Jesus die?" or "Was Jesus crucified?" That kind of information would have been entailed in the essential kerygma Paul had formerly rejected but now proclaimed.

Paul's pre-Christian questioning would have focused on issues vital to the way in which the Law and the prophets were being interpreted and acted upon. But once Paul became a Christian there would have been a whole new set of questions for him to ask concerning aspects of Christian life and faith which were relatively untouched by points at issue over whether something had or had not happened "in accordance with the scriptures." As a Pharisee Paul had sat in Moses's seat, and it thus had been for him and his fellow Pharisees to decide how the Law and prophets were to be interpreted. When any members of the covenant were interpreting the Law and the prophets in a manner contrary to Pharisaic teaching, and especially when these interpretations led to behavior that was threatening to the established world of Jewish piety, Paul, as a Pharisee, zealous for the Law, was constrained to act. And act he did. But once Paul was converted, questions such as "What happened on the night Jesus was handed over?" that is, questions concerning matters important to Christians, but which had not been problem causing to Paul the enforcer of Torah, would now have become questions of interest to Paul the Christian leader and they were perfectly legitimate questions for him to pursue. As his leadership role in the church grew, that he have a firm grasp on such matters would have assumed some place of importance, however minor, in Paul's overall preparation for mission.

In this context we should not shy away from accepting the plain meaning of what Paul writes in reference to going to Jerusalem: He went to question Peter. Paul is not making himself subservient to anyone in his decision to ask questions. This apostolic concern to "get it right" is foundational for Christian life and faith. Paul is not forensically diminishing his authority by "making inquiry" of Peter. On the contrary his use of ἱστορῆσαι in this context conceptually places Peter in the dock. Paul is the ἵστωρ. Peter is the one being cross-examined. What is at issue is the truth in a whole range of practical matters which Paul wants to discuss with Peter—none, we conclude, extending to the heart of his gospel. That much Paul appears to rule out decisively in what he says about how he received his gospel in Gal 1:1-17.

Paul in going to Jerusalem to question Peter, is moving up the stream of church tradition to its very source, that is, to those eyewitnesses who first carefully formulated it.

Paul's use of ἱστορῆσαι at this point serves very well his purpose of establishing both his apostolic independence and his apostolic authority. He is not just an independent apostle who has seen the Risen Jesus. He is an independent apostle who stands in a close relationship to Peter. By implication, everything that Paul did or said in the church after that meeting carried with it the implicit authority of both Paul and Peter. That was the risk Peter took in agreeing to the meeting. We have no way of knowing from any statement made by Peter on the subject how Peter viewed Paul's coming to Jerusalem. But the practice of risk taking out of love, even love of a potential enemy, has been endemic to Christian faith from its origin in the heart of Jesus.

And I remained with him fifteen days

The conventional critical comment on this compound phrase reflects the purpose of this phrase in Paul's overall argument in Galatians; namely to establish that he was not dependent for his authority to preach the gospel upon those who had been apostles before him. Thus Ernest de Witt Burton writes, "The mention of the brief duration of the stay is intended, especially in contrast with the three years of absence from Jerusalem, to show how impossible it was to regard him as a disciple of the twelve, learning all that he knew of the Gospel from them."[4] But if this is the case, how much more remarkable is the evidence that Paul provides! For in this case Paul's statement that he remained with Peter for fifteen days is being given under some constraint. His purpose would have been better served had he been able to write that the visit was for only one day.

We have an example in the early church of such a one-day visit which features "greeting the brethren" (Acts 21:7). Of course such visits can last several days. Thus when King Agrippa and Bernice arrived at Caesarea for a courtesy visit to Festus "They spent several days there" (Acts 25: 13-14). While visits in the early church are often for unspecified periods of time, it is not unusual to have the length of stay explicitly mentioned, and it is instructive to see Paul's visit with Peter against the background of a spectrum of visits of specified length. Thus in addition to the one-day visit of Acts 21:7, there are three instances of seven-day stays or stayovers. Thus Paul met up at Troas with some fellow workers who had gone on ahead, and they spent a week there. This is not a visit per se, but it is instructive (Acts 20:6). As Paul was returning to Jerusalem for the last time his ship put in at Tyre to unload cargo. He took advantage of the situation and spent seven days with the disciples in that city before returning to his ship (Acts 21:4). On his way to Rome Paul and those with him finally reached the port of Puteoli, where some fellow Christians invited them to remain with them seven days (Acts 28:14).

If we are to appreciate the significance of Paul's two-week stay with Peter, we cannot do better than recognize that in cultures which observe a lunar calendar important meetings or conferences fall into one or another of four basic categories. There are important one-day visits. These provide the occasion for direct face-to-face meetings between important persons. Only limited tasks can be accomplished, however, during a one-day meeting. Next we have a basic pattern of three days and two nights. The guests arrive during the first day, and after greetings and preliminary matters are taken care of, the agenda for the following day is agreed upon. What is not accomplished during the second day can be dealt with before departure on the third day. The three-day visit, meeting, or conference is very

---

[4]*A Critical and Exegetical Commentary on the Epistle to the Galatians,* ICC (Edinburgh: T. & T. Clark, 1921) 60.

efficient and often used. This basic pattern is easily expanded by adding one or sometimes two full working days. Next is the one-week meeting. This is reserved for more important meetings. For one thing it is very expensive in terms of time taken out of the busy schedules of the persons concerned, as well as the time required in making arrangements for such a long series of discussions. A great deal can be accomplished within the rhythm of the week-long meeting. It is relatively rare, however, for conferences, whether planned or unplanned, to go into a second week. Such two-week conferences, when planned, are generally planned long in advance, and are reserved for only the most far-reaching projects. A fifteen-day visit corresponds comfortably to the rhythm of a two-week conference. One could arrive on the sixth day of the week sometime before sunset which begins the sabbath and depart early on the morning following the sabbath two weeks later. Such a stay will accommodate a leisurely visit, with ample time for work and relaxation. One can expect maximum communication during such a visit. Among other things such a period of time allows for the most difficult of topics to be laid out on the table, and, providing the persons concerned are capable of it, there is time to confront decisive issues, bare mounting tensions, and confidently await lasting resolutions, all within the framework of what can be called a "double sabbath."

The point is not that Peter and Paul used their two-week visit in any such fashion. We will never know how they spent those days together in Jerusalem. The point is that two weeks for important leaders, not to say the two persons who eventually emerged as the two leading apostles of the church, is a considerable length of time for a visit. Seldom do great leaders have the luxury of such schedules. In our own time one thinks of the Camp David accords. Or we can cite the two-week visit that Dietrich Bonhoeffer made to talk with Karl Barth on his way back from his stay in the United States before he took up his role within the life of the Third Reich, which led eventually to his death.

Two weeks provided ample time for both Peter and Paul to discuss whatever was uppermost in their minds, including such topics, we must presume, as the Lord's Supper and other matters bearing upon the preaching of the Gospel, including the Resurrection.

And when we realize the full range of meanings that Paul's readers could rightfully associate with his use of ἱστορῆσαι in this context, presuming that he was careful in his choice of language, we must be open to understanding Paul as saying that he went to Jerusalem to question, examine and observe, to the end that he would leave informed and ready to report to others on the results of his inquiry.

Peter was Paul's host throughout the two-week period. As Peter's guest Paul was being afforded an unparalleled opportunity to gain an inside view of Peter's life and manners. To remain with Peter for two weeks would, of necessity, have afforded them the opportunity to share table fellowship, and it is altogether likely that they observed the Lord's Supper together in accordance with the words of institution which are preserved for us in 1 Cor 11:23-26 sometime during that two-week period. It would be interesting to know whether James was present during this presumed occasion.

We are now ready to take up the question with which we began this section on Galatians: Granted that Paul wanted to make contact with church authorities in Jerusalem (he did see James, for example), why did he go to Peter?

The Role of Peter in the Pre-Pauline Palestinian Church

In the Gospel of Matthew are preserved in their pristine oral form the following words of Jesus.

> Woe unto you, Chorazin!
> Woe unto you, Bethsaida!
>   For if the mighty works which were done in you,
>   Had been done in Tyre and Sidon
>   They would have repented long ago in sackcloth and ashes.
> But I say to you,
>   It shall be more tolerable for Tyre and Sidon
>   At the day of judgment
>   Than for you!
> And as for you, Capernaum, shalt thou be exalted into heaven?
> Thou shalt be brought down to hell!
>   For if the mighty works which have been done in you
>   Had been done in Sodom,
>   It would have remained until this day.
> But I say to you,
>   It shall be more tolerable for the land of Sodom
>   At the day of judgment
>   Than for you!   (Matt 11:21-24)

The evenhanded treatment of these three Galilean cities, all of which face a terrible fate on the day of judgment for their failure to repent in the face of the mighty works that had been done in them, does not prepare us for the exceptional role that one of the three plays in the Gospel stories of Jesus. All four Gospels feature the city of Capernaum, and give scant attention to the other two places which one would judge from the words of Jesus were the beneficiaries of his preaching and healing ministry no less than Capernaum.

The gospels, of course, tell the story of Jesus from the theological perspective of the mission to the Gentiles. In even the most Jewish of the four, the risen Jesus commands the eleven disciples to go and "make disciples of all the Gentiles" (Matt 28:19).

Indeed it is to the text of this gospel that we must go in our search for an answer to the question of how the city of Capernaum has come to play such a dominating role in the gospel story.

But first it is important for us to situate in our mind's eye the location of Capernaum in relation to other points of interest in the early church, especially the city of Damascus which lies to the northeast.

The Lake of Galilee is a great expanse of water fed by the Jordan River, which empties into the lake at its northern estuary and exits at the south to wend its way in serpentine fashion through the great Jordan valley until it finally empties into the Dead Sea. Capernaum is situated at the northern end of the lake west of the Jordan estuary. Here it occupies an outstanding position at the crossroads of both land and sea routes leading north and east from Galilee.

The main road north from Judea and southern Galilee skirted the western coast of the lake until it reached a point just west of Capernaum. There it divided. One could continue north by ascending up the river bed of Nahal Korazim by way of the village and synagogue of Korazim (following the spelling of modern topography). One would then cross the Jordan over the B'noth-Ya'agor bridge and proceed eastward through Gualanitis (Golan) to Damascus. Or one could follow the eastern branch of this road at Capernaum and proceed along the northern coast of the lake of Galilee leaving the port of Capernaum on the immediate right and thus in a short time reach the Jordan estuary. The river was crossed about one mile above the estuary via the ford at Beth-Saida (Bethsaida), which in the first century served as the capital of Philip the Tetrarch of Gualanitis, Iturea, and Trachonitis. From Beth-Saida this road turned northwards until it joined the Qu neitra-Damascus highway.[5]

As a port, Capernaum was favorably located in relation to excellent fishing grounds near the Jordan estuary, and from Capernaum people had easy access by boat to Tiberias and about thirty other fishing villages all around the lake of Galilee.[6] All in all Capernaum was well situated to be a base for the disciples as they undertook—as in time they certainly did—the making of new disciples in areas north and east of Galilee. At any rate, however it happened, by the time the evangelist Matthew undertook to compose his gospel, Capernaum had become an important city in the salvation history of the Gentile church.

It is clear that the evangelist Matthew composed his gospel while standing in the tradition of an early Christian mission that came originally out of northern Galilee. He takes as his *central key text,* compositionally speaking, a text from Isaiah. In this text, a passage that makes no reference to Capernaum is interpreted in a way that nonetheless makes Capernaum a part of God's plan of salvation for

---

[5]Baruch Sapir and Dov-Neeman, *Capernaum, History and Legacy, Art and Architecture* (Tel-Aviv, 1976) 11.
[6]Ibid.

the Gentiles.[7] According to the Hebrew-Masoretic text, this passage from Isaiah reads as follows.

> In the former time he brought into contempt the land of Zebulun and the land of Naphtali; but in the latter time he hath made it glorious, by the way of the sea, beyond the Jordan, Galilee of the Gentiles. The people that walked in darkness there have seen a great light; they that dwelt in the land of the shadow of death, upon them hath the light shined. (Isaiah 9:1-2)

The LXX version of this text in Matthew is shortened and slightly modified:

> The land of Zebulun and the land of Napthali, by the way of the sea, beyond the Jordan, Galilee of the Gentiles. The people that sat in darkness saw a great light. And to them that sat in the region and shadow of death, upon them hath the light shined.

The evangelist believes the way to understand this text is to realize that when the prophet Isaiah writes "by the way of the sea," he is referring to the sea coast of the Lake of Galilee. We know this because in the preceding verses Matthew notes that in leaving Nazareth and coming to dwell in Capernaum *by the sea* in the regions of Zebulun and Naphtali, Jesus did so in order that the word of Isaiah the prophet might be fulfilled (Matt 4:13-14).

Thus, Capernaum is important because, situated on the coast of the Lake of Galilee, it can be interpreted as being "by the way of the sea." Since there is nothing in the text of Isaiah that refers to Capernaum, one must presume that Capernaum was in some unexpressed way important to the evangelist. According to the words of Jesus, Capernaum is notable as one of three cities doomed for destruction because of its negative response to his ministry. What then has happened to reverse this judgment of Jesus so that in the gospel stories of God's salvation Capernaum plays such a positive and important role?

One might say that there is no mystery, since we know that Jesus had a ministry in Capernaum, and since Capernaum was a city on the coast of the lake of Galilee, it was natural for the evangelist to see Jesus' going to Capernaum as a fulfillment of the prophecy of Isaiah. However, it is equally clear that Jesus also had a ministry in other Galilean cities and villages, including significant evangelistic efforts in Chorazim and Bethsaida, and yet little or nothing is said about these ministries. Clearly a selective process has taken place that calls for an explanation.

---

[7]Other reasons supportive of the view that the evangelist Matthew wrote for readers who lived in Christian communities which were the fruit of early missionary activity from northern Galilee into southern Syria are given in "Some Thoughts on the Provenance of Matthew" by William R. Farmer, in *The Teacher's Yoke: Studies in Memory of Henry Trantham*, ed. E. Jerry Vardaman and James Leo Garrett, Jr. (Waco: Baylor University Press, 1964) 109-16.

Something very important concerning Capernaum must have taken place in order to account for its prominence in the gospel story. The evangelist has made this city the turning point in the whole development of Jesus' ministry. Following his baptism in the Jordan, and his return to Nazareth in Galilee, Capernaum is the next place of importance. Jesus goes to Nazareth, but nothing much of importance happens there. He goes immediately then to Capernaum where the first thing he does is to call Peter and his brother Andrew as well as James and John. He calls them from their fishing duties as his first disciples. Capernaum is the place where Jesus inaugurates his public ministry by calling disciples, three of whom—Peter, James, and John—will be with him at most of the high moments throughout his ministry. When compared to the rest of the twelve, these disciples, and especially Peter, clearly dominate the Jesus-tradition that the evangelist will use in composing his gospel.

The best way to explain this selectivity is to recognize that the story of Jesus is being told from a particular perspective, that is, that of the evangelist, or better, that of the churches for which he is writing his gospel. The best way to explain this selectivity of emphasizing Capernaum and certain of the twelve is that Capernaum and some or all of those first disciples called by Jesus were singularly important in the history of the evangelist's church.

This is not to say that the story of Jesus has been falsified. Rather it is to say that the gospels grow out of an exegetical tradition. It makes the best sense if we posit that Jesus himself inaugurated this exegetical tradition by his reading of Isaiah. Because Isaiah was important for Jesus, Isaiah was therefore important for his early disciples. The early Christians living on the coast of the lake of Galilee, including any living in Capernaum, would have been the first to understand and appreciate this Matthean hermeneutical development within the Jesus-school of Isaianic exegetical tradition. Our analysis suggests that this exegetical tradition developed in the hands of a Christian preacher in the city of Capernaum who interpreted the text of Isaiah to apply to the city in which he was preaching: "We here in this place have seen a great light." It would appear that in some such way the text of Isaiah has come to be seen in relationship to the history of the readers for whom the evangelist is writing.

Capernaum is one of many places frequented by Jesus. But this place, this particular place, because of its topographical importance, so well situatied as a base for evangelistic outreach with good road and water connections, especially between Galilee and Damascus, becomes very important to the mission that moves from Galilee towards Damascus. Capernaum is the only city Jesus is known to have frequented that is situated on the sea coast made important by the prophecy of Isaiah, and which also served travellers on their way from Jerusalem to Damascus. Capernaum was a chief port of entry for travellers from southern Syria (including Damascus) into Galilee and points south (including Jerusalem). At the same time, and for similar reasons, it was the most suitable northern base for Christian missionary activity, moving out of Galilee into southern Syria. We know that Paul's persecution of Christians took him to Damascus, and that if he ever passed through Galilee on the way he would have passed by or very near Capernaum.

The whole of early church history makes sense if Peter was important in an early Christian mission going forth from Galilee into southern Syria and if this was also the missionary church that Paul had been persecuting and from which he received the tradition he passed on to others after his conversion. This would not have precluded Peter's spending periods of time in Jerusalem, and giving leadership to the Twelve from that center.

Paul's Relationship to Peter

Looking at the matter in this way makes it possible for us to say that Paul entered into a partnership with Peter in principle the day he began preaching the faith of the church that he once ravished (Gal 1:23).

There is nothing intrinsically implausible or improbable in this way of interpreting the evidence. It certainly helps us to understand how it was possible for Paul to visit Peter in Jerusalem and to remain with him for fifteen days.

It is altogether likely that each knew a good deal about the other long before they met in Jerusalem. And it is not unlikely that there had been some communication between them during the period Paul was preaching the gospel prior to his visit to Jerusalem to visit Peter. The visit itself almost certainly would have required some communication between them as well as some kind of preunderstanding.

Paul's decision to preach in Cicilia and points farther west would have provided the occasion for him to visit Peter in Jerusalem, and for him to reach a firm apostolic understanding with that apostle to whom the risen Christ, according to the tradition he had received, had indeed appeared first. Thereafter, wherever Paul went he passed on the tradition he had received from the mission Peter had organized and inspired.

> I delivered to you first of all that which also I received: That Christ died for our sins according to the scriptures [Isaiah 53]; and that he was buried; and that he hath been raised on the third day according to the scriptures [Hosea 6:2, Jonah 2:1]; and that he appeared to Cephas; then to the Twelve; then he appeared to about five hundred brethren at the same time, of whom the majority abide with us until this day, but some have fallen asleep; then he appeared to James; then to all the apostles. (1 Cor 15:3-7)

To this litany of what he had received, which he now passes on to the Corinthians, Paul adds pertinent items from his own history with fitting theological and interpretative comments:

And, last of all, as to one born out of due time he appeared also to me. For I am the least of the apostles, one who is not [even] worthy to be called an apostle, because I persecuted the Church of God. But by the grace of God I am what I am, and his grace which I have received has not been without effect; on the contrary [because of the effect of God's grace] I labored more abundantly than all of them [i.e., the other apostles]: yet not I but the grace of God which was with me. Whether it be I or they, so we preach, and so ye believed. (1 Cor 15:8-11)

This tradition that Paul passes on, and which represents Peter as the first to whom the risen Christ appeared, raises interesting questions. The gospel of Matthew, for example, preserves a tradition according to which Jesus after his Resurrection first appeared to Mary Magdalene and the other Mary. It is argued that Paul passes on a kerygma that must have the value of legal testimony, and that since women's testimony was unacceptable in Jewish courts, it was omitted altogether in kerygmatic passages, so that it would be wrong to argue that the tradition Paul passes on conflicts with that from Matthew. In any case, it is clear that Paul is passing on a pro-Petrine tradition, that is, a tradition that developed within a church in which it was remembered that the risen Lord first appeared to Peter. That apostle to whom the risen Christ was believed to have first appeared would have had a special place in post-Resurrection churches. It is also important to note that in Paul's version of this tradition Christ's appearance to him, coming at the end of the series—"last of all"—creates a series which begins with Peter and ends with Paul. According to Paul's version this is a closed canon of Resurrection appearances. It runs the gamut of apostolic authority, from Peter to Paul. Paul is least of all, because he persecuted the church of God. But, he is also first, because where sin doth abound, there doth grace much more abound. Similarly Paul can claim to have labored more than any of the apostles, which would have included Peter. So the last shall be first—whether by one's own labor in the gospel, or by God's grace.

Paul passed on a tradition that had developed in a church in which there was already present an incipient Petrine primacy. But his churches received this tradition from him within an overall theological framework that bespoke apostolic mutuality between the first of the twelve and the Apostle to the Gentiles (Gal 2:6-9 and 2:5-16). Was this simply Paul's construction, or did it represent a bona fide apostolic agreement that had been reached between Peter and Paul before or during that fifteen-day meeting in Jerusalem?

It must have represented an implicit apostolic quid pro quo whether consciously recognized or not. In any case no one can deny the facts: Paul passed on a pro-Petrine if not an implicit Petrine-primacy tradition and Peter supported Paul's call to head the apostolate to the Gentiles. Of course, this understanding was not officially ratified by the pillars of the church in Jerusalem until fourteen years later when Paul returned to Jerusalem, and lay before those who had been apostles prior to himself the gospel he had been preaching to the Gentiles.

It has been argued that the Jerusalem conference was only possible because Peter was willing to arrange it, presumably at Paul's request, and, in any case, for the sake of the gospel.[8] According to this argument, the fundamental theological agreement reached between Peter and Paul during their fifteen-day visit fourteen years before the apostolic conference (Gal 2:1-10) and tested by fourteen years of missionary work by Paul and his associates, provided the essential components for the successful outcome of the apostolic conference. The agreement of the Jerusalem apostles to ratify the longstanding understanding between Peter and Paul, which issued in the decision to make each of them the heads of two separate but concordant missions, is the apostolic Magna Charta of the holy Catholic church, reaffirmed martyrologically by signatures made in blood by these two chief apostles during the Neronian persecution. Paul gives his readers an eyewitness report of what actually happened at this historic conference. It is one of the most remarkable statements in the New Testament:

> When they [i.e., the pillars of the Church in Jerusalem] saw that I had been entrusted with the gospel of uncircumcision, even as Peter with the gospel of the circumcision (for he that wrought for Peter unto the apostleship of the circumcision wrought for me also unto the Gentiles), and when they perceived the grace that was given unto me, James and Cephas and John, they who were reputed to be pillars gave to me and Barnabas the right hand of fellowship, that we should go unto the Gentiles, and they unto the circumcision. (Gal 2:7-9)

This dual leadership of the historical apostolate helps explain why the New Testament writings feature Peter and Paul. But the subsequent concordant martyrdom of these two apostolic heads is no less essential to the historical development that eventually led to the formation of the New Testament canon.[9]

There is a solid New Testament foundation for the recognition of Irenaeus that the founding and building up of the church in Rome by "the two most glorious [i.e., martyred] apostles Peter and Paul" (*Adv haer* 3.3.2) provides the holy Catholic church with an essential touchstone in history for the combatting of heresy. That which is not in harmony with the concordant apostolic witness of Peter and Paul sealed in blood, and witnessed to in the scriptures which have been normed by this

---

[8]William R. Farmer, "Peter and Paul: A Constitutive Relationship for Catholic Christianity," *Texts and Testaments: Critical Essays on the Bible and Early Church Fathers, a Volume in Honor of Stewart Dickson Currie,* ed. W. Eugene March (San Antonio: Trinity University Press, 1980) 219-36; and "Peter and Paul," in *Jesus and the Gospel, Tradition, Scripture, and Canon* (Philadelphia: Fortress Press, 1983) 50-63.

[9]William R. Farmer and Denis Farkasfalvy, *The Formation of the New Testament Canon* (Mahwah: Paulist Press, 1983) 7-95.

apostolic history and faith, is not catholic, and cannot be accepted as being faithful to the primitive *regula,* that is, the "truth of the gospel,"[10] by which these two apostles had agreed to norm their faith and practice (Gal 2:11-21).

Tertullian correctly saw that the norm by which the issue between Peter and Paul at Antioch was finally settled was in fact a primitive apostolic understanding based upon a theological agreement to which both Peter and Paul subscribed (*Against Marcion* 4.2.1-5). He understood this *regula* to have been laid down for the church by the apostles at the Jerusalem conference of Gal 2:1-10. Our analysis leads to the conclusion that this apostolic conference was preceded by a less-publicized, and, in some sense, preparatory meeting, a meeting that had taken place between Peter and Paul in the same city fourteen years earlier (Gal 1:18).

In his first letter to the church at Corinth Paul addresses the problem of party spirit in that church and specifically refers to four parties, that is, those who say "we belong to Paul," those who say "we belong to Apollos," those who say, "we belong to Cephas," and those who say "we belong to Christ." While Paul does not criticize Peter for contributing to this divisiveness it is clear from the fact that there were members of the Corinthian church who said "we belong to Cephas," that there was a basis for tension between Peter and Paul over the way in which their respective adherents behaved toward one another.

Just how serious this tension may have been we do not know. There is no reference in any other letter of Paul to a "Cephas party." In Paul's second letter to the church at Corinth he is at pains to criticize certain opponents at Corinth who questioned his apostolic authority and worked against him. The depth of Paul's feeling about the challenge this opposition represented to his apostleship may be measured by his use of sarcasm in referring to them derogatively as "super apostles." While there is no way these "super apostles" in 2 Corinthians can be identified with any degree of certainty as adherents of the "Cephas party" in 1 Corinthians, neither can one absolutely rule out the possibility that Paul's opponents in 2 Corinthians may have stood in some meaningful, even if undefinable, relationship to this party.

To the degree that we allow for the possibility that Paul's opponents in 2 Corinthians are positively related to the Cephas party mentioned in 1 Corinthians, the case for serious tension between Peter and Paul in the period following the apostolic conference in Jerusalem is strengthened. Certainly the incident that Paul relates in Gal 2 concerning the confrontation he had with Peter over the issue of table fellowship between Gentile and Jewish Christians in Antioch serves to underscore the undeniable fact that these two apostles could differ strongly over

---

[10]For the relationship of the apostolic norm of the "truth of the gospel" and the second-century forms of the "regula," see William R. Farmer, "Galatians and the Second-Century Development of the 'Regula Fidei,' " *The Second Century* 4 (1984): 143-70.

very important issues. However, such disagreements only serve to underscore how firm was the bond that united them. The more we make room for postconciliar tension, and the greater the place we give to this tension, the more we recognize the need for preconciliar solidarity to account for the eventual outcome. For if there is one thing that is certain in church history it is that in spite of any pigheadedness on the part of either or both these great apostles, they did stand together on the fundamental theological basis of the faith, that is, God's redemptive, sacrificial, and atoning love for sinners, and all else that is entailed in the good news of justification by faith (Gal 2:15-21).

The Pre-Pauline Tradition Concerning the Lord's Supper

Finally, in answer to the question, "By what authority does the Apostle to the Gentiles assure the Corinthian church that the tradition concerning the Lord's Supper he had received and had in turn passed on to them, originated with Jesus himself?" we answer, by the authority of those who were apostles before him. And if it be asked, did Paul have the opportunity to discuss the form, content, and credibility of this tradition with those apostles who were eyewitnesses to what actually happened in Jerusalem on the night when Jesus was delivered up? The answer is most assuredly yes.

First he could, and presumably did, discuss such matters with Peter, who, according to the Gospels (Matt 26:17-30 and parallels), was present there in Jerusalem that night in the very room where Jesus took bread and broke it. Second, Paul had further opportunity to discuss such matters with John as well as with Peter fourteen years later during the Jerusalem conference, if by that time he still had any questions. Paul's subsequent assurance to his readers in Corinth that he was passing on to them a tradition that he had received entails, under these circumstances, the presumption that this tradition is handed on to us in the scriptures as tradition that comes not only with the authority of the Apostle Paul but with that of those apostles Paul knew who had themselves been eyewitnesses to the event. We cannot be certain of this point. But it appears to us to be intrinsically probable in the light of the considerations to which attention has been brought in this essay.

The import of this conclusion is far-reaching. If Christ died for our sins according to the scriptures (1 Cor 15:3), since Isaiah 53 is the only scripture theologians can supply to explain the meaning of the tradition Paul is passing on, we must be open to the conclusion that this passage in the book of Isaiah was important for Jesus. The evidence of his words preserved in Matthew 20:25-28 (and Mark 10:42-45), where the Son of Man gives his life as a ransom for many, argues for this conclusion.

It would follow in this case that for Jesus to speak as he spoke and to act as he acted on the night he was delivered up would have been for him to have taken a crucial step in instituting the church. And a church so instituted would be a church which in a central way would live out of the mystery of this Eucharist. In other words it would be a martyrological church living out of the vicarious and atoning sacrifice of Jesus. The concordant martyrdom of the two chief apostles Peter and Paul in Rome would be inspired by the definitive faith that mysteriously comes to expression in the eyewitness tradition concerning this institutional act, and, as a rite, it would be central in the life and faith of that holy Catholic church within whose divine economy it would be the vocation of the church in Rome to represent the concordant witness of the chief apostles Peter and Paul, and to counsel with all churches which wish to remain faithful to that earliest apostolic witness: "in the night he was delivered up, he took bread. . . . " That is to say, words and deeds, as well as the death and Resurrection of Jesus Christ, would be normative for the church in relationship to this central rite as the specification by our Lord of how the concord between the Law and the prophets and the covenant that was coming into being through his death and Resurrection was to be understood and lived out; a rite in which the fulfillment of the Law and prophets is celebrated, the redeeming benefits of the atoning sacrifice of Christ are appropriated by faith, and the fruits of the Spirit that flow from the New Covenant are shared by the participants.

Presence in the Lord's Supper

1 Corinthians 11:23-26 in the Context of Hellenistic Religious History

Hans-Josef Klauck

Orientation

Meals invested with religious meaning are a universal phenomenon in the history of religions, not restricted to antiquity.[1] To insert the Christian tradition of the Lord's Supper into this panorama is quite difficult, owing to the overwhelming mass of material. It is nevertheless an important and in substance fascinating task.

From the outset it is highly advisable to avoid, as far as possible, certain constricting perspectives and fallacious prejudgments. Here, the research of an earlier generation, the circle of the History-of-Religions School,[2] which traced the origins of the Lord's Supper to Hellenistic mystery cults, can serve as paradigm.[3] In this kind of judgment there is a whole batch of problematic prejudgments, every one of

---

[1] Cf. Edgar Reuterskiöld, *Die Entstehung der Speisesakramente* (Heidelberg: Carl Winter, 1912); Fritz Bammel, *Das heilige Mahl im Glauben der Völker. Eine religionsphänomenologische Untersuchung* (Gütersloh: Bertelsmann, 1950); Manfred Josuttis and Gabriel Marcel Martin, eds., *Das heilige Essen. Kulturwissenschaftliche Beiträge zum Verständnis des Abendmahls* (Stuttgart-Berlin: Kreuz, 1980). The following essay is substantially dependent on Hans-Josef Klauck, *Herrenmahl und hellenistischer Kult. Eine religionsgeschichtliche Untersuchung zum ersten Korintherbrief,* 2nd ed. (Münster: Aschendorff, 1986), which offers a comprehensive collection of primary and secondary literature.

[2] On this, cf. most recently Gerd Lüdemann and Martin Schröder, *Die religionsgeschichtliche Schule in Göttingen. Eine Dokumentation* (Göttingen: Vandenhoeck & Ruprecht, 1987); on method in general, cf. Karlheinz Müller, "Die religionsgeschichtliche Methode. Erwägungen zu ihrem Verständnis und zur Praxis ihrer Vollzüge an neutestamentlichen Texten," *Biblische Zeitschrift* 30 (1985): 161-92.

[3] On the beginnings in Albert Eichhorn, Wilhelm Heitmüller, Alfred Loisy, G. P. Wetter, et al., see H.-J. Klauck, *Herrenmahl,* 1-2, 8-15.

which deserves critical review: (a) belief in a sacramental mediation of salvation has no foothold in the preaching of Jesus and cannot be accounted for from within the cultural world of Palestinian Judaism; (b) a Last Supper of Jesus with his disciples before his death cannot be historically grounded with sufficient certainty, and even if, contrary to expectation, it were to have happened, it would have had no impact on the later practice of the Lord's Supper; (c) available analogies, if there is so much as a single remote relationship in time or place, are always to be analyzed genetically, and in the analysis Christianity is regularly to be assigned the role of the borrower; (d) only altogether original and distinctive elements impose themselves credibly; outside influences invariably signify a deviation from the pure gospel, which—depending on orientation—is to be derived from the preaching of the historical Jesus or the message of the primitive Christian kerygma.

The manifest misapprehensions that come to expression in this still quite incomplete list have substantially contributed to the undeserved rejection of many accurate and fruitful insights from history-of-religions research. In straightforward dependence on as well as in discriminating development of the older discussion, I would essay a reformulation of the research agenda as follows: (a) analogies of diverse density between the Christian Lord's Supper and non-Christian phenomena cannot seriously be disputed. This means that examination and assessment on various levels— historical, structural, and theological—are a permanent acquisition. But comparison of this kind need not lead to the framing of genetic relationships of dependence. On the contrary, it can just as well allow the distinctive and proper profile of the data in question to come graphically to light. (b) The adoption and adaptation of foreign influences can also be assessed positively, as a sign of Christian faith's assimilative capacity, which is able to fuse diverse elements together. An exclusive fixation on the question of origins—a trait shared, of course, by not a few of the enemies, on principle, of the History-of-Religions School—distracts attention from the processes of reception and inculturation by which what is taken over is reshaped and assimilated. (c) Even if we proceed from the historically plausible premise, which I fully share, that a farewell meal of Jesus with his disciples represents the most important point of departure for the celebration of the Lord's Supper in the primitive Christian communities, the history-of-religions formulation of the state of the question even in its narrower sense as restricted to Hellenism retains its relative validity, be it only in serving to limn the contours of the cultural world in which a Gentile-Christian community adopted the Lord's Supper tradition.

Here numerous points might be added in the context of preliminary methodological remarks and in dialogue with the still to be fully mastered legacy of the History-of-Religions School. To mention only one issue, it is evident that we should not maintain a clean line of division between Hellenism and Judaism. Again, limitation to a single object of comparison—for example, the mystery cults[4] so dear to an earlier generation—can be allowed only on heuristic and technical grounds; and this limitation loses its admissibility, as a consciously and methodically controlled contraction of perspective, as soon as it is invested with absolute claims. Besides, to stay with this example, the question arises whether we know—all that exactly—just what mystery cults and the meals belonging to them actually are. Here it was partly a matter of investigators' having worked with some few standardized premises and without the requisite counter-controls respecting the sources. But a more exactly differentiated approach runs the risk of being overwhelmed by the relevant data. These include, as indispensable context, sacrificial cult generally and the sacrificial meal; the voluntary association and its social meal; the cult of the dead and its cultic meal. On the other hand, early Christian literature, which would have to be examined from the New Testament to, at least, the Didache, Ignatius,[5] and Justin's first apology, offers no fully unified picture, with the result that much depends from the start on selecting and setting up the right levels of comparison.

Time and again since the days of Eichhorn and Heitmüller, 1 Corinthians[6] has shown itself to be the most promising textual base for entry into comparative work. This ties in with the special character of the writing (its themes are dictated by practical problems) and with the specific contour of the Christian community in Corinth (its embeddedness in Hellenistic urban culture). Here too the spectrum of possible points of departure is extremely various. With reference to 1 Cor 10, the κοινωνία-conceptuality (in my opinion a Hellenistic conceptual resource, which has been brought to bear on the Last Supper tradition[7] should be investigated. The question of what exactly is meant by "the cup of demons" and "the table of demons" in 10:21, and the question of the extent to which the idea of a demonic infection of food resonates with this, leads back to the most characteristic sphere of Hellenistic history of religions. In 1 Cor 11 two aspects of the framework of the

---

[4]On the complex of themes "early Christianity and mystery religions" which largely supplies the framework for research into the Last Supper by the History-of-Religions School, see the bibliography in H.-J. Klauck, 1nn2-3, 8n1; A. J. M. Wedderburn, *Baptism and Resurrection. Studies in Pauline Theology against Its Greco-Roman Background* (Tubingen: Mohr-Siebeck, 1987); see my review in *Biblische Zeitschrift* 33 (1988): 151-53. On the mystery cults in general, see now Walter Burkert, *Ancient Mystery Cults* (Cambridge: Harvard University Press, 1987).

[5]Most instructive on this topic: Lothar Wehr, *Arznei der Unsterblichkeit. Die Eucharistie bei Ignatius von Antiochen und im Johannesevangelium* (Münster: Aschendorff, 1986).

[6]Among recent commentaries, cf. Gordon D. Fee, *The First Epistle to the Corinthians* (Grand Rapids: Eerdmans, 1987); Friedrich Lang, *Die Briefe an die Korinther* (Göttingen: Vandenhoeck & Ruprecht, 1986).

[7]Cf., among others, Hans-Josef Klauck, "Eucharistie und Kirchengemeinschaft bei Paulus," *WiWei* 49 (1986): 1-14; English summary in *Theology Digest* 35 (1988): 19-24.

Last Supper tradition proper merit keener attention: (a) a surprising light falls on the disorders and abuses occurring in the Corinthians' celebration of the Lord's Supper and condemned by Paul, if one brings them into relationship with ancient association-ordinances and with the depictions (partly caricatures) of ancient banquets:[8] (b) at 11:30, it is hardly possible to suppress the alarming suspicion that Paul is tracing physical malady and premature death back to defective behavior at the Lord's Supper. Hence the temptation to speak of "catastrophic taboo-effects"[9] and to compare them with superstitious reactions to certain food regulations in the Gentile world.

In what follows we must be content with more modest aims. We restrict ourselves in a first review to the text of 1 Cor 11:23-26, and select four facets thereof for closer analysis: (1) the transmission-of-tradition terminology in 11:23a; (2) the possible specification of genre as cult aetiology, which is open to correlation with 1 Cor 11:23b or to correction on the basis of the same text; (3) the sequence of the celebration, 11:25a providing an index to the problem; (4) the double remembrance mandate in 11:24 and 11:25. In a second, more comprehensively designed review, we shall seek to define and order forms of the presence of the Lord at the Lord's Supper.

On 1 Corinthians 11:23-26

1. Transmission-of-Tradition Terms

It has long been recognized that in 1 Cor 11:23a there exist two terms relating to the transmission of tradition: παραλαμβάνειν (to receive) and παραδιδόναι (hand on, deliver). The latter was already introduced in 11:2, and both recur prominently in 15:3 (cf. also 15:1), functioning to introduce a credo-formula. There are equivalents to these terms in rabbinic terminology: qbl (to receive) and msr (hand on, deliver). With their help, and in accord with the Pharisaic conception of

[8]As very nicely realized in Gerd Thiessen, "Soziale Integration und sakramentales Handeln. Eine Analyse von 1 Cor XI 1-34," in his *Studien zur Sociologie des Urchristentums,* 2nd ed. (Tübingen: Mohr-Siebeck, 1983) 290-317; likewise illuminating: Dennis Edwin Smith, "Meals and Morality in Paul and his World," in *SBL Papers* 20 (1981): 319-39.

[9]Thus Bammel, *Das heilige Mahl* (see n. 1, above) 152; cf. also Johannes Weiss, *Der erste Korintherbrief,* KEK 5, 9th ed. (Göttingen: Vandenhoeck & Ruprecht, rpt.1977; =1910 292: "a conception that stands closer to the Jewish retribution doctrine and pagan superstition than to the spirit of the words of Jesus."

written Torah and oral tradition operative in unison, chains of tradition take shape that make possible an unbroken line leading written and oral tradition back to their point of origin. One must be clear, however, that the texts adduced as attestations are all to be dated later—some much later—than, for example, 1 Corinthians. This holds first of all for the locus classicus, Abot 1:1: "Moses received the Torah on Sinai and delivered it to Joshua, and Joshua delivered it to the elders, and they to the prophets, and the prophets to the men of the great Synagogue."[10] One can partly fill the time gap between Paul and these texts by appealing to passages like Mark 7:3-4, 13 or Josephus, *Ant* 13.297, where we meet the words παραδιδόναι and παραλαμβάνειν or cognates in connection with the oral Torah of the Pharisees. There is already here a Grecising of Pharisaic-rabbinic academic terms, which consequently must be accorded a still earlier origin.

If we go still another step back, we come across a passage in the LXX which clearly presupposes a different frame of reference. In Wisdom 14:15, it is said in the context of a euhemeristic explanation of the fact of heathen polytheism, "And he passed on (παρέδωκεν) to his subordinates secret celebrations and initiations (μυστήρια καὶ τελετάς). Now, that is unmistakably borrowed from the language of the Hellenistic mysteries.[11]

An exclusive derivation of the Pauline terms for transmission-of-tradition from academic rabbinic terminology[12] must be qualified as, at the minimum, one-sided. The abundance and antiquity of attestations drawn from the religious hermeneutic of Hellenism can very well rival the constantly adduced Jewish texts.[13] To choose only a few examples: Plato calls teaching and learning a process of handing on and receiving (Theat 198B: παραδιδόντα . . . παραλαμβάνοντα). In the academic

---

[10]Wilhelm Bacher, *Die exegetische Terminologie der jüdischen Traditionsliteratur,* vol. 1 (Leipzig, 1899; = rpt. Darmstadt: Wissenschaftliche Buchgesellschaft, 1969) 106, comments on *msr,* "The verb is seldom found in Tannaitic texts." Cf. among other texts, CD 3:3; Mek. Exod 19:4.

[11]Respecting this passage, in an important book for our history-of-religions state of the question, see Karl-Gustav Sandelin, *Wisdom as Nourisher. A Study of an Old Testament Theme, Its Development within Early Judaism and Its Impact on Early Christianity* (Abo: Abo Akademi, 1986) 80. A Hellenistic flavor for *paralambanein* and *paradidonai* is detectable in Philo (Cher 68; VitMos 2.11; SacrAC 64.78) as well as in others, such as the above-mentioned passage in Josephus *Ant* 19.30-31. For detail cf. Wiard Popkes, *Christus Traditus. Eine Untersuchung zum Begriff der Dahingabe im Neuen Testament* (Zurich: Zwingli, 1967) 100-104.

[12]A typical example is Fee, *Corinthians* (see above, n. 6) 548n15: "While it occurs in the mysteries and in Gnosticism . . . , that is irrelevant for Paul's usage, given his rabbinical training." How certain is our knowledge of rabbinism in the first century AD, and does the judgment of "irrelevant" necessarily extend to the addressees of Paul?

[13]A comprehensive collection of passages is offered in Josef Ranft, *Der Ursprung des katholischen Traditionsprinzips* (Paderborn: Schöningh, 1931) 179-90.

terminology of philosophy both verbs stand for the transmission of authoritative oral teaching, which can also be esoteric secret tradition.[14] A metaphorical use of mystery terminology is discernible in Theon of Smyrna. In the course of a comparison he uses a five-stage model based on the mysteries, the second stage of which represents ἡ τῆς τελετῆς παράδοσις (the handing on of secret initiations) and the fourth stage of which qualifies one for the act of handing on: "What each has received in initiations he can also hand on."[15]

The Latin equivalent of παραδιδόναι is *tradere*. In the *Tusculanae Disputationes* Cicero puts on the lips of one of the speakers, "Remember what is handed on in the mysteries (*quae tradantur mysteriis*), for you indeed belong to the initiated" (Tusc. Disp. 1.29). What was handed on in the mysteries could quite concretely be, first of all, certain secret cult objects, as is the case in the mystery-inscription of Andania: "the holy men are to pass on to their successors the case and the books that Mnasistratus (the founder of the cult) has delivered; they should hand on also whatever else was assigned for the mysteries."[16] What might be referred to includes, among other things, the establishment of a cult,[17] instruction in the myth of the mysteries,[18] and the allotting of degrees of initiation.[19]

What emerges from all this? In the matter at hand there is a convergence of academic rabbinic and academic Hellenistic language. The latter exhibits a relationship to the language used in the mysteries. The choice of the terms παραδιδόναι and παραλαμβάνειν in the sphere of Hellenistic Judaism is conditioned by the language both of the mysteries and of philosophical education. With this conceptuality Paul, whether deliberately or not, accommodates the conceptual horizons of the Corinthians. The similarity of Paul's formula, introduced in this way, to mystery myths and mystery formulas must have imposed itself on them, for

> Probably the members of the community had derived from the Greek political system and its laws and from the Hellenistic mystery religions a keen sensitivity for almost magically effective formulas handed on in verbally exact fashion.[20]

---

[14]Cf. Plutarch, StoicRep 9 (1035A/B); Alex 7.3.

[15]ExpRerNat 1 (14.18;nD15.5 Hiller).

[16]SIG;s3 736 or no. 65, lines 11-13 in Franciszek Sokolowski, *Lois sacrées de cités grecques* (Paris: E. de Boccard, 1969) 122.

[17]Herodotus, *Hist.* 2.51.3.

[18]Plutarch, *Is. et Os.* 2 2 (351F): Isis delivers the sacred teaching to the initiated.

[19]Porphyrius, *Abst* 4, 16: ILS 4267.

[20]Paul Neuenzeit, *Das Herrenmahl. Studien zur paulinischen Eucharistieauffassung* (Munich: Kösel, 1960).

2. Definition of the Genre as "Cultic Aetiology"

A cultic aetiology serves the grounding and explaining, in narrative form, of a cultic rite, simultaneously reflecting its concrete performance. To make this concrete we shall illustrate it, using the example of the Homeric hymn of Demeter and the mysteries of Eleusis.[21] The goddess Demeter, searching for her daughter Persephone, makes her way into the Eleusinian royal palace. Keeping silence and fasting, she sits on a pelt-covered stool, like the adepts in the μύησις, the first level of initiation. She refuses to drink wine, but asks for a mixed drink called "Kykeon," made of pearl barley, water, and mint. The goddess partakes of it "on account of the sacred practice,"[22] or in the translation of Richardson, "for the sake of the rite."[23] We cannot really render "for the sake of the sacred practice" by a single phrase; we can only variously paraphrase it: to establish the rite, to preserve and observe it, to perform and practice it. In the mythical narrative Demeter establishes the rite and, acting at the same time as prototype of all future adepts, she herself performs what she has instituted.[24] Here for once, on the very surface of the text, the aetiological character of the mythical narrative comes to light. A passage of this kind permits the whole narrative-event so to become diaphanous that through it we can see the performance of the mystery ritual.

Ovid, with Eleusis in view, has very beautifully formulated the not always tension-free but doubtless always present homologous relation between myth and rite: "Because the goddess ends her fast as night begins, it is even today at the appearance of the stars that the initiates hold their meal."[25] It is not surprising, then, if some centuries later Clement of Alexandria cites a synthema (roughly, password or watchword) from the Eleusinian mysteries, in which (among other things) the initiate confesses: "I have drunk the mixed drink."[26]

The Last Supper texts of the New Testament, too, although they expressly relate to Jesus' last meal with his disciples, indirectly offer a glimpse of the cultic community's celebration, itself grounded in the initial event. This holds true even

---

[21]On what follows cf. N. J. Richardson, *The Homeric Hymn to Demeter,* 2nd ed. (Oxford: Oxford University Press, 1979) with text and commentary.

[22]*Hom Hym Dem* 211: δεξαμένη δ'ὁσίης ἕνεκεν πολυπότνια Δηώ.

[23]Richardson, *Homeric Hymn,* 225, who also notes other suggestions: "to save the rite," "pour fonder la rite," "a cause du rite solennel."

[24]Ibid. 226: "Demeter, in founding the rite, is also acting as the prototype of the initiates, and observing the prescription which she herself has created."

[25]Ovid, *Fasti* 4.535-36: quae quia principio posuit ieiunia noctis, tempus habent mystae sidera visa cibi.

[26]Clement of Alexandria, *Prot* 21.2 (16.18-20 GCS 56 Stählin).

to the extent that, as scholarship generally has conceded, liturgical practice has itself exercised an influence on the wording of the text.[27] One need only think of the strong tendencies towards paralleling which are at work in the history of the transmission of "the words of interpretation," and which, finally, in Justin, lead to the extreme short form: "This is my body—this is my blood" (Apol I 66,3). In this respect there are undeniable analogies to cult aetiologies in Hellenistic forms of religion.

Nevertheless, there exist numerous not inconsiderable reservations respecting the transferal of the genre-designation "cultic aetiology" to a text such as 1 Cor 11:23-26. Such reservations are in order if, in connection with this designation of genre, which does indeed relate to certain textual phenomena, a negative judgment of historicity is smuggled in and the Last Supper account is classified as a mythical founding legend. In the text itself verse 23b clearly obviates this: "The Lord Jesus on the night he was delivered up. . . . "

An index to the mythical understanding of time is a maxim from late antiquity on the interpretation of myth: "This never happened but is forever extant."[28] Despite its narrative surface structure, the myth does not report historical events, but tells of eternal, changeless being.[29] Language unfolds in chronological sequence what understanding recognizes as timeless unity. 1 Cor 11:23b is totally different. Here the ritual practice of the community is anchored in history and referred back to a fixed point in the recent, not to say most recent, past. Granted all formal and functional similarities, therein lies an essential difference from the founding legends of the mystery cults.

3. The Sequence of the Celebration

"In the same way also the cup after supper" in 1 Cor 11:25 signifies that, after eating, a similar act of blessing is performed over the cup as over the bread at the outset.[30] This means that the breaking of the bread and the blessing of the cup frame

---

[27]Established in the somewhat forgotten book of Fritz Hamm, *Die liturgischen Einsetzungsberichte im Sinne vergleichender Liturgieforschung untersucht* (Münster: Aschendorff, 1928).

[28]Ps-Sallustius, *De diis et mundo* 4.8 (8.9-11 CUFr Rochefort): *Tauta de egeneto men oudepote, esti de aei* (from the fourth century AD).

[29]Cf. also ibid., the continuation: Καὶ ὁ μὲν νοῦς ἅμα πάντα ὁρᾷ ὁ δὲ λόγος τὰ μὲν πρῶτα τὰ δὲ δεύτερα λέγει. And whereas intelligence intuits all this together, discourse speaks the first things, then the second.

[30]Against the attempt to draw τὸ ποτήριον μετὰ τὸ δειπνῆσαι together as "the after-supper cup," cf. Archibald Robertson and Alfred Plummer, *A Critical and Exegetical*

the full meal as opening rite and closing rite. So it doubtless went at Jesus' farewell meal with his disciples, which exhibited the characteristic sequence of a Jewish festal meal; so it went also in early post-Easter community practice.

Now Gerd Theissen supposes that in Corinth, too, this was still the practice, for otherwise Paul could not have cited the traditional text unchanged.[31] But that leads to a number of other problems. If the rite with the bread stands at the beginning of the meal, followed by the full meal, and the rite with the cup of wine at the end, those who came late would have participated in the cup ritual but not the breaking of the bread. To escape this conclusion one must largely eliminate the temporal aspect from the terms προλαμβάνειν ("anticipate" in 11:21) and ἐκδέχεσθαι ("wait for" one another in 11:33). One must also place the private meal of 11:21 still earlier than the rite with the bread, and limit the full meal for the poor to the bread and wine alone, since the distribution formulas of the Lord's Supper provided for these only and said nothing of the other alimentary elements.

It still seems to me a less forced way of illuminating the situation, if the breaking of the bread and the blessing of the cup, combined in a double rite, took place at the conclusion of the full meal, as in the synoptic tradition. (In Mark the gestures and words over the bread and wine follow without discernible interval the notice "while they were eating" in 14:22, and in 14:26 the meal is already finished. Luke, in 22:20, alters the wording of 1 Cor 11:23a ever so slightly, so that the bread and wine rites both take place after the meal.) Paul apparently considers it unnecessary to insert a correction into the sacred text, for his concern is not the liturgical procedure but its theological meaning. He brings the "for you" and the "new covenant" of the words of interpretation into play as critique of the Corinthians' faulty dispositions at the Lord's Supper.

We can further validate this consideration by drawing on an analogy from a Hellenistic model, if at the same time we take up in addition the still disputed question of the relationship between the Lord's Supper in 1 Cor 11 and the worship service described in 1 Cor 14. For purposes of comparison we choose the Greek symposium. In its full form it goes like this: It begins, toward evening, with a full meal. A libation marks the transition to the second principal part of the symposium. This is a libation of pure wine offered to the gods of the symposium or to the immortalized founder whose memory a cultic association celebrates with a

---

Commentary on the First Epistle of St Paul to the Corinthians, ICC, 2nd ed. (Edinburgh: Clark, rpt. 1978; = 1914) 246: "But we must not translate the 'after-supper cup,' which would require τὸ μετὰ τὸ δ. ποτήριον." Another way of expressing this would be by use of the attributive position with repetition of το: τὸ ποτήριον τὸ μετὰ τὸ δειπνῆσαι.

[31]Cf. Theissen, "Soziale Integration," 297-300, in disagreement with Neuenzeit, *Herrenmahl,* 71-72; with Theissen: Smith, *Meals and Morality,* 325; Otfried Hofius, "Herrenmahl und Herrenmahlsparadosis. Erwägungen zu 1. Kor 11, 23b-25," *ZTK* 85 (1988): 371-408 (printed in the present volume in English translation).

symposium. To this is joined the drinking bout, which in its ideal form (not, admittedly, in its normal form) had philosophic discussions and conversation as its main content.

This can already be inferred from Plato's portrayal:

> Afterwards, Socrates, having reclined on the couch and having completed his dinner with the others, and then having offered a drink offering, intoned a hymn to the god and performed the usual customs, finally turning to the drinking bout,

a bout, it should be noted, from which the obligation to drink was lifted, the flute player dismissed, and conversation established as the sole form of entertainment.[32]

In the will, fixed by inscription, of Epicteta of the island of Thera, a libation dedicated to the memory of the foundress together with her husband and two sons,[33] is the point of transition from the meal to the symposium.

It is self-evident that among Christians one proceeded with greater sobriety (cf. the appeals to sobriety in 1 Cor 15:34; 1 Thess 5:6-8). But the full meal toward evening in both is roughly the same. In the symposium the transition endowed with religious meaning has its equivalent, on the side of the Lord's Supper, in the double rite of bread and wine, inserted into the center; and in place of philosophic discussion there are the prayers, readings, exhortations, psalms, prophecies, and speaking in tongues of 1 Cor 14. The pattern, once more, in overview:

SYMPOSIUM	COMMUNITY MEETING	
(1) Festal meal (toward evening)	Full meal (toward evening)	1 Cor 11:20-22
(2) Libation of pure wine for gods or founders	Twofold rite with bread and wine, harking back to Jesus	1 Cor 10:16-17 1 Cor 11:23-26
(3) Drinking bout with conversations, etc.	Worship service with psalms, etc.	1 Cor 14

---

[32]Plato, *Symp* 4-5 (176A-E); on this and on transposition to the Christian assembly, cf. also Smith, *Meals and Morality*, 319-20, 325-26.

[33]Cf. Sokolowski, *Lois sacrées*, 230-33 = n. 135:20-23.

4. The Remembrance Mandate

The textual situation may be rapidly summarized as follows: Markan and Matthean tradition contain no remembrance mandate. Luke presents it only once, with the word over the bread (Luke 11:19). Paul has it twice, with the word over the bread and the word over the cup. At first glance this state of affairs elicits the suspicion—by analogy with use of the rule of the shorter as the more original text—that it is a matter of gradual growth, from liturgical practice; that, in others words, the remembrance mandate did not figure in the oldest Last Supper account and in the historical component of the tradition. It is not easily understandable why Markan tradition would have dropped the remembrance mandate. Just at the point at which a liturgical text recedes into the distance of a reported event—as in Mark, in the context of the passion narrative—a founder's mandate would make excellent sense as a historicising effort to ground the community's practice. Whether this point is successfully overturned by the argument that the use of the texts in the celebration of the Lord's Supper effectively replaced the remembrance mandate[34] remains for me somewhat questionable.

Our main attention in any case does not relate to this problematic. It focuses rather on the conceptual horizon to which the remembrance mandate points and against which it takes on profile. With this in mind, here is a rough survey of the history of scholarly opinion.

In his commentary Hans Lietzmann, evidently prompted by Leclerq[35] and with recourse to the material in Laum,[36] compared the formula "in commemoration of me" with the establishment by will of a cultic association to hold regular dinners in memory of its founder. He concluded somewhat tentatively that to a Gentile "converted to Christianity . . . the Lord's Supper would have appeared analogous to such memorial meals."[37]

Joachim Jeremias flatly contradicted this view. Exclusively stressing the Jewish-Palestinian background, he proposed an interpretation of the remembrance mandate which has won little agreement: "Do this, that (God) may remember me

---

[34]Cf. also the often-quoted words of Pierre Benoit, "Le récit de la Cene dans Luc II, 15-20. Etude de critique textuelle et littéraire," *RB* 48 (1939): 357-93, at 386; also rpt. in *Exégese et Théologie,* vol. 1 (Paris: Editions du Cerf, 1961) 163-203, at 195: "On ne récite pas une rubrique, on l'éxécute."

[35]Henri Leclerq, *DACL* 1/1:775-91.

[36]Bernhard Laum, *Stiftungen in der griechischen und römischen Antike. Ein Beitrag zur antiken Kulturgeschichte,* 1. Darstellung, 2. Urkunden (Leipzig-Berlin: Teubner, 1914). Cf. especially the grave bequest from Bithynia during the time of the Caesars, 2:141, no. 203: [ἐπὶ τῷ] ποιεῖν αὐτοὺς ἀνά[νη[σ]ίν μου.

[37]Hans Lietzmann, *An die Korinther,* HNT 9, 2 vols., rev. W. G. Kümmel, 5th ed. (Tübingen: Mohr-Siebeck, 1969) 57-58, with the supplement on the materials, 91-94.

(as Messiah, and so bring about his kingdom)."[38]

The more recent investigation of Fritz Chenderlin is relatively close to Jeremias both respecting the preference for the Judaic horizon of comparison and respecting the notion that with the formula or with the fulfillment of what the formula mandated, God was to be reminded of something. He nevertheless makes room for a certain analogy with the Greek meals for the dead and takes account of the transposability of many aspects of the one culture into the other:

> To anyone familiar with Greek ways even to a moderate degree, "memorial" might have suggested a cult to the dead. Such cults occasionally developed into hero worship—an institution that could easily have been seen by Christians as preeminently suited to their own special hero, Christ.[39]

The significance for New Testament tradition of the biblical-Judaic theology of remembrance bound up with the root *zkr*,[40] should by no means be contested or underplayed. On the other hand, however, there should also be kept in mind the simple fact that εἰς ἀνάμνησιν occurs only four times in the LXX, in some notoriously difficult passages, and that there is no passage in the whole of the Old Testament and Jewish material, so far as I know, that would clearly refer to a particular person and to a memorial meal. Just two examples:[41] Epicurus in his will prescribes, in addition to offerings for the dead on behalf of his relatives and the annual celebration of his birthday, that a memorial meal be held on the 20th of each month "in our memory and in memory of Metrodorus."[42] A Roman woman establishes a cultic association and a meetinghouse so that meals be held there regularly in memory of her husband: *ut in memoriam Anici Prisci c(oniugis) sui in ea semper epulentur.*[43]

---

[38]Cf. Joachim Jeremias, *Die Abendmahlsworte Jesu,* 4th ed. (Göttingen: Vandenhoeck & Ruprecht, 1967) 229-46; ET *The Eucharistic Words of Jesus,* rev. ed. trans. (from 3rd ed.) Norman Perrin (London: SCM Press; New York: Scribner's, 1966) 237-55.

[39]Fritz Chenderlin, *"Do This as My Memorial." The Semantic and Conceptual Background and Value of* Ἀνάμνησις *in 1 Corinthians 11:24-25* (Rome: Biblical Institute Press, 1982) 217; cf. 143-45.

[40]On this I name only Willy Schottroff, זכר, THAT 1:507-18; Hermann Eising, זָכַר, TWAT 2:571-93, ET TDOT 4:64-82 (with bibliography).

[41]For more detail on the meal in the cult of the dead, Klauck, *Herrenmahl,* 76-88.

[42]Εἰς τὴν ἡμῶν καὶ Μητροδόρου [μνήμνην]. Admittedly, μνήμν is missing from the account in Diog Laert, Vit. Phil. 10.18; it can be completed from Cicero, Fin 2.101: *ut et sui et Metrodori memoria colatur;* cf. Hermann Usener, *Epicurea* (Leipzig: Teubner, 1897) 165-68. Also Plutarch, Lat Viv Epic 3 (1129A) asks the Epicureans about the meaning of their gatherings and the meals they took together; according to Athenaeus, Deipn 7 (298D), one of them, centuries after Epicurus's death, bears the surname εἰκαδιστής, which derives from the practice of the memorial meal on the 20th.

[43]ILS 3091; of the many Latin statutes, cf. the *Lex Collegi Aesculapi et Hygiae,* ILS

From a theological perspective this memorial meal is, no doubt, insufficient to interpret the meaning of the Lord's Supper, but neither is it as wholly inappropriate as it is often made out to be. In the background originally stood the belief in the personal presence of the dead one and table-fellowship with him. The meal in his remembrance also bestows partial survival on him. In this context the similarity of the Last Supper rites with bread and cup to the mourning rites in Jer 16:7 deserves mention ("No one shall *break bread* for the mourner to comfort him for the dead, nor shall anyone give him *the cup* of consolation, not even at the death of his father and mother"). Also to be pondered: that against the tendencies to enthusiasm in Corinth, Paul in 1 Cor 11 would once more inculcate especially the death motif and the bond of the celebration with the historical saving act, the death of Jesus on the cross. Even the motif of comfort, dominant in the meal of mourning and the meal of remembrance, can have a certain function in the Pauline Lord's Supper, for this celebration not only knows the presence of the Lord, it is also painfully conscious of his absence (1 Cor 11:26: death and parousia).

Forms of the Presence of the Lord

In a last review we shall proceed more systematically, taking up and further developing the categories that Johannes Betz in his groundbreaking works has set at our disposal.[44] We intend to bring the exegetical facts and the result of the comparative religious examination to bear on inquiry into the idea of presence at the meal.[45] Four conceptions will essentially cover this area of inquiry. Though they sound somewhat complicated at first, on closer acquaintance they turn out not to be complicated at all. So we differentiate four forms of presence, presented here as tags, but to be invested in what follows with explanatory comment: the principal mode, personal presence; commemorative actual presence; proleptic definitive presence; and bodily real presence.

1. Principal Mode: Personal Presence

At the meal the risen Lord is personally present in his spiritual mode of being and specificially as *princeps,* that is, as head of the table and host who summons his

---

7213.
[44]Johannes Betz, *Die Eucharistie in der Zeit der griechischen Väter*: 1/1. *Die Aktualpräsenz der Person und des Heilswerkes Jesu im Abendmahl nach der vorephesinischen griechischen Patristik* (Freiburg: Herder, 1955); 2/1. *Die Realpräsenz des Leibes und Blutes Jesu im Abendmahl nach dem Neuen Testament,* (Freiburg: Herder, 1961; 2nd ed. 1964).
[45]Drawing on and developing Klauck, *Herrenmahl,* 373-74.

own to the meal. That is so self-evidently the controlling trait of the ancient understanding of the sacred meal that it is only rarely made thematic. In Corinth this kind of conception stands, for example, behind the distribution practice in the Lord's Supper. Ideally, the participants were to bring food with them, each according to his means, so contributing to the common meal. For the poor, who could bring nothing, there was nevertheless no intimation of alms. Rather, the Lord Jesus was to be the true host. All without distinction were to receive gifts from his hand.[46] That is, in essence, a dimension of the designation of the Lord's Supper as κυριακὸν δεῖπνον, "the Lordly (= belonging to the Lord) Supper" in 1 Cor 11:20: The community knows the Lord present in spirit at its celebration.

To serve as an example from the non-Christian realm we might single out the meals in the Sarapis cult. In his rapturous praise of Sarapis, Aristides (ca. AD 143/144) enlarges:

> And moreover in a special way with this god alone men celebrate sacrificial communion in the true sense of the word: They invite him to their hearth and give him the best place as lord of the meal and host. Whereas in other festival meals now this god, now that one participates, Sarapis signifies the crown that does the honors in all meals alike, in that, as symposiarch, he holds sway among those who assemble in his name. . . . So this god is the giver and the receiver of donations in one.[47]

The papyrus invitations to Sarapis meals vividly illustrate the practices corresponding to this description. The meals can take place in the sanctuary of Sarapis[48] and in many cases the god himself (through human intermediaries, of course) offers the invitation.[49] Here, as mentioned above, we meet a datum which to a considerable extent essentially constitutes the phenomenon of sacred meals. It lives on in early Christian understanding of meals and it provides the sustaining ground for other forms of the presence of the Lord.

---

[46]Cf. Ernst von Dobschütz, *Die urchirstlichen Gemeinden. Sittengeschichtliche Bilder* (Leipzig: J. C. Hinrich, 1902) 50: "The Lord himself, to whom the gifts were brought, was thus at the same time to appear as host."

[47]Aristides, Or 45.27 (360.10-20 Keil); cf. Anton Höfler, *Der Sarapishymnus des Ailios Aristeides* (Stuttgart-Berlin: Kohlhammer, 1935).

[48]POxy 110: "Chairemon invites you to dine at the meal of the Lord Sarapis in the Separeion tomorrow, i.e., on the 15th at 9 o'clock."

[49]PKoln 57: "The god invites you to dinner, which will take place in the shrine of Thoeris tomorrow, at 9 o'clock." Further examples in Mariangela Vandoni, *Feste pubbliche e private nei documenti greci* (Milan-Varese: Istituto Editoriale Cisalpino, 1964) nos. 124-47; summarized now by Maria Totti, *Ausgewählte Texte der Isis- und Serapis-Religion* (Hildesheim: Olms, 1985) nos. 124-47.

2. Commemorative Actual Presence

The exalted one, spiritually present at this meal, bears the marks of the crucified one. In the backward (commemorative) look at his death on the cross, this event becomes present here and now (*actualiter*). In Paul this thought, which was evidently in danger of being lost in Corinth, is again made central. In and through the Lord's Supper the death of the Lord is effectively proclaimed: thus 1 Cor 11:26. To master the Corinthian situation Paul draws on the ὑπὲρ ὑμῶν ("for you") of the word over the bread, which expresses Jesus' surrender of his life, and, from the word over the cup, the idea of the new covenant, based on the blood of one dying.

The mystery cults, too, in abbreviated and symbolic form ritually enact the fate of their cult deity. The goal of consecration is ritual sharing in the mythical fate of the gods. We have already caught a brief glimpse of this style of thought in the Demeter hymn, which recurs as a rite in the Eleusinian mysteries. For all the formal points of comparison, the weightiest differentiation factor, we can only repeat, lies in the understanding of time. The Lord of the Lord's Supper is not a figure of the mythical past, but Jesus of Nazareth, whose death by crucifixion, lay, at the time of Paul's writing, hardly a generation earlier.

3. Proleptic Definitive Presence

The present meal anticipates (in the form of a prolepsis, an advance realization) the eschatological meal at the end of time, and looks ahead to it. The Lord who is present is at the same time the Christ of the parousia, who at the end (*finis*) of the days will definitively come. For Paul each meal celebration must hold this prospect open "until he comes," as 1 Cor 11:26, a diminuendo of the eschatological prospect of Mark 14:25 parr., maintains. This thinking has its roots in the apocalyptic metaphor of the meal, which aims at clothing in banquet imagery the coming aeon, with the inauguration of God's reign.

Religious use of the meal metaphor is, of course, found in Hellenism, too. According to the mystery cults' expectation of the beyond, the more desirable mode of existence of souls after death, itself attributed to initiation into the mysteries and favorably contrasted with the umbral existence of the Hades of Homer, includes a sublated continuation of the mysteries meal. Whereas in Plato's *Politeia* (= *Republic*), one of the speakers finds fault with this promise among the Orphics, in a pseudo-Platonic dialogue, the *Axiochos,* symposia and festal meals without end are ordained for the pious; there the initiated preside.[50] But this meal is conceived

---

[50]Cf. Plato, Resp 363C/D; Ps-Plato, Axioch 371D. In Empedocles' view, the goal of soul-transmigration is to become a table partner of the immortals (*FVS* 31 B 147); the

as belonging to the timeless beyond, not to the apocalyptic endtime. The differences in the understanding of time reappear and take on a new quality.

4. Bodily Real Presence

Bodily real presence means that the body ($\sigma\hat{\omega}\mu\alpha$) and blood of the crucified Christ are present *really* in the alimentary elements of the meal, bread and wine. The other modes of being, too—those treated above, which encompass present, past, and future—are real, but in the bodily real presence they are compressed into one concrete point. Respecting Paul, the bodily real presence is debated among exegetes. Nonetheless, Ernst Käsemann, a witness above suspicion, finds the following clear words: "The expression 'real presence,' whatever may be said against it, hits off Paul's meaning exactly."[51] One certainly would not want to overload ontologically the $\dot{\epsilon}\sigma\tau\acute{\iota}\nu$ of the words of interpretation in the Last Supper narratives, especially inasmuch as there was no copula in any presumed Semitic prototype. Backing for this view derives, rather, from the distinctively realistic-sounding argumentation of Paul in 1 Cor 11:27-30,[52] the appeal to the κοινωνία-concept in 1 Cor 10:16, and the implicit analogy which Paul in 1 Cor 10 invokes vis-à-vis Hellenistic sacrificial meals and the meals belonging to the mysteries: These lie half-hidden behind "the cup of demons" and "the table of demons" and the danger of becoming "table-fellows" with demons.[53] Parallels, certainly not flatly identical but still remotely comparable, would be the phenomena classified in religious studies as theophagy. This, generally speaking, is a matter of material appropriation of divine life-force through participation in sacrifice and meal ceremonies. In the Dionysan-Orphic cult this level may have been reached.[54]

The exegete, too, is neither able nor willing to close his eyes in the face of the cares and needs of his own time. With the theme of the bodily real presence we reach, ecumenically speaking, an especially ticklish point. The significance that this

---

Pythagoreans hope to dine with Pluto (Aristophon Fr. 12-13 Kock).

[51]Ernst Käsemann, "Anliegen und Eigenart der paulinischen Abendmahlslehre," in his *Exegetische Versuche und Besinnungen,* vol. 1, 6th ed. (Göttingen: Vandenhoeck & Ruprecht, 1970) 11-34, at 28; ET "The Pauline Doctrine of the Lord's Supper," in *Essays on New Testament Themes,* SBT 41, trans. (from 2nd ed.) W. J. Montague (London: SCM Press, 1964) 108-35, at 128: "Thus, whatever objections may be raised against the term 'Real Presence,' it expresses exactly what Paul wants to say."

[52]Cf. Betz, *Eucharistie* 2/1:106: "the real presence midrash on the words of institution."

[53]Cf. Sandelin, *Wisdom as Nourisher* (see above, n. 11), 172: "It is a possibility that in the pagan cult against which he warns the Corinthians (1 Cor 10:19-21) Paul may see some mystery cult."

[54]For details, see Klauck, *Herrenmahl,* 106-18; a skeptical view: A. J. M. Wedderburn, *Baptism* (see above, n. 4) 320-26; Sandelin, *Wisdom as Nourisher,* 172n59.

model had for the early church and for the mediaeval doctrine of the Eucharist is obvious.

We should first of all be clear on this: Even on the assumption that real-presence statements are found as early as the New Testament, e.g., in John 6:52-58 (again, not unanimously accepted), one may still wonder about its obligatory force. Historians of religion in generations past did just this insofar as they noted that massive Hellenistic influence on the New Testament is discernible in this passage, and this on a scale that appears unacceptable. Here, however, the question very seriously arises of standards of appraisal imported from outside. The contrary procedure, namely, to hold the bodily real presence as a doctrine of faith even if it were in no wise attested in the New Testament, would be considerably more difficult to imagine.

For the most part it happens that exegetes who by reason of their confessional commitments put in doubt a bodily real presence resolutely contest its existence in the New Testament. The Statement of Convergence from Lima (1982) operates with the concept of real presence, but allows leeway on how its content is to be spelled out. The main text reads,

> The eucharistic meal is the sacrament of the body and blood of Christ, the sacrament of his efficacious presence (real presence). In manifold ways Christ fulfills his promise to be with his own to the end of time. Nevertheless the presence of Christ in the Eucharist is unique in kind. . . . The church confesses Christ's real, living, and operative presence in the Eucharist.

(For the most part the last point would also be met by personal presence.) On this the explanatory notes further specify,

> Many churches believe that through these words of Jesus and the power of the Holy Spirit, the eucharistic bread and wine become in a real, if mysterious, way the body and blood of the risen Christ. . . . Other churches affirm an efficacious presence of Christ in the Eucharist, to be sure, but do not so specifically bind this presence to the signs of bread and wine. The decision respecting whether there is room for this difference within the convergence formulated in the text itself is left up to the churches.[55]

The question arises of how much difference a convergence can bear and still remain a convergence. The critical point on which theological work must be continued lies precisely here. It may not be altogether pointless to observe, from the viewpoint of the Catholic exegete, that the doctrine of transsubstantiation represents

---

[55]*Taufe, Eucharistie, und Amt. Konvergenzerklärungen der Kirchenverfassung des ökumenischen Rates der Kirchen,* 5th ed. (Paderborn: Bonifatius, 1983) 21.

only one way of thematizing what is meant by the bodily presence of the Lord.[56] The doctrine of transsubstantiation was formulated in the course of the Middle Ages. The Council of Trent designates it as a particularly apt and particularly proper formula:

> *quae conversio convenienter et proprie a sancta catholica Ecclesia transsubstantiato est appellata* (DS 1642); *quam quidem conversionem catholica Ecclesia aptissime transsubstantiationem appellat* (DS 1652).
>
> This change is appropriately and properly called by the Catholic church "transsubstantiation" (DS 1642); and this change the Catholic church most aptly calls "transsubstantiation" (DS 1652).

Nevertheless, given a carefully deployed dogmatic hermeneutics, this by no means precludes the possibility, in my opinion, that with time other models may be found and developed to interpret the sacramental event which, as such, remains in the last analysis beyond our reach.

The analogies, various in scope, that may be drawn on to illuminate the total makeup of the early Christian Lord's Supper in Paul and beyond, should not be allowed to create the impression that the Lord's Supper was assembled, mosaic-like, out of the available elements, and that it owes its origin to just such a conscious act of construction. The whole remains a creative synthesis, unique and underived. In it early Christianity adequately expresses its faith in the eucharistic presence of its Lord.

---

[56]Cf. the brief but significant remarks of Xavier Léon-Dufour, *Abendmahl und Abschiedsrede im Neuen Testament* (Stuttgart: Katholisches Bibelwerk, 1983) 177-81; orig. *Le partage du pain eucharistique selon le Nouveau Testament* (Paris: Seuil, 1982). Far more negative respecting traditional conceptions of real presence, cf. Markus Barth, *Das Mahl des Herrn: Gemeinschaft mit Israel, mit Christus und unter den Gästen* (Neukirchen-Vluyn: Neukirchener Verlag, 1987) 85-98 and passim.

The Lord's Supper
and the Lord's Supper Tradition

Reflections on 1 Corinthians 11:23b-25

Otfried Hofius

The Lord's Supper paradosis (= tradition), which Paul in 1 Cor 11:23-26 cites as having been delivered to himself and passed on by him to the Corinthians, is to be classified form-critically as a *cultic aetiology*.[1] That means: The sacred text 1 Cor 11:23b-25, connected by ὅτι-recitativum to the introductory formula in 11:23a and commented upon by Paul in 11:26, normatively establishes, while simultaneously reflecting, the liturgical practice of the early Christian communities.[2] Paul

---

[1]See, among others, Paul Neuenzeit, *Das Herrenmahl. Studien zur paulinischen Eucharistieauffassung* (Munich: Kösel, 1960) 96ff.; Ferdinand Hahn, "Die alttestamentlichen Motive in der urchistlichen Abendmahlsüberlieferung," *EvT* 27 (1967): 337-74, at 339; Helmut Merklein, "Erwägungen zur Überlieferungsgeschichte der neutestamentlichen Abendmahlstraditionen," *BZ* 21 (1977): 88-101, 235-44, at 99-100; idem, in *Studien zu Jesus und Paulus* (Tübingen: Mohr-Siebeck, 1987) 157-80, 168ff.; Rudolf Pesch, *Das Abendmahl und Jesu Todesverständnis* (Freiburg: Herder, 1978) 53-66; Hans-Josef Klauck, *Herrenmahl und hellenistischer Kult. Eine religionsgeschichtliche Untersuchung zum ersten Korintherbrief* (Münster: Aschendorff, 1982) 197-98; Christian Wolff, *Der erste Brief des Paulus an die Korinther*, vol. 2. *Auslegung der Kapitel 8-16* (Berlin: Evangelischer Verlagsanstalt, 1982) 84; Friedrich Lang, *Die Briefe an die Korinther* (Göttingen: Vandenhoeck & Ruprecht, 1986) 150. Following a first full citation, commentaries on 1 Cor will be cited by authors' names alone.

[2]With reference to the Pauline introductory expression in 11:23a the following should be noted. The termini technici παραλαμβάνειν (= Heb. *qibbēl*; Aram. *qabbēl*) and παραδιδόναι (= Heb. *māsar*; Aram. *mĕsar*) have, apart from the famous passage in Abot 1:1, an especially interesting parallel in TanhB Gen, *br'šyt* ¶10. R. Shemuel b. Nachman (Pal. ca. 260) communicates to R. Jonathan b. El'azar (Pal. ca. 220), in a whisper, an esoteric tradition concerning the creation of the world and adds the remark, "As I received in a whisper, so I have passed it on to you in a whisper (*kšm šqyblty . . . kk msrty lk . . .*). Adolf Schlatter notes this reference in *Paulus, der Bote Jesu. Eine Deutung seiner Briefe an die Korinther*, 4th ed. (Stuttgart: Calwer, 1969) 320n1.

expressly traces the tradition back to the κύριος himself,[3] who, in virtue of the introductory formula, established the meal "on the night on which he was delivered up (by God)."[4] That we in fact have here pre-Pauline traditional material emerges clearly from the distinctive linguistic features of the text.[5] A convincing proof that the Apostle has himself encroached on the wording of the tradition delivered to him has not thus far been adduced.[6] Evidently, we have to do here with a tradition, "fixed in wording" "which Paul cites unchanged."[7] We are in the dark regarding the path taken by the tradition in its pre-Pauline phase, and the attempts to illuminate it do not carry us beyond noteworthy, perhaps, but ultimately indemonstrable conjectures.[8] Guaranteed ascertainments respecting the original form of the *verba*

---

[3]The expression ἀπὸ τοῦ κυρίου in 11:23a indicates the originator of the tradition (distinct from indicating the tradents, which is done by the use of παρά + gen; see Gal 1:12; 1 Thess 2:13; 4:1; 2 Thess 3:6). On this cf. Joachim Jeremias, *Die Abendmahlsworte Jesu,* 4th ed. (Göttingen: Vandenhoeck & Ruprecht, 1967) 195; ET *The Eucharistic Words of Jesus,* rev. ed. trans. (from 3rd ed. corr.) Norman Perrin (London: SCM Press; New York: Scribner's, 1966; Philadelphia: Fortress Press, 1977) 202-203.

[4]The passive παρεδίδετο describes the act of God and the verb is used in the sense of Rom 4:25; 8:32. Cf. Isa 53:12.

[5]See Jeremias, *Abendmahlsworte* 98 (ET *Eucharistic Words,* 104). But the reference to the words "my body" in 11:24b (as foreign to Paul) should be removed, for in Rom. 7:4 also τὸ σῶμα τοῦ Χριστοῦ designates not the community but the body of Jesus which had been delivered up on the cross (against Jeremias, ibid.).

[6]This holds also for the remarks of Jeremias, ibid., 99, cf. also 160 (ET 105, cf. also 166-67); and Heinz Schürmann, *Der Einsetzungsbericht Lk 22,19-20* (Münster: Aschendorff, 1955) 24ff.; 40-41. As to the prepositional attributive τὸ ὑπὲρ ὑμῶν in 11:24b, placed after the noun τὸ σῶμα, it should be said that the expression τὸ σῶμα τὸ ὑπὲρ ὑμῶν, contrary to a widespread view held also by Jeremias, ibid., 160 (ET 166-67), can be retroverted without difficulty into Hebrew as well as into Aramaic. Proof of this is offered in my essay, "Τὸ σῶμα τὸ ὑπὲρ ὑμῶν 1 Cor 11,24," *ZNW* 80 (1989): 80-88.

[7]Pesch, *Abendmahl,* 59n1.

[8]Pesch, *Abendmahl,* 34-51, proposes the thesis that the cultic aetiology in 1 Cor 11:23b-25 is derivable from the narrative account in Mark 14:22-25, and on the basis of this narrative seems to have been adapted to "independent usage free of contextual relation" (51). "The cultic aetiology passed on by Paul . . . is, so far as we can see, already constituted in the primitive, Aramaic-speaking Jerusalem community on the basis of the narrative report of the Last Supper of Jesus with the twelve (Mark 14:22-25) with a view to governing the celebration of the Lord's Supper, and probably had already been translated into Greek for the Greek-speaking community of Hellenistic Christians" (59).

Peter Stuhlmacher, "Das neutestamentliche Zeugnis vom Herrenmahl," *ZTK* 84 (1987): 1-35, arrived at another view: The Pauline text in 1 Cor 11:23b-25, as likewise the Lukan text in Luke 22:14-20, "goes back to the proto-Lukan passion tradition probably originating in Antioch" (13-14; cf. 19, 25, 33-34). The line of transmission of the tradition of the Eucharistic narrative "leads . . . from Jesus to the Jerusalem passion tradition as it is preserved in Mark, and from here to the proto-Lukan passion narrative, from which Paul's text in 1 Cor 11:23ff. is taken" (19n17). Stuhlmacher's essay is found now in his

testamenti are equally beyond reach.[9] Respecting, in particular, the quest of the most original wording of both of the "words of bestowal,"[10] it must remain open whether Paul's version here (1 Cor 11:24b, 25b) or that offered in Mark's gospel (Mark 14:22b, 24b) merits the nod of acknowledgment[11] or whether we must grant that in both texts we already have before our eyes adaptations and transformations of an original form.

This study quite deliberately foregoes dealing with the problematic issues just now briefly evoked; it will not, then, take up anew the quest of the original form of the *verba testamenti* and their tradition history, nor enter into a comparative investigation of the different New Testament eucharistic narratives. Our interest is turned exclusively to the tradition of the Lord's Supper (1 Cor 11:23b-25) and to the context (1 Cor 11:17-34) in which the tradition is set and on which it is brought to bear. Our concern is accordingly to discuss three inseparably connected issues: what *function* is assigned the tradition of the Lord's Supper in the context of 1 Cor 11; how Paul in this connection understood the *declarations* of the text that he cited; and what inferences can be drawn regarding *the liturgical form* of the Lord's Supper, on the one hand from the tradition, and on the other from its context.[12]

I

In the context of 1 Cor 11:17-34 Paul, by citing the Lord's Supper paradosis,[13] reveals the basis of the sharp reprimand to which he gave vent in 11:17, the content

---

Jesus von Nazareth—Christus des Glaubens (Stuttgart: Calwer Verlag, 1988) 65-105.

[9]So, e.g., it is not unambiguously to be decided whether the anamnesis mandate in 1 Cor 11:24c,25c (cf. Luke 22:19c) belongs to the oldest tradition of the *verba testamenti* or not.

[10]The current designation of the word over the bread and the word over the cup as "words of interpretation" (= *Deuteworte*) is highly questionable. I take the term "words of bestowal" (= *Gabeworte*) to be decidedly more appropriate; O. Bayer settled on this term with good reason in *Promissio. Geschichte der reformatorischen Wende in Luthers Theologie* (Göttingen: Vandenhoeck & Ruprecht, 1971) 212n62 (cf. 289-90, 349). On the other hand, the word *Spendeformel* ("administration-formula"), which he also suggests as an alternative formula, is hardly serviceable.

[11]That the decision falls in favor of Mark's version, given this alternative, is still a long way from being established. See my essay referred to in n. 6, above.

[12]I wish to thank my colleague and friend Gert Jeremias for several conversations that were helpful to me in my reflections on these sets of questions.

[13]The words οὐκ ἐπαινῶ in 11:17 and 11:22 are a litotes: "I reproach most severely."

of which he specified in 11:20, and emphatically repeated in 11:22.[14] The assembly of the community for table-fellowship[15] leads in Corinth—so the Apostle declares in 11:17—"not to the advantage but to the detriment" of the members of the community.[16] This, as Paul specified in 11:20, is because it is "not possible,"[17] owing to the behavior of certain members of the community at community worship assemblies, to hold the Lord's Supper—the meal, that is, which the Lord has established, but which he also ever prepared anew for his community and at which he is himself the host.[18] That means: The meal ceremony performed by the Corinthians is in reality not the κυριακὸν δεῖπνον, for if the Lord's Supper is not rightly celebrated, then it is not celebrated at all.[19] Paul's tone is very sharp as he speaks of an eating and drinking of the sacramental gifts that takes place ἀναξίως, i.e., in an inappropriate and unworthy manner, which represents, as such, a sin "against the body and blood of the Lord" (11:27b)[20] and so necessarily elicits the Lord's condemnation and punishment (11:29; cf. 11:34).[21]

---

[14]As the connection through γάρ in 11:23a shows, the paradosis of 11:23b-25 together with the Pauline interpretation in 11:26 serves to ground what is said in 11:17-22. To the γάρ there corresponds the ὥστε of 11:27a (taken up again in 11:33a), which makes it clear that everything said in 11:27-34 is to be conceived as the inescapable consequence of the tradition of the Lord's Supper.

[15]With respect to συνέρχεσθαι as terminus technicus for the worship assembly (1 Cor 11:17, 18, 20, 33, 34; 14:23, 26) cf. Philo Vita contemplativa 65-66, and 1QSa 2.17, 22 (y'd in Nif. on the assembly of the members of the community for the community meal).

[16]Cf. Philip Bachman, Der erste Brief des Paulus an die Korinther, KNT 7, 3rd ed. (Leipzig and Erlangen: Deichert, 1921; 6) 362.

[17]οὐκ ἔστιν with inf. denotes here the objectively given impossibility.

[18]Cf. Wolff (see n. 1 above), 80; also ibid., 56, on 1 Cor 10:21.

[19]So Calvin, In Epist, I ad Corinth, Comm., ad loc. ("non fieri quod rite non fit"). I have cited from Ioannis Calvini in Novi Testamenti Epistolas Commentarii, vol. 2. Epistolae ad Corinthios, ed. A. Tholuck, 4th ed. (Berlin: Eichler, 1854) 170.

[20]ἔνοχος ἔσται is not meant as an eschatological future and is not to be related to the last judgment as "judgment threat"; against Ernst Käsemann, "Anliegen und Eigenart der paulinischen Abendmahlslehre," in Exegetische Versuche und Besinnungen, vol. 1, 2nd unrev. ed. (Göttingen: Vandenhoeck & Ruprecht, 1960; 0) 11-34, at 23; ET "The Pauline Doctrine of the Lord's Supper," in Essays on New Testament Themes, SBT 41, trans. (from 2nd ed.) W. J. Montague (London: SCM Press, 1964) 108-35, at 121-22. Rather, Wolff, 94, is correct: "Becoming guilty of the body and blood of the Lord is . . . an already given state of affairs deriving from inappropriate behavior." On ἔσται cf. LXX Gen 26:11; LXX Lev 20:9; 1 Macc 14:45; Matt 5:21 (legal terminology).

[21]κρίμα (11:29, 34) refers not to the last judgment, but to the condemnation and punishment occurring in the present, which is traced back to sacrilegious behavior. What κρίμα concretely means Paul explains in 11:30. Vv. 11:31-32 also preclude the meaning of last judgment.

What concretely the issue was regarding Paul's grievances can only be inferred from the remarks found in 1 Cor 11:17-34. In 11:18 the Apostle declares that in the worship assembly (ἐν ἐκκλησίᾳ)[22] divisions (σχίσματα) come to light. The context leaves no doubt at all that here the σχίσματα of 1 Cor 1:1-4 are not being referred to, but "breaches" conditioned by diversities in social standing among members of the community.[23] A more exact specification of the still quite general data in 11:18 essentially depends on how we are to picture the liturgical course of worship assemblies in Corinth.

With respect to this question a *consensus plurium* has been reached,[24] which may be stated summarily as follows: The tradition quoted by Paul presupposes, as the phrase μετὰ τὸ δειπνῆσαι in 11:25a indicates, a worship service in which the breaking of the bread and the distribution of the cup are separated from each other by a regular full meal. In Corinth, to be sure, a not insubstantial change in the liturgical sequence had already been made: the rite of the bread and the rite of the cup had been joined together and situated at the end of the worship assembly, so that now the full meal (i.e., the meal later called the "agape") preceded the sacramental eating and drinking (i.e., the ritual later called the "Eucharist").[25] The practice in Corinth, which Paul criticized in the sharpest terms as unworthy, was accordingly seen in the way that H.-J. Klauck, for example, compactly describes it in his commentary:

At the supper hour . . . people come together in an appropriate room. . . . The more well-to-do members of the community, who could dispose of their time more freely, meet earlier. They bring with them provisions for the meal that are meant to suffice for all, but they begin to dine and soon find themselves in a merry mood. Slaves and wage-laborers, who are not free to leave the household of their master or their places of employment any sooner, discover at their late arrival that of the full meal, to which they have nothing of their own to contribute, scanty remains at best are left. At the conclusion of the meal

---

[22]Cf. 1 Cor 14:19, 28, 35.

[23]Cf. Günther Bornkamm, "Herrenmahl und Kirche bei Paulus," in *Studien zu Antike und Urchristentum* (Munich: Kaiser, 1959) 138-76, 141-42; Wolff, 79; Lang, 148.

[24]See, e.g., Bornkamm, "Herrenmahl," 143-44, 154-55; Neuenzeit, *Herrenmahl,* 70ff., 115-16; Hahn, "Motive," 339; Jeremias *Abendmahlsworte,* 114-15, 241 (ET *Eucharistic Words,* 121, 250-51). Hans Conzelmann, *Der erste Brief an die Korinther,* KEK, 11th ed. (Göttingen: Vandenhoeck & Ruprecht, 1969) 234 (cf. also 228n18, 229n23) (ET *1 Corinthians. A Commentary on the First Epistle to the Corinthians,* Hermeneia, trans. James W. Leitch [Philadelphia: Fortress Press, 1975]); Klauck, *Herrenmahl,* 295; idem, *1. Korintherbrief,* 2nd ed. (Würzburg: Echter, 1987) 81ff.; Wolff, 77ff., 86.

[25]Lang, 148-49, 153, also adopts this liturgical sequence.

stands the sacramental rite of bread and wine. The Corinthians of better social standing ease their own consciences and those of others with the argument that no one is excluded from the sacraments and that alone is what finally matters.[26]

Though, since its proposal, this view has won wide recognition and the dignified status of an assured result lifted above all doubt, it still calls for critical review. Here two questions should be mentioned: 1. Does the phrase μετὰ τὸ δειπνῆσαι in 1 Cor 11:25a really permit the conclusion that in the earliest church there was a liturgical *ordo* for the celebration of the Lord's Supper, which exhibited the sequence "bread rite—full meal—cup rite"? 2. Do the remarks of 1 Cor 11:17-34 in fact allow the inference that at the time of the composition of 1 Corinthians the full meal preceded the sacramental ritual made up of the bread rite and the cup rite, and are the abuses censured by Paul understood in line with the situation described by H.-J. Klauck? In the two following sections of our investigation we shall have to occupy ourselves in detail with these two questions.

II

The first question demands discussion, for Rudolf Pesch and Peter Stuhlmacher have expressly contested the view that the words μετὰ τὸ δειπνῆσαι in 1 Cor 11:25a refer to a type of early Christian meal in which the full meal is opened with the eucharistic rite of the bread and closed with the eucharistic rite of the cup.[27] Both exegetes construe the phrase μετὰ τὸ δειπνῆσαι not as adverbial, but as a prepositional attributive modifying to ποτήριον,[28] and they understand the expression τὸ ποτήριον μετὰ τὸ δειπνῆσαι (= "the cup after eating"[29] / "the cup after the meal"[30] to the effect that by this expression the third Passover cup is quite

---

[26]Klauck, *1 Korintherbrief,* 81; for details, idem., *Herrenmahl,* 291ff. See further, e.g., the depiction in Bornkamm, *Herrenmahl,* 141ff.; Wolff 77, 81; Lang, 148-49.

[27]Pesch, *Abendmahl* 44-45, 62ff.; idem, *Das Markusevangelium,* HTKNK, vol. 2 (Freiburg-Basel-Vienna: Herder, 1977; 0) 370, 373. Stuhlmacher, *Herrenmahl*; idem, "Biblische Theologie als Weg der Erkenntnis Gottes," *Jahrbuch für Biblische Theologie* 1 (1986): 91-114, at 100n49; also Lang, 151.

[28]Pesch, *Markusevangelium,* 2:370: "The expression μετὰ τὸ δειπνῆσαι belongs to τὸ ποτήριον and does not describe any detail of the procedure." Stuhlmacher presupposes the same judgment, when he understands the formula as "the cup 'after the meal' " (*Herrenmahl,* 9-10 [= 72, 74]; "the cup passed around after the meal," 14 [= 77]).

[29]So Pesch, *Markusevangelium* 2:373 (= *Abendmahl,* 44); *Abendmahl,* 64.

[30]So Stuhlmacher (see n, 28).

emphatically meant.[31] On the basis of this understanding of text and referent respecting the words μετὰ τὸ δειπνῆσαι, Peter Stuhlmacher firmly states: "Of an early Christian celebration of the Lord's Supper at which the bread is distributed at the outset and the cup only after the full meal (Günther Bornkamm), we know nothing at all!"[32] The original Christian practice assumed by Bornkamm and others "is not historically attested anywhere in the early Christian sphere of tradition";[33] we have to do here with "a pure construct of exegetical research based on three Greek words which [in fact] are meant to enlighten catechumens of the diaspora, uninstructed in Jewish customs, on which cup was involved in Jesus' handling of the cup!"[34]

The interpretation that Pesch and Stuhlmacher propose of the phrase μετὰ τὸ δειπνῆσαι is, as is now to be shown, not viable. Even linguistically it is impossible. If the words μετὰ τὸ δειπνῆσαι were intended as a prepositional attributive modifying τὸ ποτήριον, and if this use of the attributive was for the purpose of stressing that the cup referred to was the third of the four cups prescribed for the Passover meal, then the article would have necessarily had to stand before the prepositional phrase:[35] τὸ ποτήριον τὸ [!] μετὰ τὸ δειπνῆσαι.[36] On the basis

---

[31]Pesch, *Markusevangelium* 2:373 (= *Abendmahl,* 44): "The expression μετὰ το δειπνῆσαι has (in the first place) nothing to do with the performance of the Lord's Supper, its sequence, its liturgical regulation, but denotes the third cup at the end of the Passover meal." Stuhlmacher, "Herrenmahl," 14 [= 77]: The Pauline text establishes, respecting "the cup that Jesus took: it was the (third) cup (of the four required for Passover), taken 'after the meal.' "

[32]Stuhlmacher, *Herrenmahl,* 14 [= 77].

[33]Ibid. 14n13 [= 101n13].

[34]Ibid. For Stuhlmacher the words μετὰ τὸ δειπνῆσαι refer to the "farewell Passover . . . which Jesus held together with the twelve (on the night on which he was delivered up)" (ibid.). To that extent, but only to that extent, would there be in this expression a reference to a meal at which the bread transaction and the cup transaction were separated from one another by a full meal.

[35]See Blass-Debrunner-Rehkopf, *Grammatik des neutestamentlichen Griechisch* (BDR) ¶269.2 and ¶272; further, L. Radermacher, *Neutestamentliche Grammatik,* HNT 1/1, 2nd ed. (Tübingen: Mohr-Siebeck, 1925) 117; E. Bornemann and E. Risch, *Griechische Grammatik* (1973) ¶150; E. G. Hoffmann and H. von Siebenthal, *Griechische Grammatik zum Neuen Testament* (Riehen/Schweiz: Immanuel-Verlag., 1985) ¶136a (1.b). One of the possible exceptions (see BDR ¶269.1, ¶272.2) is not relevant to 1 Cor 11:25a. On the contrary: precisely when "the cup after the meal" (e.g., the *qidduš*-cup) is to be emphatically differentiated from the other cups of the Passover meal, the article must absolutely be present (see BDR ¶269.2!). A. T. Robertson and Alfred Plummer, *A Critical and Exegetical Commentary on the First Epistle of St Paul to the Corinthians,* ICC, 2nd ed. (Edinburgh: T. & T. Clark, 1914) 246, have rightly said, "We must not translate, 'the after-supper cup," which would require τὸ μετὰ τὸ δειπνῆσαι ποτήριον." Klauck rightly

of grammar, then, the translation "the cup after the meal" in 1 Cor 11:25a is positively excluded.[37] Nor can the translation be at all justified by arguing that τὸ ποτήριον μετὰ τὸ δειπνῆσαι is a "liturgical technical" expression corresponding to a "Jewish *terminus technicus*," namely, to the expression "the wine after eating."[38]

The expression "the wine after eating"[39] is admittedly found in m. Ber. 6:5; still, it is by no means a "Jewish *terminus technicus*," but an *ad hoc* formula coined in halakic discussion.[40] It should likewise be remarked that the phrase "the wine after eating" denotes the wine served with dessert at a dinner party.[41] This wine accordingly has as little to do with the ποτήριον of the Lord's Supper as it does

---

gives his approval to this in *Herrenmahl*, 310n152, and adds appropriately, "A repetition of το after ποτήριον would also be possible with the attributive position (thus: το ποτήριον τὸ μετὰ τὸ δειπνῆσαι).

[36]An unproven and also unprovable (because doubtless false) claim is made when Pesch, *Abendmahl*, 44, explains his own view as follows: "The word order clearly speaks for . . . this interpretation. If a reference to the action . . . after the meal had been intended, the formulation would have had to be μετὰ τὸ δειπνῆσαι ὡσαύτως καὶ το ποτήριον or ὡσαύτως μετὰ τὸ δειπνῆσαι καὶ τὸ ποτήριον." How the references then adduced by Pesch support this statement has remained wholly mysterious to me. The attestation of Luke 12:5, which he especially emphasizes, shows the grammatically correct position of the prepositional attributive, and would require, analogously to 1 Cor 11:25a, the formula τὸ ποτήριον τὸ μετὰ τὸ δειπνῆσαι ποτήριον.

[37]This should also be said in opposition to Neuenzeit, *Herrenmahl*, 71, who asserts that the formula in 1 Cor 11:25a "can equally have intended to designate 'the cup after the meal,' therefore the cup of blessing of the Jewish festal meal."

[38]So Pesch, *Abendmahl*, 45: "With τὸ ποτήριον μετὰ τὸ δειπνῆσαι the third cup can be designated in liturgical-technical fashion in analogy to the attested Jewish terminus technicus, the 'wine after eating' (m.Ber. 8.8)." Similarly in Hermann Patsch, *Abendmahl und historischer Jesus* (Stuttgart: Calwer Verlag, 1972) 72: "Perhaps τὸ ποτήριον μετὰ τὸ δειπνῆσαι is a Jewish terminus technicus for the 'wine after eating' (*yyn 'hr hmzwn*) (m.Ber. 8.8)." The reference to m.Ber. 8.8 is an error, which Pesch and Patsch have taken over from Gustaf Dalman, *Jesus-Jeschua* (Leipzig: Hinrichs, 1922; rpt. Darmstadt: Wissenschaftliche Buchgesellschaft, 1967) 138n13. The correct reference would be m.Ber 6.5.

[39]Alongside the expression "the wine before the meal," which designates the wine served with appetizers before a dinner party. On this see Paul Billerbeck, *Kommentar zum Neuen Testament aus Talmud und Midrash* (Munich: Beck, 1922–1928; 7th unrev. ed. 1978) 4/2:616).

[40]This cannot be a terminus technicus any more than the expressions, likewise appearing in m.Ber 6.5, "the savories before the meal" (*hprprt šlpny hmzwn*) and "the savories after the meal" (*hprprt šl'hr hmzwn*). The alleged "Jewish terminus technicus" has in the meantime also found its way into a commentary (Joachim Gnilka, *Das Evangelium nach Markus*, EKKNT 2, vol. 2 [Zürich-Einsiedeln: Benziger, 1979] 241), and no doubt will—thus wondrously brought to life—remain alive and well in NT scholarship.

[41]See Billerbeck 4/2:634.

with the third cup of the Passover meal. But especially to be pondered linguistically is the fact that in Hebrew the expression "the wine after eating" displays the prepositional attributive joined to the noun by the relative particle *še: hyyn šl'hr hmzwn*.[42] To this there would correspond in Greek the joining of the attributive by the article (therefore: ὁ οἶνος ὁ [!] μετὰ τὸ δειπνῆσαι). We find an adverbial use of the expression "after dinner" in, for example, m. Ber. 8:8 (*b'lhm yyn l'hr hmzwn*), "wine is served (to the diners) after dinner."[43] In this clause the phrase *l'hr hmzwn* is to be classified as adverbial. The expression μετὰ τὸ δειπνῆσαι in 1 Cor 11:25a exactly corresponds to it. The conclusion to be drawn from these linguistic considerations: It is certain that the words μετὰ τὸ δειπνῆσαι do not belong adjectivally—i.e., as prepositional attributive—to το ποτηριον; rather, they belong adverbially to ἔλαβεν εὐχαριστήσας, to which ὡσαύτως relates as complementary predicate.[44]

Considerations of content should be set cheek by jowl with the result of the linguistic inquiry. If one takes the text of the paradosis in 1 Cor 11:23b-25 as it stands, no reference of any kind to the Passover meal is in evidence.[45] There is no reference whatever of this kind even in the mention of the cup that Jesus took "after supper," over which he spoke a thanksgiving, and which he then distributed to his table-fellows (11:25a). In short, the Pauline tradition gives us a description of Jesus' Last Supper that exhibits the typical elements of a Jewish meal.[46] The words ἔλαβεν ἄρτον καὶ εὐχαριστήσας ἔκλασεν in 11:23b, 24a describe in charact-

---

[42]Likewise, ibid., "the wine before the meal" = *hyyn šlpny hmzwn*. Cf. also the usages cited in n. 40, above.

[43]Cf. also m.Ber. 6.6 and see b.Ber. 42b-43a on the diversity of construction with the adnominal (attributive) and adverbial use of prepositional expressions respectively.

[44]This is the sense in which *all* ancient translations understand the text: Vulgate, *similiter et calicem, postquam coenavit*; Peshitta, *hkn' mn btr d'hšmw 'p ks' yhb*; Sahidic, *auō ouapot on ĕnteihe mĕnĕnsa treuouōm*; Bohairic, *pairēti on pikeaphot menensa pidipnon*. The old liturgies understand the text likewise, as, e.g., the *Euchologion* of Serapion (13.14) shows: ὁ κύριος Ἰησοῦς Χριστὸς λαβὼν ποτήριον μετὰ τὸ δειπνῆσαι ἔλεγεν . . . ; see *Prex Eucharistica. Textus e variis liturgiis antiquioribus selecti*, ed. A. Hänggi and I. Pahl, 2nd ed. (Fribourg: Universitätsverlag, 1968) 130. Cf. further ibid., 120 (Papyrus 465 of the John Rylands Library at Manchester); 126 (Papyrus of Dêr-Balizeh); 248 (Greek James-Anaphora); 364 (Greek Gregory Anaphora).

[45]With a view to 1 Cor 11:25a Schlatter, *Paulus, der Bote Jesu*, 324, correctly remarks: Whether Paul takes the meal referred to by δειρπνῆσαι "to be the Passover meal is not discernible." It is different with the Lukan Long Text, Luke 22:14-20, where the description is clearly oriented to the sequence of a Passover meal.

[46]Cf., above all, Jeremias *Abendmahlsworte*, 103-105; also 166-70 (ET *Eucharistic Words*, 108-11; 174-78).

eristically Jewish terminology[47] the rite of the blessing *before* the meal, the so-called *birkat ham-mô ṣ î.* With the "breaking" of the bread, which the one who speaks the blessing thereupon distributes to the diners, the meal is opened.[48] The *birkat ham-māzôn,* the blessing after the meal, brings the meal to an end. The words ὡσαύτως καὶ τὸ ποτήριον μετὰ τὸ δειπνῆσαι in 11:25 speak of this prayer. The adverb ὡσαύτως (in like manner) is, as we remarked above, to be complemented by the predicate ἔλαβεν εὐχαριστήσας ("in like manner [he took] the cup after supper [and spoke the blessing, (i.e., the prayer of thanksgiving)], saying . . . ").[49]

The gesture alluded to here—corresponding to the distribution of the bread implied in ἔκλασεν (11:24a)—includes Jesus' handing round the cup to his table-fellows. It is no accident that, in contradistinction to anarthrous ἄρτον in 11:23b, the article stands before ποτήριον.[50] The article is chosen because with reference to the ποτήριον there is question of the cup specified for the thanksgiving prayer, which thus has a fixed liturgical function and bears a name bringing just this function to expression: "the cup of praise" (or, as custom has formulated it, "the cup of blessing, the blessing cup").[51] In Hebrew the terminus technicus is *kôs šel běrākāh,*[52] in Aramaic, *kāsā děbirkětā'.*[53] The Greek equivalent is attested in 1 Cor

---

[47]See esp. j.Ber. 8.12a.53: "He (R Abbahu) gave him (R. Zeʿira) the bread to break, saying: Take and speak the blessing!" (*yhb lyh ʿgwlh dqṣy* [read *dyqṣy*] *'mr lyh sb byhk*). Cf. further j.Ber. 6.10a.56-57, 74. I cite the Jerusalem Talmud from the Krotoschin edition (1865/1866). On the translation of *brk* by εὐχαριστεῖν, see Jeremias, 106, 167, 170. (ET: 115, 175, 177.)

[48]Cf. b.Ber. 46a: "to begin" (*šrʾ*), i.e., "to begin the meal," is identical with "to break bread" (*bṣʿ*). Terms for the breaking of bread are Heb. *bṣʿ* (b.Ber. 39b, 46a, 47a; b.Sabb. 117b; b.Hul. 7b); Aram. *qṣʾ* (j.Ber. 6.10a.73, 8.12a.53; j.Sabb. 6.8d.6). Less frequently, Heb. *prs* (b.Roš Haš. 29b; cf. Aram. *prs* (Tg.J. 1 Sam 9:13).

[49]Cf. outside Mark 14:23 (λαβὸν ποτήριον εὐχαριστήσας) the Jewish parallel in j.Ber. 7.11b.74: R. Yaʿaqob b. Acha "took the cup and recited the blessing and said" (*nsb . . . ks' wbyrk w'mr*). See further the common form of the command spoken after the meal was completed: "Take (the cup) and recite the blessing" (*sb bryk*); e.g., j.Ber. 7.11c.6, 8.12a.54; Lev Rab. 9:3 to 7:11. Jeremias lined up the rabbinic material, *Abendmahlsworte,* 169 (ET *Eucharistic Words,* 177), explaining that by the "taking (up)" of the ποτήριον "is . . . meant the raising of the cup about one handsbreadth above the table, an action which introduced the grace."

[50]So also Luke 22:20; but Mark 14:23 = Matt 26:27 differ.

[51]Cf. Jeremias, *Abendmahlsworte,* 106 (ET *Eucharistic Words,* 113). "The use of the article before ποτήριον (noticeable in virtue of its asymmetry with anarthrous ἄρτον in v. 23) points to the ritual 'cup of blessing' (1 Cor 10:16)."

[52]j.Ber. 7.11c.70, 75; 11d.2; b.Ber. 50b, 51a, 51b, 55a; b.šabb. 76b; b.Erub. 29b; b.Pesah 105b, 106a, 107a, 109b, 119b; b.Sota 38b; b.B. Mes. 87a; b.B. Bat. 97b; b.Hul. 87a; Gen Rab. 8:15 to Gen 1:28; Midr. Ps 134 ¶2 to v. 2; Pirqe Mashiah, BhM 3.76; Seʿudat Gan ʿEden, BhM 5.46; Pesquita hadatta, BhM 6.47.

[53]b.Ber. 51b (several times); b.Pesah 103a; b.Sukk. 49b.

10:16 (τὸ ποτήριον τῆς εὐλογίας) and in Jos. As. 8:9; 19:15 (ποτήριον εὐλογ-ίας). The cup of blessing, which in rabbinic literature, when the context is clear, can be designated simply as "the cup,"[54] is always and exclusively the cup of wine over which the blessing after the meal is recited.[55] In the Passover meal this is the third of four prescribed cups (m.Pesah 10.7).[56] Nevertheless, the cup of blessing was by no means used exclusively for the Passover meal or even for a Jewish festival meal;[57] in Jewish table-custom it belonged rather "to every meal at which wine was drunk."[58] That did not have to be a festival meal at all, as the following references sufficiently attest.

j.Ber. VII 11b 73ff.

R. Ze'ira, R. Ja'aqob b. Acha, R. Hiyya b. Ba and R. Hanina "sat (together) and ate (with one another)" (*hww ytbyn 'klyn*). After the common meal "R. Ja'aqob took the cup and recited the blessing" (*nsb ks' wbyrk*).

j.Ber. 8.12a.52ff.

R. Ze'ira goes to see R. Abbahu in Caesarea and meets him "just as he was about to eat." R. Abbahu invites his visitor in to dine with him and asks him to

---

[54]So, e.g., j.Ber. 7.11b.59, 74; 11c.6; Qoh Rab. 7 ¶24 to v. 12; Exod Rab. 25:10 to 16:4 (of the meal of the time of salvation: *nwtnyn ldwd hkws*, "one gives David the cup [that he may recite the grace after the meal]").

[55]Ps 116:13 is occasionally referred to the cup of blessing, and only to it ("the cup of salvation will I raise . . .": b.Ber. 51b; b.Pesah 119b par Se'udat Gan 'Eden, BhM 5.46; Exod Rab. 25:10 to 16:4. Cf. today's thanksgiving after the meal: Sidur Sefat Emet (with German trans. by S. Bamberger), Basel, 1956 = 1964, 279.

[56]Cf. Jeremias, *Abendmahsworte*, 81n8, 104-105 (ET *Eucharistic Words*, 87n8, 110-11).

[57]In exegetical literature one often chances upon the wholly unexplained concept of the Jewish "festal meal" and upon the view that the "cup of blessing," apart from the Passover meal, is only customary at the festal meal. The reason for this may lie in the fact that Paul Billerbeck dealt with the daily blessing *before* and *after* the meal in the framework of the excursus, "An Ancient Jewish Festal Meal" (4/2:611-39: blessing before the meal, 621-22; blessing after the meal, 627ff.). Billerbeck himself formulates as follows: "after each (solemn) meal in common grace was said over the cup of blessing" (4/1:58).

[58]So correctly Leonhard Goppelt, *Theologie des Neuen Testaments*, vol. 2. *Vielfalt und Einheit des apostolischen Christuszeugnisses* (Göttinger: Vandenhoeck & Ruprecht, 1976) 477; cf. idem, ποτήριον, TWNT 6:155ff., 3-4 (= TDNT 6:149ff., 3-4). On the other hand, it is inaccurate to say, with Gerhard Delling, *TRE* 1:49, 5ff., that the *kôs šel běrākāh* "introduced the further drinking of wine by the dinner guests."

break the bread.[59] After eating (*mn d'klyn*) R. Abbahu once again asks of his guest: "Take (the cup) and recite the blessing!" (*sb bryk*).[60]

Lev Rab. 9:3 to 7:11

R. Yannai receives a guest in his house, invites him to dine, and after eating requests that he take the cup and recite the blessing (*sb bryk*).

b. Ḥul. 87a

Rabbi dines with a single guest. "After they had eaten and drunk," (*l' h r š'klw wštw*), they performed the thanksgiving prayer over the cup of blessing.

In none of these cases is there question of a "feast-day meal";[61] it is just an everyday meal.[62] At an ordinary meal, too, the repast was opened by the bread rite and, if wine was available, closed with the cup rite.[63]

Our inquiries up to this point have led us to a twofold conclusion: (a) the words μετὰ τὸ δειπνῆσαι ποτήριον in 1 Cor 11:25a are clearly to be specified as adverbial; their belonging attributively to ποτήριον is entirely ruled out on grammatical grounds. (b) In the tradition represented by 1 Cor 11:23b-25 nothing points to the particularities of a Passover meal; the ritual acts described in 11:23b, 24a and 11:25a correspond rather to the formal grace before and after meals typical of a Jewish repast.

Before we draw the conclusion from these findings, 1 Cor 11:25 is still open to two possible interpretative missteps to be briefly taken up and dismissed.

The first is to relate ὡσαύτως to the adverbial μετὰ τὸ δειπνῆσαι, and thus find expressed in 11:25a the notion that Jesus took up and distributed both the bread

---

[59]See n. 47 above.

[60]This narrative very richly attests (for the ordinary meal) the following sequence: bread rite—meal—cup rite. The phrase *mn d'klyn* (lit. "after they had eaten") exactly corresponds in substance to the μετὰ τὸ δειπνῆσαι of 1 Cor 11:25a.

[61]There is reference to a feast-day meal, e.g., in j.Ber. 7.11b.59 (with context) par. Qoh Rab. 7 ¶24 to v. 12, as in the descriptions of the banquet of the time of salvation (b.Pesah. 119b among others).

[62]Likewise also j.Ber. 7.11c.5ff.; b.Ber 51b; b.Hul. 86b.

[63]The following judgment of Stuhlmacher, *Herrenmahl*, 14n13 [= 101n13] is therefore to be corrected: "The only truly attested meal celebrations at which acts connected with the bread and those connected with the cup were separated in the way suggested by Bornkamm, are the Passover and the Jewish festal meal."

and the cup *after* the meal.[64] The impossibility of an interpretation of this sort is first of all manifest from the fact that the breaking of the bread is the fixed ritual *opening* of the meal. Added to this is the linguistic consideration that ὡσαύτως καί is invariably related to the immediately following expression.[65] The clause "similarly after the meal he also took the cup" would have to have read (if the Greek text were to be unambiguous): ὡσαύτως καὶ μετὰ τὸ δειπνῆσαι τὸ ποτήριον.[66] The formulation in 1 Cor 11:25a allows for only *one* interpretation: "in the same way [he] also [took] the cup—(and this, to be precise) after the meal. . . . "

A second faulty interpretation results if one refers τὸ δειπνῆσαι exclusively to the eating of the previously mentioned eucharistic bread.[67] For, the verb δειπνεῖν

---

[64] This interpretative error underlies the following suggestion of Wolff, 91: "The notice 'after eating,' which characterizes the cup as the one passed around after eating, and which allows the inference of an original meal between the bread transaction and the cup transaction, could be understood on the basis of the 'likewise also' to the effect that the distribution of the wine took place 'likewise,' like that of the bread, 'after eating.' "

[65] See 2 Macc 2:12; 3 Macc 7:19; Prov 20:4; 27:15, 20; Ep Jer 60; T. Lev. 17:7; 1 Tim 5:25. The same goes for ὡσαύτως δὲ καί: Jdt 15:5; Tob 7:10 S; 2 Macc 2:14; 15:39; 3 Macc 6:33; Ep Jer 21, 27, 70; Ep. Arist. 158, 197, 309; Mark 14:31; Luke 20:31; Rom 8:26.

[66] Possible, but not unambiguous, would be also: ὡσαύτως μετὰ τὸ δειπνῆσαι καὶ το ποτήριον (cf. respecting the connection of the simple ὡσαύτως to an adverb immediately following: Josh 6:8; Esth 9:13). Also not unambiguous is the formulation such as is found in Luke 22:20a: καὶ τὸ ποτήριον ὡσαύτως μετὰ τὸ δειπνῆσαι. Here ὡσαύτως *can* relate to the adverb ("and the cup likewise after the meal"); it *can* just as well, however, belong to τὸ ποτήριον ("and in the same way the cup—[and this, to be precise,] after the meal"). If in other words ὡσαύτως is referred to a nominal subject or object, it either immediately precedes this subject or object (1 Chron 28:16; Ezek 40:16; Matt 25:17; 1 Tim 2:9), or it immediately follows it (Deut 12:22; 15:22; Ezek 42:5; Mark 12:21; 1 Tim 3:8, 11; Titus 2:3, 6). On this second possibility, cf., above all, the reference (mentioned by Delling, *TRE* 1:51, 23-24) from Xenophon *Anab* 7.3.22: ἀναλόμενος τοὺς ἑαυτῷ παρακειμένους ἄρτους διέκλα κατὰ μικρόν καὶ ἐρρίπτει οἷς αὐτῷ ἐκόκει, καὶ τὰ κρέα ὡσαύτως ("he took the bread lying before him, broke it into small pieces, and threw it to the guests, as it pleased him; and likewise the meat"). As ὡσαύτως is here related to τὸ κρέα so in Luke 22:20a it can very well belong to τὸ ποτήριον. That the Lukan formulation, which does not correspond to that in 1 Cor 11:25, depicts a secondary meal custom of a later time, "which has transposed the eucharistic breaking of the bread to the eucharistic cup at the end of the meal (Schürmann, *Einsetzungsbericht*, 34), is, therefore, by no means certain.

[67] This interpretative error is found, for example, in Pesch, *Abendmahl,* 62: "Even if μετὰ τὸ δειπνῆσαι were itself a temporal designation, it would suffice to think of the eating of the eucharistic bread." In support of this thesis, Pesch, 63, claims (appealing to Gerd Thiessen), "The Lord's Supper as a full meal was a meal consisting only of bread." In fact, this claim is far from substantiated. And even if it were correct, still not *all* the bread that was eaten as a full meal was "eucharistic bread." For *eucharistic* bread is only

(to dine, to eat a meal) is used as a rule of a real meal,[68] and the phrase μετὰ τὸ δειπνῆσαι itself has parallels in Greek literature that unambiguously speak of a full meal.[69] That in biblical Greek "to eat bread" is not ἄρτον δειπνεῖν but ἄρτον ἐσθίειν or ἄρτον φαγεῖν[70] should also be observed.[71]

To formulate the result thus far, we should say, the Lord's Supper paradosis handed on by Paul in 1 Cor 11:23b-25, presupposes, as the words μετὰ τὸ δειπνῆσαι clearly attest, a meal between the bread rite and the cup rite.[72] But if this tradition is to be seen as a "sacred cultic formula,"[73] a cultic aetiology reflecting, codifying, and grounding the liturgical performance or, as Peter Stuhlmacher formulates it, "a piece of ritual in narrative form,"[74] then the liturgical sequence of the meal celebration in the earliest church *must* have corresponded to it. This holds in any case for the zone from which the tradition hails and in which it is transmitted. Historically, there cannot be the slightest doubt about the existence of a Lord's Supper celebration at which a full meal took place between the bread rite and the cup rite.

III

At this point we take up the second question formulated above (at the end of section one) which bears on the situation in Corinth as Paul in 1 Cor 11:17-34 has

---

the bread that belonged to the rite of grace before the meal and then was distributed to the table partners.

[68]Cf. in LXX Tob 7:9 S; 8:1; Prov 23:1; Dan 11:27; further: Ep Arist 180; Test Job 15:2; Josephus *Ant.* 2.312; Luke 17:8; Rev 3:20.

[69]Plutarch, *Quaest. conv.* 3.1.1 (Mor. 645D); Polybius, *Hist.* 10.49.2; Athenaeus, *Deipnosoph.* 5.179d, 9.410b, c; cf. also Philo *Vita contemplativa* 83 (*meta to deipnon*) and, in substance, Did. 10:1 (*meta to emplēsthēnai*). In rabbinic literature the expressions *l' h r hmzwn* in m.Ber. 8.8 (cf. b.Pesah 105b); *mn d'klyn* j.Ber. 8.12a.54; *l'hr š'wklyn wšwtyn* b.Pesah 119b; *l' h r š'klw wštw* b.Hul. 87a. correspond to it.

[70]See the concordances. Besides, one comes across the expression ἄρτον τρώγειν twice in John's gospel (John 6:58; 13:18).

[71]The phrase ἄρτον δειπνεῖν in Hesiod, Op. 442 means not simply to eat bread, but "make a meal on [of?] bread" (Liddel/Scott 375a).

[72]So rightly also Gerd Theissen, "Soziale Integration und sakramentales Handeln. Eine Analyse von 1 Cor XI 17-34," in his *Studien zur Soziologie des Urchristentums*, 2nd ed. (Tübingen: Mohr-Sieback, 1983) 290-317, at 299.

[73]Ibid.

[74]Stuhlmacher, "Herrenmahl" 3 [= 67]; cf. 34 [= 97].

it in view. Does the Apostle presuppose a worship assembly at which—in contradistinction to the original practice—a full meal preceded the sacramental meal made up of the bread rite and the cup rite? At the time of the composition of 1 Corinthians was the phrase μετὰ τὸ δειπνῆσαι (11:25a) accordingly "only an antiquated liturgical formula"[75] to which liturgical practice had long since ceased to correspond? These questions, in my opinion, call for a decided no.[76]

Specifically, the questions would be answerable in the affirmative only on condition that the interpretation of the two verses 11:21 and 33, which provides the foundation of the current *consensus plurium,* had to be acknowledged as accurate. This interpretation understands 11:21 to say that the well-to-do members of the community "anticipate," i.e., already begin eating before the poor are present; and the interpretation correspondingly finds in 11:33 the Apostle's admonition that the wealthy members are supposed to "wait for" the poor members. In both cases, however, there exists in my view an interpretative misstep, for προλαμβάνειν in 11:21 does not mean "anticipate, take in advance" and the directive ἀλλήλους ἐκδέχεσθε in 11:33 does not mean "wait for one another"! Both these assertions must now be supported in detail.

First Cor 11:21 reads, ἕκαστος γὰρ τὸ ἴδιον δεῖπνον προλαμβάνει ἐν τῷ φαγεῖν, καὶ ὃς μὲν πεινᾷ ὃς δὲ μεθύει. But if one translates προλαμβάνειν here by "goes ahead" (as in RSV: "For in eating, each one goes ahead with his own meal, and one is hungry and another is drunk"), there result three quite substantial problems.

(1) One must grant an imprecise use of the word ἕκαστος ("each one") and offer an explanation for it, e.g., "The word chosen, 'each one,' is an exaggeration (as in 14.26, as well) and denotes those who by reason of easy circumstances do not have to work, and so met early, and who provided most of the food for the Lord's Supper."[77]

(2) The expression ἐν τῷ φαγεῖν (at the [common] meal) cannot be taken literally, since the rich begin to eat before the poor arrive, so that a communal φαγεῖν cannot take place at all.[78]

---

[75]So Bornkamm, *Herrenmahl,* 155.

[76]Well-grounded demurrals to the view represented by Bornkamm and others are advanced by, e.g., Theissen, "Soziale Integration," 289ff.; Christoph Burchard, "The Importance of Joseph and Aseneth for the Study of the New Testament: A General Survey and Fresh Look at the Lord's Supper," *NTS* 33 (1987): 102-34, esp. 127.

[77]Wolff, 81; cf. Klauck, *Herrenmahl,* 293: "*hekastos* . . . is used, as in 14:26, imprecisely, in the sense of: each who is in a position to." Also Theissen, 294, similarly assesses *hekastos.*

[78]Cf. Johannes Weiss, *Der erste Korintherbrief,* KEK 5, 9th ed. (Göttingen:

(3) Between the preceding sentence ἕκαστος . . . τὸ ἴδιον δεῖπνον προλαμβάνει ἐν τῷ φαγεῖν and the following description, ὃς μὲν πεινᾷ ὃς δὲ μεθύει, connected to the above by a consecutive καί, one must assume an incongruity: inasmuch as ἕκαστος can refer only to the well-to-do, ὃς μὲν . . . ὃς δέ cannot be understood as unpacking ἕκαστος.[79]

By way of response to these three problems, the following should be said in all brevity.

(1) ἕκαστος in 14:26 may perhaps be "exaggerated";[80] but both in Paul himself and elsewhere in the New Testament as well, where an ἴδιος appears next to ἕκαστος (as in 11:21!),[81] ἕκαστος is always to be understood literally and so, quite precisely, in a comprehensive sense.[82]

(2) The words ἐν τῷ φαγεῖν take on unforced meaning only if we see denoted thereby the "communal" eating and understand 11:21 in such wise that "everyone" is present at the meal; all members of the community, then, eat at the same time.[83]

(3) On the linguistic side, ἕκαστος can only be a collective concept under which ὃς μέν and ὃς δέ are ordered; such is the case in the comparable construction of Rom 14:5: ὃς μὲν κρίνει ἡμέραν παρ' ἡμέραν, ὃς δὲ κρίνει πᾶσαν ἡμέραν· ἕκαστος ἐν τῷ ἰδίῳ νοΐ πληροφορείσθω.[84] "One man (ὃς μέν) esteems one day as better than another, while another man (ὃς δέ) esteems all days alike. Let everyone (ἕκαστος) be fully convinced in his own mind" (RSV).

The states of affairs thus presented exclude, in my opinion, the option that προλαμβάνειν in 1 Cor 11:21 have the sense of "to anticipate, to go ahead." Rather,

---

Vandenhoeck & Ruprecht, rpt.1977; =1910) 281.

[79]The tortuous and not completely harmonizable paraphrase in *EWNT* 3:380-81 here speaks for itself: "Each anticipates (at the gathering for the Lord's Supper) his own meal," i.e., before all are there, so that there are then those (at the Lord's Supper itself) who are (still) "hungry" and others (already) "drunk."

[80]Theissen, "Soziale Integration," 294, also names 1 Cor 1:12 in addition to 1 Cor 14:16. In both places, however, ἕκαστος can easily be taken *literally*.

[81]Rom 14:5; 1 Cor 3:8; 7:2, 7; 12:11; 15:23, 38; Gal 6:5; Matt 25:15; Luke 6:44; John 16:32; Acts 2:6, 8; Jas 1:14.

[82]The same goes for the sentence of Eratosthenes (frag. 16) cited by Theissen, 295: καὶ ἐξ ἰδίας ἕκαστος λαγύνου παρ' αὐτῶν φέροντες πίνουσιν. See further the passage from Johannes Malalas cited in n. 92.

[83]For this understanding—and against the widespread interpretation of the Corinthian siutation—v. 20 also speaks: συνερχομένων οὖν ὑμῶν ἐπὶ τὸ αὐτὸ (!); cf. 14:23.

[84]Analogous referent: 1 Cor 7:7, ἕκαστος ἴδιον ἔχει χάρισμα ἐκ θεοῦ, ὁ μὲν (v. 1, ὃς μέν) οὕτως, ὁ δὲ (v. 1, ὃς δὲ) οὕτως. Cf. finally also Matt 25:15, where ᾧ μέν . . . ᾧ δέ . . . ᾧ δέ is all brought together in ἑκάστῳ.

it will have to be translated: "At the (common) meal each (par)takes (of) his own food." The translation of προλαμβάνειν with "to (par)take (of)"[85] is linguistically unobjectionable. The verb has two basic meanings: "to take in advance" (*vorher-nehmen*) and "to take (out)/bring forth" (*hervornehmen*). Hence, the verb can so be used that *pro* in a temporal sense is stressed; this is the case in the New Testament[86] in Mark 14:8. It can also be used, however, *without* stress on the temporal aspect, of which, in the New Testament, Gal 6:1 provides an example (προλαμβάνεσθε = be taken).[87] The compound form προλαμβάνειν is directly identical with the uncompounded form in Sib. Or. 3.569, where προλαμβάνειν τέλος is used in the sense of λαμβάνειν τέλος (Sib. Or. 211.741): to come to an end. But with respect to 1 Cor 11:21, it is especially significant that προλαμβάνειν is found on a stele of the Asclepius sanctuary in Epidaurus in the sense "to take (food)/to partake of (food).[88] The stele reads,

Just as I arrived in the sanctuary, he (the god) commanded me, . . . to partake of cheese and bread (τυρὸν καὶ ἄρτον προλαβεῖν, . . . to partake of lemon skins (κιτρίου προλαμβάνειν τὰ ἄκρα), . . . to partake of milk with honey (γάλα μετὰ μέλιτος προλαβεῖν).[89]

The phrase τὸ δεῖπνον προλαμβάνειν in 1 Cor 11:21 is therefore identical in meaning with the phrase τὸ δεῖπνον λαβεῖν in T. Job 15:1 (V).[90] If προλαμβάνειν in 1 Cor 11:21 is understood in this sense, what the verse states should be specified as follows: At the common meal (ἐν τῷ φαγεῖν) each partakes of *his own* meal, i.e., each consumes what belongs *to him*[91] and what *he himself* has brought with

---

[85]So, e.g., Walter Bauer, *Wörterbuch zum Neuen Testament,* 5th ed. (Berlin: A. Topelmann, 1958) 1404, s.v. 2.a; Conzelmann, 226, 229n22; Theissen, "Soziale Integration," 300. See also J. H. Moulton and G. Milligan, *The Vocabulary of the Greek Testament Illustrated from the Papyri and Other Non-Literary Sources* (London: Hodder and Stoughton, 1930; rpt. Grand Rapids: Eerdmans, 1976) 542b s.v.

[86]The verb occurs here only three times: Mark 14:8; 1 Cor 11:21; Gal 6:1.

[87]So also: Wis 17:16; Pap Oxy. 928 8-9.

[88]1170, 7,9,15. Text and translation of the stele of Apellas (ca. AD 160) also in R. Herzog, *Die Wunderheilungen von Epidauros,* Philologus, Suppl. 22/3 (Leipzig, 1931) 43-45.

[89]Translation according to Herzog, 44.

[90]The sons of Job "daily took their (own) meal after caring for the poor" (ἐλάμβανον . . . τὸ δεῖπνον αὐτῶν).

[91]On ἴδιος = "belonging to the individual," see John 10:3; 1 Cor. 7:4; cf. also 1 Cor 12:11; Gal 6:5.

him.[92] Ἔκαστος refers therefore to all those who came together for the meal, and who are divided into two groups, the well-to-do[93] and the have-nots (οἱ μὴ ἔχον- τες, 11:22b).[94] Since each consumes what he himself brought, the upshot is that at the common meal "one goes hungry, the other feasts" (11:21b).[95] Paul, then, pre- supposes in fact that "the luxuriantly feasting and those going hungry are simulta- neously gathered together at supper."[96] The abuses that he denounces are abuses at the common meal![97] Precisely therein lie the σχίσματα (11:18), that during the worship assembly (ἐν ἐκκλησίᾳ) rich and poor are together in one space and yet, separated by social groups, eat what each respectively was able to bring. Since the well-to-do feast in the presence of and before the eyes of the hungry poor, they

---

[92]Cf. Bachmann, 364: "what each individual brought with himself"; Hans Lietzmann, *An die Korinther* 1/2, 5th ed. (Tübingen: Mohr-Siebeck, 1969) 56: "his own meal that he brought with him." J. J. Wettstein, *Novum Testamentum Graecum* 2 (Amsterdam, 1752 = Graz, 1962) 148, respecting 1 Cor 11:21, refers to Johannes Malalas, *Chronographia* 7: Ἐν τοῖς συμποσίοις τοῖς λεγομένοις φιλικοῖς ἔκαστος τῶν συνερχομένων εἰς τὸ συμπόσιον τὸ ἴδιον αὐτοῦ βρῶμα καὶ πόμα μεθ᾽ ἑαυτοῦ κομίζει, καὶ εἰς τὸ κοινὸν πάντα παρατίθεται, καὶ ἐσθίουσι κρατήσαντες τὸ ἀρχαῖον ἔθος ἔως τοῦ νῦν (see PG 97 [1865] 288B). Cf. Xenophon, Mem. 3.14.1.

[93]This group is represented by those "who have houses," 11:22a (cf. 11:34a).

[94]The interpretation of Theissen, "Soziale Integration," 293, differs: "Those who dispose of their ἴδιον δεῖπνον (and ἔκαστος, v. 21, refers to them) stand apart from the "μὴ ἔχοντες, those who have no food."

The often-instructive comments of Theissen yield, in my opinion, a too-complicated analysis of the Corinthian situation. The "Lord's Supper" appears as an extraordinary event, as a type of feast-day meal. But the word δεῖπνον designates not simply—nor indeed in the first instance—a banquet organized on festive occasions (so, e.g., Mark 6:21; 12:39 parr.; Luke 14:16-17, 24; John 12:2; 1 Cor 10:27 v. 1; Dan 5:1 Θ; Ep. Arist. 217; Jos. As. 3:4; 18:2; 21:8); it is in the first instance a fixed term for the usual daily meal, which is taken in the evenings (so, e.g., Luke 14:12; John 13:2, 4 [see v. 30]; 21:20; 4 Macc 3:9; T. Abrah. [B] 4:3; 5:1; T. Job 15:1; Mart. Pol. 7:1). Thus, the δεῖπνον of 1 Cor 11:17-34 refers either to "the evening table fellowship of the community" (Johannes Behm, διεῖπνον, δειπνέω, TWNT 2:34 = TDNT 2:34) or (more likely) the meal celebration held every Sunday (cf. 1 Cor 16:2; Acts 20:7; Did 14:1).

[95]Μεθύειν is used by metonymy; cf. the explanation by H.-D. Wendland, *Die Briefe an die Korinther*, 13th ed. (Göttingen: Vandenhoeck & Ruprecht, 1972) 96: "Paul says very sharply: the poor are hungry and the rich carouse." On the use of μεθύειν by metonymy, cf. in the LXX Ps 36(35):9 and Hos 14:8; see also Hesychius of Alexandria, *Lexicon*, ed. M. Schmidt (Jena, 1867) s.v.

[96]Formulation of Wolff, 81, who doubts this and, as evidence, adds, "Otherwise he would not have omitted to mention in his following remarks the factor of brotherly sharing." Now, Paul does not leave this motif untouched, as 11:33 shows (on this see below).

[97]Cf. Lucian, *Saturnalia* 22, 23 as well as the material listed by Klauck, *Herrenmahl*, 294.

"shame" the μὴ ἔχοντες (v. 22).[98] This is exactly how "the social distinctions in the community make their appearance in especially crass fashion at the Lord's Supper," and the poor, thanks to the callous behavior of the rich, are "once more reminded of their oppressive situation."[99]

Our interpretation of 11:21 must now prove its worth by the exegesis of 11:33; for, it is precisely by reference to 11:33 that scholars ground both the translation of the verb προλαμβάνειν in 11:21 as "to go ahead" and the related view of relations within the Corinthian community. So, for example, Christian Wolff: "The temporal dimension contained in προ- has its justification from 11:33, which permits the inference that it was not taken for granted to hold off the beginning of the evening meal until all were assembled."[100] The point of departure for this option is that the words συνερχόμενοι εἰς τὸ φαγεῖν ἀλλήλους ἐκδέχεσθε in 11:33 should be translated, "If you are gathered together to eat, then wait for one another (i.e., until all are present)"! But one may doubt that this translation is accurate. The verb ἐκδέχεσθαι does not have only—nor indeed primarily—the meaning "to await" (*expectare*), but rather in the first instance and above all has the meaning "to receive" (*excipere*).[101] Ἐκδέχεσθαι with the accusative of person can accordingly mean "expect someone" (e.g., 1 Cor 16:11), "wait for someone" (e.g., Acts 17:16); but it also means "receive someone"[102] (especially to receive as host),[103] "welcome someone,"[104] "accept someone,"[105] "take someone under one's charge,"[106] or "take

---

[98]Wettstein, 148, relates καταισχύνετε τοὺς μὴ ἔχοντας (11:22) with good reason to b.Pesaḥ 82a; b.Taʿan. 31a; b.M. Qam. 27a; and Schlatter, 319n1, likewise refers to Taʿan 4:11 (better, 4:8). According to these texts, the humiliation of those who have nothing takes place whenever the differences between those who have and those who do not becomes evident in one and the same situation or at a coincident or simultaneous function.

[99]I adopt the formulation from Wolff, 81.

[100]Wolff, 81.

[101]That this state of affairs is not even alluded to is the problem of the article ἐκδέχομαι by Bauer, *Wörterbuch,* 472. The exegete who for 1 Cor 11:33 draws merely on Bauer's dictionary will necessarily be led astray.

[102]LXX Hos 9:6; Phil, Post. 39; Josephus, *JW* 5.215; *Ant.* 3.149. Cf. c. acc. rei "to receive something": Philo, Opif, 34 (antonym ἀνείργειν "to keep back"); see also in LXX Isa 57:1; Sir 6:33. Both passages are to be materially complemented by an acc. rei.

[103]John 4:45 D; P.Teb 33.7 (Liddel-Scott, 503b s.v., gives as a translation "entertain"); Josephus *Ant.* 15.343; 16.6.131, 140 (here ἅπαντας ἐξεδέξατο καταγωγαῖς καὶ τραπέζαις [!] . . .). Cf. also the references cited in the following notes.

[104]3 Macc 5:26; Philo, Post. 136; Josephus, *JW* 2.1.297; 3.32; 6.140; 7.70, 74; *Ant* 7.351; 11.340; 12.138; 13.104, 148. Cf. c. acc. rei, "to receive something": Sir 32:14; Ep.Arist. 205; T.Job 4:10; Philo, Post. 12; Flacc 147; Josephus, *Ant.* 7.102; 12.157; 13.78.

someone under one's wing."[107]

In view of this lexical evidence, nothing prevents us from translating the phrase ἀλλήλους ἐκδέχεσθε in 1 Cor 11:33 as "care for one another!"[108] "receive one another warmly!"[109] "grant one another table fellowship!" "show hospitality to one another!" This way of construing the text is supported by the considerations that follow.

(a) The phrase συνερχόμενοι εἰς τὸ φαγεῖν in 11:33 presupposes, as does the usage ἐν τῷ φαγεῖν, as well, that *all* members of the community are present for the meal. The command συνερχόμενοι εἰς τὸ φαγεῖν ἀλλήλους ἐκδέχεσθε stands, in other words, in antithesis to the statement of 11:18: συνερχομένων ὑμῶν ἐν ἐκκλησίᾳ ἀκούω σχίσματα ἐν ὑμῖν ὑπάρχειν.[110] The ἀλλήλους ἐκδέχεσθε demanded by Paul is thus the exact opposite of the blameworthy state of affairs of σχίσματα ἐν ὑμῖν ὑπάρχειν.[111]

(b) The directive in 11:34a (εἴ τις πεινᾷ, ἐν οἴκῳ ἐσθιέτω), which follows 11:33, provides no argument for the meaning of the words ἀλλήλους ἐκδέχεσθε that we have rejected. In short, it would be a basic misunderstanding to wish to interpret it, "The hungry rich should eat their fill in their own homes before the beginning of the worship service, so as to be able to wait at the service until the poor members of the community have made their appearance." Rather, as already intimated in the question of 11:22a (μὴ γὰρ οἰκίας οὐκ ἔχετε εἰς τὸ ἐσθίειν καὶ πίνειν·) the directive bears on the strict distinction between private meal and

---

[105]So in LXX Ps 118:122; Micah 2:12; Nahum 3:18. Cf. c. acc. rei "take something": Prov. 1:30 (α′, θ′, σ′ ; in θ′ and σ′ there appears as antonym παροξύνειν in the meaning "to despise" or "to reject"); Sir 6:23 (antonym, ἀπαναίνομαι, "to refuse," "to hold back"); Sir 18:14.

[106]LXX Gen 44:32 (cf. also LXX Gen 43:9).

[107]Soc 349.1; 830.15 (ἐκδέχεται ἡμᾶς μικροὺς ὄντας καὶ ὀρφανούς).

[108]Cf. προσλαμβάνεσθε ἀλλήλους, Rom 15:7. The προσλαμβάνεσθαι is meant only inclusively (cf. Rom 14:1, 3), whereas ἐκδέχεσθαι in 1 Cor 11:33 specifically relates to the meal situation.

[109]The composite is therefore used, as in John 4:45D, in the sense of the unprefixed δέχεσθαι = "to receive hospitably." (For the unprefixed usage, see Matt 10:14, 40-41; Mark 6:11; Luke 9:5, 53; 10:8, 10; John 4:45; Col 4:10; Heb 11:31.) On the identity of meaning of the compound with ἐκ- and the unprefixed form in Paul, cf. e.g., ἐκδιώκειν (1 Thess 2:15) / διώκειν (Rom 12:14; 1 Cor 4:12; 15:9; Gal 1:13, 23; 4:29; 5:11; Phil 3:6); ἐκπειράζειν (1 Cor 10:9a) / πειράζειν (1 Cor 10:9b); ἐκπίπτειν (Rom 9:6) / πίπτειν (1 Cor 13:8); ἐξαποστέλλειν (Gal 4:4,6) / ἀποστέλλειν (Rom 10:15; 1 Cor 1:17; 2 Cor 2:17); ἐξεγείρειν (1 Cor 6:14) / ἐγείρειν (1 Cor 6:14; 2 Cor 1:9; 4:14; etc.).

[110]The gen. abs. presupposes here, as also in v. 20, the presence of *all* in the worship assembly. On this cf. 1 Cor 14:23, 26.

[111]Cf. 12:25, ἵνα μὴ ᾖ σχίσμα ἐν τῷ σώματι ἀλλὰ τὸ αὐτὸ ὑπὲρ ἀλλήλων μεριμνῶσιν τὰ μέλη.

Lord's Supper. The community's gathering for worship—this is Paul's point—is not the place to satisfy one's hunger and eat one's fill. For that there are houses; that one can and should do at home.[112]

As the linguistic analysis of 11:21 and 11:33 has shown, neither of the two passages requires the supposition that in Corinth the bread rite and the cup rite were joined together and followed the ordinary meal as sacramental act proper. There are accordingly good grounds for concluding that the sequence of the meal celebration presupposed in 1 Cor 11:17-34 corresponds exactly to the Lord's Supper paradosis: "The cup is passed 'after the meal'; it is therefore separated by the entire meal from the sacramental bread standing at the beginning."[113]

In Corinth, too, the Lord's Supper celebration exhibits the original sequence: the eucharistic bread rite—the ordinary meal—the eucharistic cup rite.[114] When, in

---

[112]With the question of 11:22a and the instruction in 11:34a Paul by no means wishes to give the advice that, if necessary, the full meal is to be separated from the sacrament and to be held in private homes (where then the rich would be under their own authority!), contrary to Jeremias, *Abendmahlsworte*, 114-15 (ET *Eucharistic Words*, 121); Conzelmann, 230; Klauck, 82; et al.

[113]So correctly Leonhard Goppelt, *Die apostolische und nachapostolische Zeit* (Göttingen: Vandenhoeck & Ruprecht, 1962) 145. Of the same view are, e.g., Weiss (see n. 78, above) 293; Lietzmann, 58; idem, *Messe und Herrenmahl. Eine Studie zur Geschichte der Liturgie*, 3rd ed. (Berlin: de Gruyter, 1955) 228.

[114]In no way does 1 Cor 10:16 contradict this. For the sequence contained in this verse, "cup—bread," does not reflect an established liturgical use; rather it is simply and solely conditioned by the context of the argument represented there. The right position is represented, e.g., by Wolff, 51-52: 1 Cor 10:16, as noted here, has nothing to do with the liturgical procedure described in Did. 9:9-10. The cup mentioned in Did. 9:2 is, in other words, *not* "the cup of blessing" (τὸ ποτήριον τῆς εὐλογίας, 1 Cor 10:16 = *kôs šel běrākāh/kāsā' děbirkětā*): this cup, after all, is *always* mixed, blessed, drunk *after* the meal has been completed; like the ποτήριον of Luke 22:17-18, it refers rather to a cup over which—*before* the breaking of the bread, i.e., before the grace that opens the meal—the blessing of the wine is spoken. This cup is the so-called *qiddûš-cup*, which in the rabbinic sources is quite clearly differentiated from the "cup of blessing" (see esp. j.Ber. 7.11c.70-71, where *kāsā' děqiddûšā* appears next to *kôs šel běrākāh*; cf. further b.Pesah 103a; also 102a,b). The "cup" of Did. 9:2 and Luke 22:17-18 can only derive, moreover, from the Passover meal (just as the sequence in Did. 9:1–10:5 and in Luke 22:14-20 agrees with that of the Passover meal). In N.T. times the wine *Qiddûš* before the blessing over the bread is attested only for the Passover meal; see Jeremias, *Abendmahlsworte*, 20-23 (ET *Eucharistic Words*, 26-29). The cup mentioned in Luke 22:17-18 is, therefore, the *Qiddûš* cup of m.Pesah 10.2 (= *ks' qm'*, "the first cup" b.Pesa h 103a); the ποτήριον of Luke 22:20, on the contrary, is the "cup of blessing," of which m.Pesa h 10.7 speaks (= *ks' dbrkt'*, b.Pesa h 103a). The two cups are not identical!

That there is no question in Did. 9:2 and in Luke 22:17-18 of the "cup of blessing," but of the cup used for the wine *qiddûš* is also indicated by the following observation. The blessing connected with the wine *qiddûš* reads, "Blessed art Thou, Yahweh, our God, King of the world, who createth the fruit of the vine" (see, e.g., m.Ber. 6.1; t.Ber. 4.3;

11:22, Paul issues the rebuke συνερχομένων οὖν ὑμῶν ἐπὶ τὸ αὐτὸ οὐκ ἔστιν κυριακὸν δεῖπνον φαγεῖν, he has in mind the gathering for a worship service encompassing these three acts and not merely, say, a sacramental act exclusively limited to the rites of bread and cup. Whence it follows that κυριακὸν δεῖπνον is a designation for the entire meal celebration consisting of bread rite, full meal, and cup rite.[115] This celebration is constituted as "the Lord's meal" by "the bread of the Lord" (ὁ ἄρτος τοῦ κυρίου) and "the cup of the Lord" (τὸ ποτήριον τοῦ κυρίου),[116] i.e., by the two sacramental acts that enclose the common meal and thus give it, too, its essential character. This is exactly why Paul, having in view the scandalous abuses that he deplores in Corinth, can argue from the Lord's Supper paradosis. A κυριακὸν δεῖπνον is fundamentally and exclusively the kind of meal celebration that corresponds in all of its components to the constitutive sacramental acts that the Lord Jesus himself has ordained and whose meaning finds valid expression in the sacred words of the κύριος spoken at the founding of the meal.[117]

---

b.Pesaḥ 103a, 106a). Jesus' word in Luke 22:18 draws unmistakably on this blessing, and the prayer in Did. 9:2 clearly shows itself to be a Christian interpretation of the same text.

[115]We are thus given the explanation of why in the Ἀποστολικὴ Παράδοσις of Hippolytus (composed ca. 215 in Rome) the common meal following the blessing of the light, i.e., the agape meal already separated from the sacrament, bears the name "cena dominica": B. Botte, *La Tradition apostolique de Saint Hippolyte. Essai de reconstruction,* 4th ed. (Münster: Aschendorff, 1972; 68.8 (= ¶27). That corresponds to ¶19 or ¶49 of the so-called Egyptian Church Order; see F. X. Funk, *Didascalia et Constitutiones Apostolorum,* vol. 2 (Paderborn: Schöningh, 1905; rpt. Turin, 1970) 113.6. Cf. Lietzmann, *Messe und Herrenmahl,* 197ff. Ps-Oecumenius refers the words κυριακὸν δεῖπνον of 1 Cor 11:20 to the agape meal, differentiated from the sacrament; see K. Staab, *Pauluskommentare aus der Griechischen Kirche,* 2nd ed. (Münster: Aschendorff, 1984) 440.11-12. Among the Fathers, however, the dominant interpretation of the expression relates it to the sacrament of the Eucharist.

This material is conveniently available in *Textos Eucaristicos Primitivos,* ed. J. Solano, vol. 1, 2nd ed. (Madrid: BAC, 1978), vol. 2 (Madrid: BAC, 1954). See 1:162-63, no. 225 (Cyprian, Ep. 63.16); 181-82, no. 250 (idem., De opere et eleemosynis 15); 404, no. 615 (Basilius, Reg., brevius tractatae 310); 612-13. no. 876f. (John Chrysostom, In 1 Cor Hom. 27.2.3); 2:116-17, no. 201 (Augustinus, Ep. 54.7); 479-80, no. 800 (Theodoret of Cyrus, Comm. in 1 Cor., on 11:20); in addition see Severian of Gabala in Staab, *Paulus-kommentare,* 262.9ff.

[116]1 Cor 11:27. The genitive τοῦ κυρίου belongs not only to τὸ ποτήριον, but to τὸν ἄρτον as well.

[117]The emphatic reference to the κύριος in 11:23a (again taken up in 11:26, 27, 32) brings the following point to expression: the κύριος Ἰησοῦς, who instituted the Lord's Supper on the night before his crucifixion, is *now,* as risen and glorified, the Lord present in his community, which awaits his parousia: he is the abiding guarantor of the validity of the tradition going back to him and so at the same time the binding authority respecting the performance of the meal he instituted. Cf. Wolff, 83; Klauck, 82.

IV

If with this we turn to the statements of the Lord's Supper paradosis itself, we should first of all ponder the words of bestowal: They read τοῦτό μού ἐστιν τὸ σῶμα τὸ ὑπὲρ ὑμῶν (11:24b) and τοῦτο τὸ ποτήριον ἡ καινὴ διαθήκη ἐστιν ἐν τῷ ἐμῷ αἵματι (11:25b). The subject of the word on the cup (τοῦτο τὸ ποτήριον) stands by metonymy for the content, i.e., for the wine in the cup (vessel-content metonymy). Parallel to that, the pronominal subject of the word on the bread refers to the bread mentioned in 11:23b, 24a (τοῦτο accordingly = οὗτος ὁ ἄρτος).[118] In both words of bestowal, of course, it is not simply the respective elements that are referred to. What is meant is the bread over which the blessing at the beginning of the meal was recited and that then was broken, distributed, and eaten. And what is meant is the wine over which the prayer of thanksgiving is said, and from which then all drink. The "elements" are therefore not to be separated from the act of solemn blessing nor from the act of distribution and communion.

Both for the word over the bread and for the word over the cup, the predicate introduced by ἐστιν bears on the totality of "element," blessing, distribution, and communion, which is conceived as a unity. To understand this ἐστιν, a glance at the parallel in 1 Cor 10:16 is instructive. Here the formula κοινωνία ἐστίν appears, and κοινωνία with the genitive of thing expresses real participation (i.e., the real gaining of a share/having of a share) in the reality named in the genitive.[119] According to 1 Cor 10:16 the eucharistic bread and the eating of this bread gives a "share" in the σῶμα τοῦ Χριστοῦ; the eucharistic cup and the drinking of the cup give a "share" in the αἷμα τοῦ Χριστοῦ.[120] The words of bestowal in the Lord's Supper paradosis mean to be understood no differently: The eucharistic bread bestows, and with the eating of this bread one receives, a share in the σῶμα of Jesus given over to death;[121] the eucharistic cup bestows, and with the drinking from it one receives, a share in the καινὴ διαθήκη (new covenant) which is

---

[118]Τοῦτο is in the neuter by grammatical attraction to the neuter predicate nominative, τὸ σῶμα.

[119]Cf. Wis 8:18; 2 Cor 8:4; Phil 3:10.

[120]On the Jewish conceptual background, namely, that eating and drinking bestow a share in the gifts of salvation, see Jeremias, *Abendmahlsworte,* 224-29 (ET *Eucharistic Words,* 232-37).

[121]The attributive τὸ ὑπὲρ ὑμῶν in v. 24b refers to the self-surrender unto death. For particulars, see below.

established in the αἷμα (blood) of Jesus shed on the cross.[122]

A formal as well as material analogy—indeed, it seems to me the only real formal and material analogy—to 1 Cor 10:16 and to the two words of bestowal in the Lord's Supper paradosis is found in the words of Jos. As. 16:14: τοῦτο τὸ κηρίον ἐστὶ πνεῦμα ζωῆς, this honeycomb is the spirit of life.[123] The honeycomb referred to here—the manna to be understood as heavenly food of angels[124] identical with the "blessed" ἄρτος ζωῆς (bread of life) and the "blessed" ποτήριον ἀθανασίας (cup of immortality) of Jos. As. 8:5; 15:5.[125] The predicate ἐστί brings to the fore the motif of *giving-a-share,* as the words that follow on the passage cited above confirm: ὅτι κηρίον ζωῆς ἐστι τοῦτο, καὶ πᾶς ὃς ἂν φάγῃ ἐξ αὐτοῦ οὐκ ἀποθανεῖται εἰς τὸν αἰῶνα χρόνον (for this is the honeycomb of life and whoever eats of it shall never die). The "blessed" bread and the "blessed" cup mediate to whoever receives them the πνεῦμα ζωῆς, the renewing and life-giving spirit of God (cf. Jos. As. 8:9). In Jos. As. 16:14 we are therefore unquestionably in the presence of a word of *bestowal,* and not merely a word of *interpretation.*[126]

The gift of which the word on the bread in 1 Cor 11:24b speaks is a participation in the σῶμα of Jesus. As in Romans 7:4, so here also (and then similarly in 11:27 and 29)[127] σῶμα means the body of Jesus Christ given over to death on the cross,[128] and the prepositional attributive τὸ ὑπὲρ ὑμῶν specifies Jesus' self-surrender unto death as expiatory and reconciliatory event.[129] To this event the word

---

[122]The sense of the expression ἐν τῷ ἐμῷ αἵματι in v. 25b is causal; see Jeremias, *Abendmahlsworte,* 162 (ET *Eucharistic Words,* 169).

[123]On the interpretation of Jos. As. 16:14 in detail, as well as on the relation of this passage to Jos. As. 16:16, see Burchard, "The Importance of Joseph and Aseneth," 114ff.

[124]See Christoph Burchard, *Joseph und Aseneth* (Gütersloh: Mohn, 1983) 605, as well as 679, note on 16:8.

[125]Cf. also Jos. As. 8:9; 16:16; 19:5.

[126]Jos. As. 16:14, like the words of bestowal of the Lord's Supper paradosis, differ not inconsiderably from those of Exod 24:8: "See, the blood of the covenant" (*hinnēh dam habbĕrît . . .*) or from the well-known words of the Passover liturgy: "See, the bread of affliction (*hā lahmā' 'anyā'*) that our fathers ate in Egypt." Both these texts are readily cited as analogies to the words of bestowal, but are they? In them blood is *interpreted* as "the blood of the covenant," or, alternatively, bread as the "bread of affliction" of the fathers; we do *not* have here words of bestowal!

[127]On v. 29, see below, n. 224.

[128]The same holds for τὸ σῶμα τοῦ Χριστοῦ in 1 Cor 10:16b.

[129]Cf. Rom 5:6,8; 8:32; 14:15; 1 Cor 1:13; 2 Cor 5:14-15; Gal 2:20; 1 Thess 5:10; also 1 Cor 8:11 (here διά c. acc.). On Paul's views of expiation and reconciliation, see O. Hofius, "Erwägungen zur Gestalt und Herkunft des paulinischen Versöhnungs-

over the cup likewise refers, for αἷμα designates here (and in 11:27)—as in Rom 3:25; 5:9—the expiatory blood of Jesus shed on the cross.[130] The word on the bread (σῶμα) and the word on the cup (αἷμα) thus both speak of the *expiatory death* of Jesus Christ.[131] But here the word over the cup emphasizes that through this expiatory death the καινὴ διαθήκη (new covenant) has been realized:[132] the eschatological act and order of salvation which—in fulfillment of the promise of Jer 31(LXX 38):31-34—has as its object the forgiveness of sins and the communion with God thereby established.[133] Whoever eats the eucharistic bread and drinks the eucharistic cup receives and so has a share in the salvation that has been settled by the expiatory death of Christ.

The eucharistic bread of which the Lord's Supper paradosis speaks is the bread that Jesus gave to his disciples on the night before his death; and the eucharistic cup

---

gedankens," *ZTK* 77 (1980): 186-99; idem, "Gott hat unter uns aufgerichtet das Wort von der Versöhnung (2 Kor 5:19)," *ZNW* 71 (1980): 3-20; idem, "Sühne und Versöhnung: Zum paulinischen Verständnis des Kreuzestodes Jesu," in *Versuche, das Leiden und Sterben Jesu zu verstehen,* ed. W. Maas (Munich-Zurich: Schnell & Steiner, 1983) 25-46.

[130]The same hold for τὸ αἷμα τοῦ Χριστοῦ in 1 Cor 10:16a. Also: outside the genuine Pauline epistles, references to the blood of Jesus regularly express the expiatory efficacy of his death: see Acts 20:28; Eph 1:7; 2:13; Col 1:20; Heb 9:12, 14; 10:19, 29; 12:24; 13:12; 1 Pet 1:2, 19; 1 John 1:7; 5:6, 8; Rev 1:5; 5:9; 7:14; 12:11.

[131]Cf. the juxtaposition and conjunction of the two notions of Christ's "body" and "blood" in Col 1:20, 22 as well as in the epistle to the Hebrews (σῶμα, 10:5, 10; αἷμα, 9:12, 14; 10:19, 29; 12:24; 13:12).

[132]On this and on the relation to Exod 24:3-8 (esp. v. 8), see Hartmut Gese, "Die Herkunft des Herrenmahl," in his *Zur biblischen Theologie. Alttestmentliche Vorträge* (Munich: Kaiser, 1977; = 2nd ed. Tübingen: Mohr-Siebeck, 1983) 107-27, at 123. With respect to Exod 24:3ff. itself, see idem, "Die Sühne," in ibid., 85-106, at 98-99. That the "blood of the covenant" in Exod 24:8 has expiatory force is stated in Tg. Onq. and Tg. Ps-J. (not, however, in Tg. Neof. and Tg. Sam); the thought is already presupposed in Jub 6:11ff. (cf. 6:2).

[133]Cf. Jeremias, *Abendmahlsworte,* 218n2 (ET *Eucharistic Words,* 226; also 178 #13). As later in the epistle to the Hebrews (Heb 10:11-18), so already in the tradition of the Lord's Supper cited by Paul (and Luke), reference to the promise of the new διαθήκη of Jer 31(38):31-34 focuses exclusively on the theme of forgiveness of sins and the resultant realized communion with God, not at all on the notion of law written on the heart (31:33). Cf. on this Ernst Kutsch, *Neues Testament—Neuer Bund?* (Neukirchen-Vluyn: Neukirchener Verlag, 1978) 97ff. (on Hebrews); 112, 119, 135, 150 (on the word over the cup).

That in the expression καινὴ διαθήκη there exists a reference to Jer 31(38):31ff. is occasionally called in question: see, e.g., Delling, *TRE* 1:55:1ff.; Wolff, 86. Should these demurrals be well grounded, it would follow that the phrase "the *new* διαθήκη" ought to be interpreted, with Delling, *TRE* 1:54:49 as "the eschatologically valid establishing of salvation" (cf. Wolff, 87n117).

that is mentioned here is the cup of blessing that he offered them on that night. For Paul it is the *very same* bread and the *very same* cup wherever the church celebrates the Lord's Supper in a way that accords with its founding. That is shown by the formula ὁσάκις . . . ἐὰν ἐσθίητε τὸν ἄρτον τοῦτον [!] καὶ τὸ ποτήριον πίνητε in 11:26a[134] and by allusion to "the bread of the Lord" and "the cup of the Lord" in 1 Cor 11:27a and it is confirmed by 1 Cor 10:17.[135] Each Lord's Supper, wherever and whenever it is celebrated, is a continuation of the Last Supper of Jesus. That is why the community receives the bread that gives a share in the body of Christ and the cup that gives a share in the divine saving act realized in Christ's blood.

With respect to the much-discussed question of the relation between the subject and the predicate nouns of the two words of bestowal, this is unquestionably *not* that of an identity in the mode of substance. For, just as the cup or its content *is not* the new covenant in the sense of subtance, neither is the bread in a substantial sense the body of Christ.[136] If one cannot speak of a substantial identity of bread and body of Christ on the one hand, and of wine and blood of Christ on the other, still neither are the eucharistic gifts for Paul—to borrow a formulation from Justin—κοινὸς ἄρτος (ordinary bread) and κοινὸν πόμα (ordinary drink).[137] Rather, they are, as the Apostle himself explains in 1 Cor 10:3-4, πνευματικὸν βρῶμα and πνευματι-

---

[134]If P[46] and other witnesses added a τοῦτο after ποτήριον, this—so far as the intended referent is concerned—was an altogether proper change.

[135]See Burchard, "The Importance of Joseph and Aseneth," 124. The sentence in 1 Cor 10:17 is a comment on 10:16, which is meant to explain why, in the Lord's Supper, insofar as we eat of the "broken" bread, we have a share in the σῶμα of Christ, i.e., in his saving death: "Because it is *one* bread, we, the many, are *one* body, for we all share in the one bread." Burchard: "All of us who eat at a [Lord's] Supper, no matter when or where, eat the one bread, i.e., the one which Christ had declared to be 'my body for you' in the night in which he was betrayed."

We shall not go into further detail on 1 Cor 10:17, apart from commenting that it seems to me an error to see in this verse the heart of the larger context and to refer the expression ἐν σῶμα to the church as the "body of Christ." On this last, see the well-grounded considerations offered by Wolff, 54, 110ff.

[136]There is in my opinion no support at all for the claim in Klauck, *Herrenmahl,* 374, that Paul holds the "bodily real presence" explained as follows: "Body (σῶμα) and blood of the crucified Christ are present really in the alimentary elements of the meal, bread and wine." The conception of the Apostle has nothing to do, even remotely, with "Hellenistic theophagy." Contrary to Klauck, ibid., in my opinion, Paul knows no *special* real presence of Christ at all in the Lord's Supper, which would be different from his permanent real presence in his community.

[137]Justin, Apol 1.66.2.

κὸν πόμα, i.e., gifts of a supraterrestrial, heavenly origin and nature.[138] Only on these grounds do they unite with Jesus Christ and bestow a share in his "body" and "blood," i.e., in the salvation realized by his expiatory death. But how, we should ask, do bread and wine become what by nature they are not? What lends them, and how do they gain, this supernatural, sacramental, quality?

A first pointer towards an answer is found in the words τοῦτο ποιεῖτε of the twice-given anamnesis (= remembrance) mandate (11:24c, 25c). The verb ποιεῖν here signifies a definite ritual procedure[139] to be repeated regularly. It is more precisely specified by the pronoun τοῦτο. In the bread rite this pronoun refers to the "taking," "giving thanks," and "breaking" mentioned in 11:23b-24a; in the cup rite it refers to the "taking," i.e., lifting up, introduced by ὡσαύτως in 11:25a, and to the "giving thanks." On the other hand, it does not simultaneously refer also to the eating of the bread and the drinking from the cup.[140] In other words, the τοῦτο is strictly related to the two ritual acts of grace *before* and *after* the meal.[141]

Now, presumably we may see in these rites the liturgical act that removes bread and cup from the realm of the profane and confers a "spiritual" character on them. The text of 1 Cor 10:16 favors this supposition. For there we find described the carrying out of the τοῦτο ποιεῖτε,[142] namely, in the words "the bread *that we break*" (τὸν ἄρτον ὃν κλῶμεν) and "the cup of blessing *that we bless*" (τὸ ποτήριον τῆς εὐλογίας ὃ εὐλογοῦμεν). Both turns of phrase unmistakably point to the table-prayers recited at a Jewish meal over the bread at the beginning and over the *kôs šel běrākāh* at the end. But, as the by no means pleonastic term ὁ εὐλογοῦμεν[143] shows, what is thought of here are not traditional Jewish table-

---

[138]This is how I understand πνηευματικός in this passage; cf. Weiss, 251; Lietzmann, 45; Eduard Schweizer, πνεῦμα, πνευματικός, TWNT 6:435 (= TDNT 6:437). For a further aspect, see below, n. 209.

[139]Cf. the use of ποιεῖν in the following O.T. passages (LXX): Exod 12:17, 47-48; 13:5; 29:35; Lev 8:34; 16:34; Num 9:2-6, 11-15; 15:11-14, 24; 16:6; 28:24; 29:39; Deut 16:1, 10; see also 1QS 2.19; 1QSa 2.21.

[140]Correctly, Weiss, 287: the τοῦτο ποιεῖτε in v. 25c summons "not the drinking of the cup; for it reads, 'do this, as often as you drink it. . . .' " With respect to ὁσάκις ἐὰν πίνητε in 11:25c, here I would observe only that in this expression I am able to recognize no reference to a sub-una celebration of the Lord's Supper. (The contrary view is held, e.g., by Schlatter, 324-25; Jeremias, *Abendmahlsworte,* 108 (ET *Eucharistic Words,* 115); Pesch, *Markusevangelium* 2:357-58; *Abendmhahl,* 49-50, 56-57.) On this I refer the reader to Klauck, *Herrenmahl,* 317-18; Wolff, 91.

[141]Cf. Jeremias, *Abendmahlsworte,* 241 (ET *Eucharistic Words,* 251).

[142]So Jeremias, ibid.

[143]In the rabbinic texts the construction *brk* (Piel) + *'l* (e.g., m.Ber. 6.1ff.; 7.5; 8.1, 6, 8; m.Pesaḥ. 10.2, 7), which in Greek corresponds to the (semitizing) formulation εὐλογεῖν ἐπί of Luke 9:16D. The usage before us in 1 Cor 10:16a—εὐλογεῖν c. acc., cf. Mark 8:7; Luke 9:16—has its Hebrew parallels (*brk* [piel] c. acc.) in 1 Sam 9:13 (in Targ. Jon.

prayers, but specifically Christian thanksgiving prayers[144] with which the Lord's Supper is opened and closed. These prayers said over the bread and cup are acts of blessing which are of a consecratory character.[145] Through them bread and wine become what by nature they are *not*: "spiritual food" and "spiritual drink" (1 Cor 10:3-4), i.e., they bear and mediate what, in accordance with the words of bestowal in the Lord's Supper paradosis, is given by the Lord in and through them and received from his hand.[146]

That the words of bestowal would themselves have been cited as part of the bread and cup rite,[147] and that a certain consecratory power would have been ascribed to them, Paul's remarks on the Lord's Supper contain no indication at all.[148] On the other hand the supposition that the eucharistic prayers over bread and cup had a consecratory character receives important confirmation through the later testimony of Justin.[149] Above all, however, this supposition is supported by the interesting comparative material from the Jewish-Hellenistic writing "Joseph and Aseneth," which Christoph Burchard has thoroughly analyzed,[150] and which induces

---

referred to table grace) as well as in 1QSa 2.19-20.

[144]Cf. Goppelt, ποτήριον, TWNT 6:156.28-157.1 (= TDNT 6:156.24ff.).

[145]Cf., on this and what follows, Goppelt, *Theologie* 2:477-78.

[146]That Christ himself is the one who distributes the sacramental gifts emerges from 1 Cor 10:4.

[147]So, e.g., Schlatter, 320, 322-24; Bornkamm, *Herrenmahl,* 155; Pesch, *Abendmahl,* 55.

[148]Cf. Weiss, 284, 293. One can even argue justifiably that the Last Supper paradosis did not have to be recited at the celebration of the meal: C. K. Barrett, *A Commentary on the First Epistle to the Corinthians,* Black's/HNTC (London: Black; New York: Harper, 1968) 264; Burchard, "The Importance of Joseph and Aseneth," 125-26. In part V below, it will be shown that even the καταγγέλλειν of 11:26 does not call for the recitation of the words of institution.

[149]Justin, Apol 1.65.5; 66.2. Jeremias *Abendmahlsworte,* 101n1 (ET *Eucharistic Words,* 107n1), finds in Apol 1.66.2 a testimony to the "liturgical use of Jesus' words of interpretation in the celebration of the Eucharist." But that would hardly be correct. The words τὴν δι᾽ εὐχῆς λόγου τοῦ παρ᾽ αὐτοῦ εὐχαριστηθεῖσαν τροφήν more likely refer to one of the epicleses entreating the Logos of God, as is found in the *Euchologion of Serapion* (13.15), *Prex Eucharistica,* 130. Cf. also Irenaeus, Adv. haer. 5.2.3.

[150]Burchard, "The Importance of Joseph and Aseneth," 110-11; cf. also idem, *Joseph und Aseneth* (see n. 124, above) 604ff. In Jos. As. 8:5; 15:5 we meet the expressions ἄρτος εὐλογημένος ζωῆς, ποτήριον εὐλογημένον ἀθανασίας and χρίσμα εὐλογημένον ἀφθαρσίας (cf. also 8:9; 16:16; 19:5). The genitive attributives "designate the effect caused by eating, drinking, and anointing" (Burchard, "The Importance of Joseph and Aseneth," 111); εὐλογεῖν means the liturgically prescribed blessing, and "it is this which seems to give bread, cup, and ointment the effect of causing ζωή, ἀθανασία, and ἀφθαρσία" (112).

him to conclude that for Paul and the community in Corinth, it was the eucharistic blessings spoken over bread and cup "which gave the bread and the cup their sacramental quality."[151] Respecting the wording of these prayers Burchard remarks, "The eucharistic blessings must have had some appropriate wording, but we do not know what it was, unless Did 9-10 permits a guess."[152] Here, however, the Didache does not carry us further, since the table-prayers reported in Did 9:1–10:5 yield "not one syllable in remembrance of the death (of Jesus),"[153] and in them we are not dealing with eucharistic prayers, but with prayers offered before and after the agape feast, which preceded the sacrament.[154] But some points of reference to the character and content of the "eucharistic blessings" may be retrieved, I believe, from the anamnesis mandate of 11:24c, 25c and from its Pauline interpretation in 1 Cor 11:26.

V

In accordance with the anamnesis mandate the rite of the consecratory prayers before and after the meal takes place εἰς τὴν ἐμὴν ἀνάμνησιν, "in remembrance of me." In the light of the two words of bestowal, that can only mean "in remembrance of" the crucified one, who gave up his body to death for his own and by whose expiatory death (= blood) the economy of eschatological salvation is established. It is therefore a matter of remembering Jesus Christ and his saving work.[155] But the crucified one, as the κύριος title of the Lord's Supper paradosis (11:23b) and of the Pauline context (11:23a; 11:16, 17, 32) clearly enough brings to expression, is the risen and exalted one, who appears in the Lord's Supper "as the present Lord and allows the members of the community to take part in it."[156] "The remembrance of the Lord is accordingly the 'recollection' of the basic events

[151]Burchard, "The Importance of Joseph and Aseneth," 126.
[152]Ibid.
[153]Lietzmann, 58.
[154]Martin Dibelius, "Die Mahlgebete der Didache," in his *Botschaft und Geschichte,* vol. 2 (Tübingen: 1956) 117-27; Jeremias, *Abendmahlsworte,* 111 (ET *Eucharistic Words,* 118); Goppelt, *Die apostolische und nachapostolische Zeit,* 31, 145. The sacramental meal does not begin before the responsorium of Did. 10:6.
[155]So, appropriately, Justin, Dial c. Tryph. 41.1; 70.4; 117.3. The "anamnēsis" occurs according to Justin in the form of eucharistic prayers over bread and cup; see ibid., and also Apol. 1.65.3; 67.5.

[156]Ferdinand Hahn, "Herrengedächtnis und Herrenmahl bei Paulus," in his *Exegetische Beiträge zum ökumenischen Gespräch. Gesammelte Aufsätze,* vol. 1 (Göttingen: Vandenhoeck & Ruprecht, 1986) 303-14, at 305.

of Good Friday and Easter in the light of the certainty that this Lord lives and grants us his presence."[157]

Hence the Lord's Supper is *not* "a 'memorial meal' for someone departed";[158] the anamnesis mandate does *not* require of the disciples "to cherish and preserve the memory of Jesus" and not to forget him.[159] This by itself rules out, in my opinion, the notion that the expression εἰς τὴν ἐμὴν ἀνάμνησιν has anything to do with the ancient meals in memory of the dead and their founding.[160] The idiom εἰς τὴν ἐμὴν ἀνάμνησιν has its parallels in Hebrew *lĕzikkārôn*,[161] and it must be understood on the basis of the Old Testament and Jewish concept of worshipful "remembering."[162] In certain traditions of the Old Testament what is expressed by *zikkārôn* is

> the relation of a later generation to events that took place in the past, but remain foundational for salvation in the present, of which the acts performed in the cult make clear to the individual worshipper that he too is included in them, affected by them, and meant through them.[163]

Discussion of a remembrance of this kind is especially to be met in statements about Passover, which is performed as a celebration "in memory of" Israel's redemption from Egyptian slavery.[164] But on other feast days, too,[165] and at every

---

[157]Ibid.

[158]Contrary to Lietzmann, *Messe und Herrenmahl*, 223.

[159]So correctly, Jeremias, *Abendmahlsworte*, 245 (ET *Eucharistic Words*, 255).

[160]Contrary to Lietzmann, *An die Korinther*, 1/2:57-58; idem, *Messe und Herrenmahl*, 223. Cf. Jeremias's convincing critique, *Abendmahlsworte* 230-35 (ET *Eucharistic Words*, 238-43). The more recent attempt of Klauck, *Herrenmahl*, 314ff. (cf. 83ff.), respecting the anamnēsis mandate to show, besides the influence of the O.T. *zkr*, also a dependence on the founding testaments of Hellenistic meals in commemoration of the dead, in my opinion, falls short of persuasiveness.

[161]See, e.g., Exod 12:14; 13:9; b.Ber. 49a; Midrash Konen (BhM II 39).

[162]Cf. Delling, *TRE* 1:53:3ff.

[163]W. Schottroff, *'Gedenken' im Alten Orient und im Alten Testament*, 2nd ed. (Neukirchen-Vluyn: Neukirchener Verlag, 1967) 316.

[164]Exod 12:14; 13:3, 9; Deut 16:3; Jub 49:7-23; Josephus, *Ant.* 2.317; j.Pesa h 10.37d, 34, 17; *Mêmar Marqah* 1 ¶9 (J. MacDonald, *Memar Marqah* [Berlin: Töpelmann, 1963] 1.22.12; 23.4); cf. also Methodius, *Symp.* 9 ¶239 (SC [1963] 268). On the liturgical performance of "remembering," see m.Pesa h 10.5-6, and the corresponding parts of the Passover haggada; in addition, the evening prayer recited during the Passover celebration: *Gebetbuch für das Pessachfest*, ed. W. Heidenheim (Basel: Goldschmidt, 1970) 1:19.

Sabbath Qidduš,[166] indeed in daily prayer,[167] the memory of the foundational saving event—redemption from Egypt—has its firm place. In view of these facts, one will hesitate to see in the phrase εἰς τὴν ἐμὴν ἀνάμνησιν simply an analogy to the "remembering" at Passover,[168] and to derive it exclusively from the Passover meal. Rather, one must think also of the use of *zkr* to denote the "representative remembering of Yahweh's saving acts,"[169] as we find it in the Old Testament psalms. In Ps 77:12 we read the suppliant's self-summoning:

> I will call to mind the deeds of Yahweh,
> yea, I will remember Thy wonders of old.

Ps 105:5 sounds the call to remembering praise:

> Remember the wonderful works that he has done,
> his miracles, and the judgments he uttered!

Inasmuch as one "remembers" the great deeds of God,[170] one "remembers" Yahweh himself. This is shown in the words of Ps 6:6 in which, as in the anamnesis mandate of the Lord's Supper paradosis, the idea of "remembrance" is bound up with a personal object:

> For, in death there is no remembrance of Thee,[171]
> in Sheol who can give Thee praise?[172]

---

[165] b.Ber. 49a.

[166] See, in the contemporary Sephardic rite, *Prières journalières à l'usage du rite séfardi*, ed. A. ben Baruch Créhange (Tel Aviv, 1976) 255; in the Ashkenazi rite, Sidur Sefat Emet (see n. 55, above) 100.

[167] m.Ber. 1.5; cf. Jub. 49:7.

[168] So, e.g., Bachmann, 369n1; likewise—bound up, to be sure, with the thought of the abolition of the Passover meal—John Chrysostom, in Matt. Hom 82.1 (*Textos Eucaristicos* 1:551-52 #789) and, in dependence on this, Peter of Laodicea (*Textos Eucaristicos* 2:805-806, #1412).

[169] W. Schottroff, THAT 1:516.

[170] Cf. further Ps 111:4; 145:7.

[171] *'ên bammāwet zikrēkā*. Whereas LXX (ὁ μνημονεύων σου) obviously reads *zokrēkā*, σ' (ἀνάμνησίς σου), α' (μνήμη σου), and Targ. (*dwkrnk*) agree with MT.

[172] On "remembering" with personal object, see also Midrash Konen (BhM II 39): the angels are created "for the remembrance of God, to praise his name" (*lzkrwn 'l lšbh 't šmw*).

Now, it is noteworthy that in the psalms the idea of proclaiming can appear side by side with that of remembering. Thus, in Ps 105:1 the imperatives of "proclamation" correspond to the previously mentioned call in v. 5 ("Remember the wonderful works that he has done . . . "):

> O give thanks to Yahweh, call on his name,
> proclaim his deeds among the peoples!
> Sing to him, sing praises to him,
> tell of all his wonderful works!

"Remembering" (*zkr*, Ps 105:5a) is therefore realized in "proclaiming,"[173] that is, in the praise-filled proclamation of the great acts of God, as in the psalm's following detailed depiction, vv. 7-45.[174] In Ps 145 there is a correspondence between, among other phrases, "to declare Thy mighty acts" (v. 4b),[175] "to recount Thy great deeds" (v. 6b),[176] and "to proclaim the memory of Thy great goodness" (v. 7a).[177]

In the Septuagint we should also note Ps 70:15-17 where the following phrases appear in close proximity: τὸ στόμα μου ἐξαγγελεῖ τὴν δικαιοσύνην σου (v. 15a, my mouth shall proclaim Thy righteousness), μνησθήσομαι τῆς δικαιοσύνης σου (v. 16b,[178] I will remember Thy righteousness), and ἀπαγγελῶ τὰ θαυμάσιά σου (v. 17b, I will announce Thy wonders). In all these passages the idea of "remembering" is unpacked by that of "proclaiming."[179] Here, though, "to proclaim" does not signify an act of preaching, but solemn liturgical proclamation, the hymnic praise of God and his saving action. In this sense the Psalms speak, with a series of verbs,[180] of the "proclaiming" of the acts of God,[181] or of his "wonderful

---

[173]*yd'* (hiphil) v. 1b; *śyh b,* v. 2b.

[174]Similarly in Ps 77, the "remembering" referred to in v. 12 is realized in the narrative of vv. 14-21.

[175]*ngd* (hiphil).

[176]*spr* (piel).

[177]*zēker rab-tûbĕkā yabbî'û.*

[178]In the Hebrew text stands *zkr* (hiphil) = to confess (in song), to praise; cf. Isa 12:4; 1 Chron 16:4.

[179]Cf. also Sir 42:15, where in view of God's showing his Lordship in creation it is said, "I shall remember the works of God, and what I have seen, I shall proclaim." Here we come across in *parallelismus membrorum* the conjunction of *zkr*/μιμνῄσκεσθαι with *spr*/*(piel)*/ἐκδιηγεῖσθαι.

[180]Hebrew: *bśr* (piel) Ps 96:2 (par. 1 Chron 16:23); *yd'* (hiphil) Ps 89:2; 105:1; Isa 12:4; *ngd* (hiphil) Ps 9:12; 30:10; 40:6; 71:17,18; 92:3; 145:4; *spr* (piel) Ps 9:2; 26:7; 66:16; 71:15; 75:2; 96:3 (par. 1 Chron 16:24); 107:22; 118:17; 145:6. Greek: ἀναγγέλλειν LXX Ps 9:12; 29:10; 91:3; 95:3; 1 Chron 16:23; Isa 12:4; ἀπαγγέλλειν LXX Ps 39:6; 70:17,18; 88:2; 104:1; 144:4; διηγεῖσθαι LXX Ps 9:2; 25:7; 65:16; 74:2; 144:6;

deeds"[182] his "great acts,"[183] his "mighty works,"[184] his "faithfulness,"[185] his "righteousness,"[186] his "salvation,"[187] his "majesty."[188]

The bond between the concepts of "remembering" and "proclaiming" as we meet it in the psalms, is to be found *also* in 1 Cor 11:23ff., for there Paul interprets the anamnesis mandate of vv. 24c and 25c in his *commentary* of v. 26 as follows: "For[189] as often as you eat this bread and drink this cup you proclaim[190] the death of the Lord until he come(s)." As the words ὁσάκις . . . ἐὰν ἐσθίητε τὸν ἄρτον τοῦτον καὶ τὸ ποτήριον πίνητε take up the words ὁσάκις ἐὰν πίνητε from 11:25c, so the words τὸν θάνατον τοῦ κυρίου καταγγέλλετε ἄχρι οὗ ἔλθῃ stand in parallel to the words τοῦτο ποιεῖτε εἰς τὴν ἐμὴν ἀνάμνησιν in 11:24c and 25c.[191] The ἀνάμνησις of Christ consequently takes place in the "proclaiming" of the death of Christ.[192] That here, too, the resurrection of the Lord

---

ἐκδιηγεῖσθαι LXX Ps 117:17; ἐξαγγέλλειν LXX Ps 70:15; 106:22; εὐαγγελίζεσθαι LXX Ps 95:2.

[181]Ps 9:12; 105(104):1; 107(106):22; 118(117):17; cf. also 66:(65):16. Further, Isa 12:4.

[182]Ps 9:2; 26(25):7; 71(70):17; 75(74):2; 96(95):3 par. 1 Chron 16:24; cf. also Ps 40(39):6.

[183]Ps 145(144):6.

[184]Ps 145(144):4.

[185]Ps 30(29):10; 89(88):2; 92(91):3.

[186]Ps 71(70):15,18-19.

[187]Ps 96(95):2; par 1 Chron 16:23.

[188]Ps 96(95):3; par. 1 Chron 16:24.

[189]On γάρ used inferentially, cf. Rom 8:22; 15:27; 1 Cor 1:26; 9:19; 2 Cor 5:4; Heb 12:3.

[190]Καταγγέλλετε is *indicative*, not imperative. "The community has its attention called to . . . what regularly takes place during celebration of the Lord's Supper" (Wolff, 91). As the indicative expression shows, the celebration of the Lord's Supper in Corinth is apparently correct from the liturgical standpoint. Cf. also the in no way ironically intended statement in 11:2. In vv. 17-34 Paul does not rebuke the Corinthians for not having preserved the tradition of the Lord's Supper; what he finds fault with is that the well-to-do by their scandalous behavior totally contradict it.

[191]Hence, the Peshitta translates verse 26, "remember the death of our Lord, until he comes."

[192]This is how the Anaphora of the papyrus of Dêr-Balizeh, fol. 2 verso, 26ff., understands the text: ο[σάκις] ἐὰν ἐσθίητε τὸν ἄρτον τοῦτον, πίνητε δὲ τὸ ποτήριον τοῦτο, τὸν ἐμὸν θάνατον καταγ[γ]έλλεται (= καταγγελλετε), τὴν ἐμὴν ἀνάμν[ησιν πο]ιεῖτε. C. H. Roberts and B. Capelle, *An Early Euchologium. The Dêr Balizeh Papyrus enlarged and reedited* (Louvain: Muséon 1949) 28; cf. *Prex Eucharistica*, 126. See also the *verba institutionis* in the Coptic Anaphoras of Cyril (*Prex Eucharistica*, 137), of Basil (E.

is included cannot be doubted in view of the κύριος title and the mention of the parousia (ἄχρι οὗ ἔλθῃ).[193]

But the idea of "proclaiming" (καταγγέλλειν) ought to be understood from the language of the Old Testament psalms.[194] Thus, the "proclaiming" of the death of Christ takes place not through the celebration of the Lord's Supper as such,[195] nor through a ritual act consisting simply of the breaking of the bread and the pouring of the wine;[196] for "καταγγέλλειν is always a matter of the word."[197] Nor should we think of the recitation, with perhaps an explanation attached, of the Lord's Supper paradosis,[198] nor of the words of bestowal,[199] nor of the preaching of the word accompanying the meal,[200] nor of the public reading of the passion story.[201] Rather, the Old Testament evidence quite decisively speaks for the view that καταγγέλλειν is to be interpreted as the eucharistic prayers spoken over bread and cup.[202] By these prayers, which in the form of praise proclaim the crucifixion (and Resurrection) of Jesus as the saving act of God, the community assembled for the meal performs the ἀνάμνησις of its Lord.

If in this way we understand the idea of "remembrance," as we ought, from

---

Renaudot, *Liturgiarum orientalium collectio,* vol. 1 [Frankfurt and London, 1847; rpt. Gregg, 1970] 15), and of Gregory (ibid., 30).

[193]The old liturgies are accordingly quite right in frequently complementing the tradition with a reference to the resurrection. So, e.g., the Greek James Anaphora: καὶ τὴν ἀνάστασιν αὐτοῦ ὁμολογεῖτε (*Prex Eucharistica,* 248).

[194]Καταγγέλλειν in Symmachus Ps 40(39):6 appears as the rendering of Hebrew *ngd* (hiphil). Cf., in addition, in LXX 2 Macc 9:17, καταγγέλλειν τὸ τοῦ θεοῦ χράτος.

[195]Thus, e.g., Hahn, "Herrengedächtnis," 309.

[196]Thus, e.g., Wilhelm Bousset, *Der erste Briefe an die Korinther,* 132; Weiss, 288-89, 293; Lietzmann, *Messe und Herrenmahl,* 222n1; Lietzmann, *An die Korinther* 1/2:58.

[197]Wolff, 91; earlier, Julius Schniewind, TWNT 1:70:22ff. (= TDNT 1:70ff.).

[198]So, e.g., Wolff, 92 (cf. 56-57). But Wolff also holds, as possible, that the text refers to "a detailed eucharistic prayer."

[199]So Jeremias, *Abendmahlsworte,* 100-101 (ET *Eucharistic Words,* 107): "recitation of the words of interpretation followed by an exposition."

[200]So, e.g., Conzelmann, 238. Καταγγέλλειν admittedly for Paul elsewhere (with the exception of Rom 1:8) signifies preaching (1 Cor 2:1; 9:14; Phil 1:17-18; cf. Col 1:28); but there it is missionary preaching, *not* preaching during the community service. Furthermore, the preaching of the word in the community's worship service would have preceded the meal, which was introduced by the holy kiss; see Jeremias, *Abendmahlsworte,* 112 (ET *Eucharistic Words,* 118-19).

[201]So the considerations offered by Stuhlmacher, "Herrenmahl," 22, 34 (= 84, 96-97); likewise, earlier Barrett, 264, 270.

[202]This is the sense in which, e.g., Bornkamm, *Herrenmahl,* 159-60, and Schürmann, *Einsetzungsbericht,* 33, understand the expression.

OldTestamentlinguisticusage,twomisunderstandingsareavoidedfromtheoutset. First, the ἀνάμνησις is no mere recalling of an event of the past, which, as such, has necessarily faded away; it is therefore not simply an intellectual process by which the "rememberer" retrojects himself into the distant past and "represents" to himself, that is, makes himself conscious of, what happened long ago. Second, neither is the ἀνάμνησις a sacramental "representation" in this sense, that the remembering first retrieves what in itself is past, bringing it into the present and allowing it so to become effective here and now.[203] In the horizon of Old Testament thought, rather, the ἀνάμνησις should be described as the praise-filled "representation" of that which happened *once,* but thereby and at the same time *once and for all,* and which, as an event of all-inclusive expiation[204] from Good Friday and Easter, affects and includes all those assembled for the Lord's Supper, and so for them, prior to all "remembering," independently of all remembering, is already determinative of being. That means the ἀνάμνησις of Christ and his saving work proclaims the once-only event of salvation, on which faith is based, as present reality determining the being of the faithful.[205]

The consecratory eucharistic prayers presupposed by Paul are, as we can now hold, ἀνάμνησις of Jesus Christ in the form of the praise-filled proclamation of his death on the cross and his Resurrection. One may ask whether an epicletic moment was proper to these prayers. Obviously, we should not be thinking of a mutation-epiclesis, such as is found later in practically all Eastern anaphoras, but an epiclesis of the sort we encounter in Hippolytus and in the Eastern Syriac Apostle-Anaphora.[206] In the anaphora of the Ἀποστολικὴ Παράδοσις[207] the words of institution end with the following: *Quando hoc facitis, meam commemorationem facitis* ("When you do this, you make commemoration of me"). Immediately attached to these words is this prayer:

---

[203]Cf. the exceedingly problematic formulation of Klauck, *Herrenmahl,* 316: "The commemorating act retrieves the past into the present as saving event that benefits those celebrating."

[204]See Hofius, "Sühne und Versöhnung" (see above, n. 129) 37ff.

[205]This state of affairs is reflected in the Anaphoras of the Eastern Church in that the anamnēsis *also* includes the sessio Christi ad dexteram Patris and his parousia. Thus, the liturgy of Chrysostom (*Prex Eucharistica,* 226) reads, Μεμνημένοι τοίνυν . . . πάντων τῶν ὑπὲρ ὑμῶν γεγενημένων, τοῦ σταυροῦ, τοῦ τάφου, τῆς τριημέρου ἀναστάσεως, τῆς εἰς οὐρανοὺς ἀναβάσεως, τῆς ἐκ δεξιῶν καθέδρας, τῆς δευτέρας καὶ ἐνδόξου πάλιν παρουσίας. . . .

[206]In these texts the bread and cup rites form a unity, so that the epiclesis refers to bread and cup as one.

[207]I cite the text according to *Prex Eucharistica,* 81; cf. Botte, *La Tradition apostolique* (n. 115, above) 16.

Memores igitur mortis et resurrectionis eius, offerimus tibi panem et calicem, gratias tibi agentes, quia nos dignos habuisti adstare coram te et tibi ministrare. Et petimus, ut mittas Spiritum tuum sanctum in oblationem sanctae ecclesiae; in unum congregans, des omnibus qui percipiunt [de] sanctis in repletionem Spiritus sancti, ad confirmationem fidei in veritate, ut te laudemus et glorificemus per puerum tuum Iesum Christum: per quem tibi gloria et honor Patri et Filio cum sancto Spiritu in sancta Ecclesia tua et nunc et in saecula saeculorum. Amen.

Remembering therefore his death and Resurrection, we offer Thee the bread and the cup, thanking Thee that Thou hast considered us worthy to stand before Thee and to serve Thee. As we beg that Thou send Thy holy Spirit onto the offering of the holy church; gathering them together, give to all who receive of [these] holy [gifts] the fullness of the holy Spirit to confirm their faith in truth, that we may praise Thee and glorify Thee through Thy servant Jesus Christ, through whom be glory and honor to Thee, Father, and to the Son with the holy Spirit in Thy holy church both now and forever. Amen.

In the eastern Syriac Apostle-Anaphora[208] the epiclesis, together with the praise with which it concludes, reads,

O Lord, let Thy holy Spirit come and rest upon this sacrifice of Thy servant and bless and sanctify it: that it give to us, Lord, pardon for transgressions and forgiveness of sins, great hope of the Resurrection from the dead and new life in the Kingdom of Heaven with all those who have been pleasing to Thee. And for the whole great wonderful work of salvation accomplished for us we thank Thee and praise Thee without ceasing with loud voice and unveiled countenance in Thy church, which is ransomed through the precious blood of Thy Christ. We bring praise and honor, glorification and adoration to Thy living, holy, and life-giving name, and now and always and for all eternity. Amen.

That the liturgy of the Lord's Supper in the Pauline communities could have known an entreaty of this kind for the descent of the Holy Spirit on the eucharistic bread and the eucharistic cup is a notion we are permitted to entertain, thanks to the designation of the sacred gifts as "spiritual food" and "spiritual drink" (1 Cor 10:3-4). In short, it is by no means excluded that the epithet πνευματικός referred not simply to the heavenly supernatural character of the eucharistic gifts, but at the

---

[208]Syrian text: *Liturgia sanctorum apostolorum Adaei et Maris* (Urmia, 1890). English translation with text-critical notes and short commentary: B. D. Spinks, *Addai and Mari—the Anaphora of the Apostles: A Text for Students,* Grove Liturgical Study 24 (Bramcote Notts, 1980). Below I provide a translation of the epiclesis (Liturgia 20); cf. the Latin translation in *Prex Eucharistica,* 380.

same time also to the work of God through his Spirit.[209] Then it would be this action of the Spirit—invoked in the eucharistic prayers—that lends the natural elements of bread and wine their sacramental character.

VI

One essential element of the clause in 1 Cor 11:26 has so far not been treated: the phrase ἄχρι οὗ ἔλθῃ, "until he come(s)." These words are not a simple time-reference,[210] but contain, as Joachim Jeremias has convincingly shown, an aspect of the "final clause": the death of the Lord is proclaimed "until (things have reached the point that) he comes, until (the goal is reached, that) he come(s)."[211] Inasmuch as the community proclaims before God the death of Jesus Christ in the Lord's Supper, they beg for the parousia of their Lord and therewith the eschatological consummation of salvation.[212] Hence, there doubtless exists an inner relation between the words ἄχρι οὗ ἔλθῃ and the Maranatha in the liturgy of the Lord's Supper, which is attested for us in 1 Cor 16:22 and Did. 10:6.[213] We shall have to think, however, not only of this liturgical call, but also and above all of the eucharistic prayers over bread and cup directed to *God* and, so, of the ἀνάμνησις

---

[209]Cf. Bachmann, 330; Schlatter, 288-89; Wolff, 41.

[210]As is the case, e.g., in Gen 49:10; 4Qpatr 3-4; 1QS 9.11; CD 12.23; 20.1.

[211]Jeremias, *Abendmahlsworte,* 244 (ET *Eucharistic Words,* 253-54). See, in addition, O. Hofius, " 'Bis dass er kommt' I Kor xi.26," *NTS* 14 (1967/1968): 439-41. In this short essay I have specified two O.T. texts, Isa 62:1 and 62:6-7 as attesting, in intercessory expressions, "until" in a final (purpose/result) sense. One could multiply examples: ParJer 2.3, "Whenever the people sinned, Jeremiah scattered dust on his head, and prayed for the people *until* their sins were forgiven" (καὶ ηὔχετο ὑπὲρ τοῦ λαοῦ, ἕως ἂν ἀφεθῇ αὐτῷ ἡ ἁμαρτία); b.Ber. 32a (on Exod 32:10): Moses spoke to God: "Lord of the world, I will not leave you alone *until* you have forgiven and pardoned them" (*'yn 'ny mny h k 'd štmhwl wtsl h lhm*); ibid. on Exod 32:11): "He stood before the Holy One—blessed be He—in prayer, *until* he had appeased him (*'d šh h lhw*); Pesiq. 16.9: Moses "did not cease to curry favor with (God) for them *until* he called them 'my people' " (*lw zz m h bbn 'd šqr' 'wtn 'my*). See further Lam 3:49-50; t.Yoma 5(4).6 (190.15-16) par. b.Yoma 86a; Abot R. Nat. (Rec. A) 9; also 1QS 10.19f.

[212]Cf. Jeremias, ibid.

[213]The imperative sense "Our Lord, come!" is nailed down by Rev 22:20b (ἔρχου κύριε Ἰησοῦ), but also by the context in Did. 10:6. For the Palestinian linguistic zone only the formulation *māran 'ătā'* is grammatically possible; see Hans-Peter Rüger, "Zum Problem der Sprache Jesu," *ZNW* 59 (1968): 113-22, at 120-21; idem, *TRE* 3:607; Klaus Beyer, *Die aramäischen Texte vom Toten Meer* (Göttingen: Vandenhoeck & Ruprecht, 1984) 124. In Greek accordingly the division of μαραναθά into μαρὰν ἀθά is correct! (Μαράνα θά is correspondingly false.)

performed in these prayers. Joachim Jeremias was altogether right in seeing this,[214] even though his linguistic understanding of the anamnēsis mandate ("Do this, *that God remember me,*")[215] cannot be upheld. The clause in 1 Cor 11:26, taking up and commenting on the anamnēsis mandate in 1 Cor 11:24c, 25c undeniably suggests that together with the praise-filled remembrance of the saving act of the expiatory death and resurrection of Jesus Christ, the community has simultaneously implored God's final definitive act: the sending of the Lord for the eschatological consummation of salvation.[216]

A corresponding prayer, so far as I know, has unfortunately not been transmitted to us in the liturgies of the ancient church of the East.[217] In the Ambrosian liturgy, however, there is one in the Anaphora intended for Maundy Thursday. In it the *verba testamenti* are concluded with a text stylized as words of Jesus:

> *Mortem meam praedicabitis, Resurrectionem meam annuntiabitis, adventum meum sperabitis, donec iterum de caelis veniam ad vos.*[218]

> Ye shall proclaim my death, ye shall announce my resurrection, ye shall hope for my coming until again I come to ye from heaven.

The prayer immediately following reads,

> *Haec facimus, haec celebramus tua, Domine, praecepta servantes, et ad communionem inviolabilem, hoc ipso quod corpus Domini sumimus, mortem dominicam nuntiamus. Tuum vero est, omnipotens Pater, mittere nunc nobis unigenitum Filium tuum, quem non quaerentibus sponte misisti. . . .*[219]

> We do and celebrate these things, O Lord, observing Thy mandates, and unto inviolable communion [with him], by the fact that we receive the body of the Lord, we announce the death of the Lord. It is truly for Thee, omnipotent

---

[214]Jeremias, *Abendmahlsworte,* 242ff. (ET *Eucharistic Words,* 251ff.).

[215]Ibid. 242 (ET, 252), italics from Jeremias.

[216]Cf. the following O.T. evidence. In Ps 9 there appears next to the proclamation of the acts of God (9:2, 12), the entreaty for his definitive act of judgment (9:18-20); Ps 96 joins the proclamation of God's saving acts (96:2-3) to the prospect of the eschatological "coming" of the universal judge (96:12-13).

[217]On the other hand, the Maranatha survives above all in the Anaphoras of Syrian-Antiochean type: in the acclamation with which the community responds to the *narratio institutionis:* "Thy death, O Lord, we remember; Thy resurrection we confess; and we await Thy second coming. . . . " *Prex Eucharistica,* 266, 271, 279, 286, 289, 295, 300, 304, 307, 312, 316, 343).

[218]*Prex Eucharistica* 450.

[219]Ibid., 453. Cf. the rite today: Messale ambrosiano festivo (Casale Monferrato, 1986) 533.

Father, to send us now Thine only-begotten Son, whom Thou hast freely sent to those who had not besought Thee.

It may be that the last sentence, under the sign of a particular sacramental theology, was made to refer to the coming of Christ at the Lord's Supper. Originally, however, this sentence, as echoing the words *adventum meum sperabitis, donec iterum de caelis veniam ad vos* (ye shall hope for my coming until again I come to ye from heaven), must have been an entreaty for the sending of the Son in the parousia.

VII

If, in conclusion, we turn again to the question of the *function* that falls to the Lord's Supper paradosis cited by Paul in the context of 1 Cor 11:17-34, we should say: In the light of this tradition and especially of the two words of bestowal, clearly the behavior that Paul finds fault with on the part of the well-to-do Corinthians radically contradicts what Jesus founded. If the founding of the Lord's Supper has "its essence in the conscious and rigorous relation to Christ and his death,"[220] then the same holds necessarily—as 11:26 expressly underscores—for each repetition concordant with Christ's founding act. The eucharistic actions that encompass the meal and make it κυριακὸν δεῖπνον give a share in the expiatory death of Jesus Christ and in the salvation realized by that death. Accordingly, they are at the same time a pledge of participation in the consummation of salvation, which in the eucharistic prayers is implored by the petition for the Lord's parousia.

But if this is the character of the eucharistic acts, then, by the bread rite at the beginning of the κυριακὸν δεῖπνον, to which the cup rite at the end corresponds, the celebration of a meal is opened at which the participants are fundamentally unable to leave Christ and his saving act out of consideration. That means that no one who has eaten the eucharistic bread and will drink from the eucharistic cup may so act as if the full meal enclosed by the eucharistic acts were the individual's private affair, and so something at which each might do as he pleased. At "the table of the Lord" (1 Cor 10:21) there assembles the ἐκκλησία τοῦ θεοῦ (11:22), which has its distinctive character from the ὑπὲρ ὑμῶν (for you), of which the word over the bread speaks. Indeed, it is just this ὑπὲρ ὑμῶν that—transcending social differences—binds all the members of the community together, calls the attention of each to the other, and makes each responsible for the other.

In a word, it is the crucified Christ himself who does this. Inconsiderateness, indifference, and lovelessness towards the "brother for whom Christ died"[221] are

---

[220]Bachmann, 370.
[221]1 Cor 8:11; cf. Rom 14:15.

consequently nothing short of a denial of the ὑπὲρ ὑμῶν (for you), an unheard-of disregard for Christ's saving expiatory death, and hence an inconceivable sin against Christ himself.[222] Whoever knows the meaning of the two sacramental acts that enclose the meal and give it its essential character is in principle unable to act as the Corinthians rebuked by Paul do; and whoever acts in this way makes it plain that he does not know or grasp what these acts mean.[223]

Hence, Paul speaks of receiving the eucharistic gifts "in an unworthy manner" (ἀναξίως, v. 27), because the one who receives does not recognize or appropriately esteem the essence and significance of these gifts (v.29).[224] The disregard implied here of the sacramental gifts signifies a sin "against the body and blood of the Lord," and brings down on the community the present punishment of the Lord (vv. 27, 29).[225] If Paul cites the tradition that has come to him from the Lord and is obligatory for the church, he does so "to enforce respect for the bread and the cup

---

[222]Wolff, 94, quite rightly explains, "Paul argues here . . . as in 8:11-12 (cf., similarly, 14:15), that what is at stake is losing sight of the saving work of Christ." The argumentation in 1 Cor 11:17-34 derives at all points from christology and soteriology, *not,* that is, from ecclesiology.

[223]Weiss, 283, conjectures—not without reason—that the Corinthians "were only mechanically participating in" the meal begun by the breaking of the bread and the blessing spoken over the cup after the meal. That the Corinthians, as is often asserted (e.g. Bornkamm, *Herrenmahl,* 141ff.) were "sacramentalists," who overvalued the rites connected with bread and cup, strikes me (despite 1 Cor 10) as implausible and, moreover, cannot be derived from the wording of 1 Cor 11:17ff. On the contrary, Paul rebukes the heedless rich for profaning the sacrament (vv. 27, 29). Rightly judging the matter are also, for example, Calvin, 170; C. F. G. Heinrici, *Das erste Sendschreiben des Apostels Paulus an die Korinthier* (Berlin: Hertz, 1880) 338-39, 342; Weiss, 283, 285, 292.

[224]That is the meaning of the words μὴ διακρίνων τὸ σῶμα (11:29), which explains the ἀναξίως of 11:27. Τὸ σῶμα stands as pars pro toto for the τὸ σῶμα καὶ τὸ αἷμα; meant thereby (as in the tradition in 11:24b, 25b, 27) are the "body" and the "blood" of *Christ* (and not, say, the church as "body of Christ"). With respect to the formula διακρίνων τὸ σῶμα, there are linguistically (i.e., from the meaning of the verb) two possible senses: (a) "to differentiate the body" (cf. 1 Cor 4:7); (b) to judge the body rightly, to evaluate the body properly (cf. 1 Cor 14:29; Matt 16:3). In the first sense, the meaning is, one does not differentiate "the bread as 'the body' of the Lord from ordinary bread" (so, e.g., Weiss, 283); in the second (in my opinion, preferable) sense this meaning is included, but at the same time it is made still more precise: one does not appreciate the real significance of the eucharistic bread, which consists in its giving a share in the death of Jesus Christ "for you" (cf., e.g. Wolff, 95).

[225]If one presupposes in Corinth the sequence "full meal—sacrament," the idea is more than slightly thrown out of kilter, as the following remark of Wolff (77) shows: "He who *beforehand* at the meal proper has failed to give thought to his brother, who then *afterwards* eats and drinks of the bread and wine in an unworthy manner, commits an offence against the Lord's saving gifts" (my emphases).

in order to avoid κρίμα."[226] This is the exact meaning of the demand in v. 28: "Let each examine himself and only then eat of the bread and drink of the cup!"[227] It is the demand to test self-critically whether one has truly understood and takes seriously what happens in the sacramental acts, and whether one acts worthily towards the Lord and honors him in whose saving death this act gives a share.[228]

---

[226]So rightly Burchard, "The Importance of Joseph and Aseneth," 126.

[227]On ἄνθρωπος = "each," "everyone," "each one," cf. 1 Cor 4:1; 7:26; on καὶ οὕτως logically referring backward, see Rom 11:26; 1 Thess 4:17.

[228]Cf. also the words spoken in 1 Cor 16:22 with reference to the celebration of the Lord's Supper: εἴ τις οὐ φιλεῖ τὸν κύριον, ἤτω ἀνάθεμα.

The Eucharist

The Sacrament
of the Economy of Salvation

Alkiviadis C. Calivas

Literary documents on the lives of saints often contain important information on Christian life, liturgy, and doctrine. One such document, which dates back to AD 304, at the height of the fierce persecutions initiated by the Emperors Diocletian and Maximian, is an eyewitness account describing the trial of a group of Christians in a town of North Africa. Of particular interest is the brief testimony of two of those martyrs. Their words concerning the Eucharist provide us with a succinct statement that, I believe, sums up the Orthodox Church's understanding of the Sacrament.

Then Saturninus, the priest, was arraigned for combat.

The proconsul asked, "Did you, contrary to the orders of the emperors, arrange for these persons to hold an assembly?"

Saturninus replied, "Certainly. We celebrated the Eucharist."

"Why?"

"Because the Eucharist cannot be abandoned."

As soon as he said this, the proconsul ordered him to be put immediately on the rack. . . .

Then Felix, a son of Saturninus and a reader in the church, came forward to the contest. Whereupon the proconsul inquired of him, "I am not asking you if you are a Christian. You can hold your peace about that! But were you one of the assembly; and do you possess any copies of the Scriptures?"

"As if a Christian could exist without the Eucharist, or the Eucharist be celebrated without a Christian!" answered Felix. "Don't you know that a Christian is constituted by the Eucharist, and the Eucharist by a Christian? Neither avails without the other. We celebrated our assembly right gloriously. We always convene at the Eucharist for the reading of the Lord's Scriptures."

Enraged by the confession, Anulinus ordered Felix to be beaten with clubs. . . .[1]

The testimony of these two ancient martyrs serves to highlight the significance and uniqueness of the Eucharist in the life of the church. The Eucharist is, at once, the source and summit of her life. In it the church is continuously changed from a human community into the body of Christ, the temple of the Holy Spirit, and the people of God.[2]

Worship is the most profound activity of the people of God; and the sacraments, most especially the Eucharist, are at the very heart of the church's worship.

Throughout history the worship of the church has been the expression and guardian of divine revelation. Not only did it express and represent the saving events of Christ's life, death, resurrection, and ascension to heaven but it also was for the members of the church, the living anticipation of the kingdom to come. In worship, the church, being the body of Christ, enlivened by the Holy Spirit, unites the faithful, as adopted sons and daughters of God the Father.[3]

Dogma and prayer, faith and worship are inseparable; and the Eucharist, being truly Christ, is the focus and content of both worship and faith. Thus, writes St. Irenaeus, "our manner of thinking is conformed to the Eucharist, and the Eucharist confirms our manner of thinking."[4] Theology, in the first place, is lived and taught liturgically and doxologically.

The Eucharist at the Center of the Church's Life

The powers of the kingdom already experienced in the church are manifested through the sacraments which are offered in faith. The Eucharist is the final and greatest of the sacraments, "for in it we obtain God Himself and God is united with us in the most perfect union," according to St. Nicholas Kavasilas.[5]

---

[1]Cited in M. H. Shepherd, Jr., *The Worship of the Church* (New York 1963) 3-4. The original text may be found in PL 8.688ff. ("Acts of St. Saturninus and Companions").

[2]See Calivas, "Reflections on the Divine Liturgy," *The Greek Orthodox Theological Review* (1983): 213ff.

[3]"Report No. 1 from the Orthodox Consultation on Confessing Christ through the Liturgical Life of the Church Today," in *Baptism and Eucharist, Ecumenical Convergence in Celebration,* Faith and Order paper no. 117, ed. Max Thurian and Geoffrey Wainwright (WCC Publications, 1983).

[4]*Against Heresies* 4.18.5.

[5]St. Nicholas Kavasilas, *The Life in Christ* 4.3.

The Eucharist is at the center of the church's life, because it "completed all the other sacraments,"[6] and "recapitulates the entire economy of salvation."[7] Baptism, by bringing us into the glorified life of Christ and making us part of His deified humanity, integrates us into the church, his body, and thus, inaugurates in us a new life. This "new life" (Rom 6:4) is constantly renewed, preserved, nurtured, and increased by the Eucharist. The Eucharist imparts life; and the life it gives is the life of God Himself.[8] The relationship between the Eucharist and life is grounded in the words of the Lord as recorded in the Gospel of John:

> Jesus then said unto them, "Truly, truly, I say to you, it was not Moses who gave you the bread from heaven; my Father gives you the true bread from heaven. For the bread of God is that which comes down from heaven, and gives life to the world." They said to him, "Lord, give us this bread always."
>
> Jesus said to them, "I am the bread of life; . . . I am the bread which came down from heaven . . . I am the living bread which came down from heaven; if anyone eats of this bread, he will live for ever; and the bread which I shall give for the life of the world is my flesh.
>
> " . . . Truly, truly, I say to you, unless you eat the flesh of the Son of man and drink his blood, you have no life in you; he who eats my flesh and drinks my blood has eternal life, and I will raise him up at the last day. For my flesh is food indeed, and my blood is drink indeed. He who eats my flesh and drinks my blood abides in me, and I in him. . . . so he who eats me will live because of me. . . . he who eats this bread will live forever." (John 6:32-58)

Jesus Christ, who is our true and everlasting life,[9] makes his own life to rise up in us in the Eucharist.[10] The whole God—Father, Son and Holy Spirit—is offered to us, "for wheresoever one person of the Trinity is, the whole Trinity is there," according to St. John Chrysostom.[11] At the same time, as our liturgical tradition reminds us, the whole man is offered to God: "Let us commit ourselves and one

---

[6]Ibid., 4.2,3.

[7]St. Theodore the Studite, Antirrheticos 2, cited in C. Andronikof, "Assembly and Body of Christ: Identity or Distinction," in *Roles in the Liturgical Assembly,* ed. M. J. O'Connell (Pueblo, 1981).

[8]See J. D. Zizioulas, *Being as Communion* (St. Vladimir's Seminary Press, 1985) 78-82.

[9]St. Ignatios of Antioch, *Smyrnaeans* 4; *Magnesians* 1.

[10]St. Nicholas Kavasilas, *The Life in Christ,* 4.17.

[11]St. John Chrysostom, *Hom. in Rom.* 13.8, 76.929.

another and our whole life to Christ our God."[12] Thus salvation is accomplished by God, but in cooperation with humanity.

The Eucharist as Food

Clement of Alexandria refers to the Eucharist and the nourishment that proceeds from it in these words:

> The Logos becomes everything to His little ones: Father, and Mother, and Teacher, and Nourisher! "Eat my flesh" He says, "and drink my blood." The Lord supplies these as the foods most appropriate for us. . . . O paradoxical mystery! He commands us to put off the old, fleshly corruption, and the old nourishment as well, to partake of another, new way of life, that of Christ, to receive Him and store Him up in ourselves. . . . Through Him we have come to trust in God, and have taken refuge at the Father's breast causing forgetfulness of care.[13]

In establishing the Eucharist during the course of a Jewish ritual meal, Christ conformed to a familiar practice already filled with human and sacred values. Jewish custom required that a blessing be pronounced over the bread at the beginning of every solemn meal and over the cup of wine mixed with water at the end of the meal. At the mystical supper Jesus gave a radically new meaning to the food and drink of the sacred meal. He identified Himself with the bread and wine. He gave his flesh as food.

> Now as they were eating, Jesus took bread, and blessed, and broke it, and gave it to the disciples and said, "Take, eat; this is my body." And he took a cup, and when he had given thanks he gave it to them, saying, "Drink of it, all of you; for this is my blood of the covenant, which is poured out for many for the forgiveness of sins." (Matt 26:26-28)

The sacred meals of the Old Testament, which signify a variety of meanings (encounter, communion, hospitality, memorial, sacrifice, covenant) are the incomplete and imperfect figure (*typos*) of the Eucharist. The eucharistic meal perfected and surpassed the *typos*. God enters into such a communion of life that he feeds humanity with his own being, while still remaining distinct.[14] In the words of St. Maximos the Confessor, Christ transmits divine life to us. The author of life

---

[12]A petition of the Small Litany in the Orthodox Liturgy.

[13]*Paedagogus* 1.42.3, 43.1, 3.

[14]See G. Wainwright, *Eucharist and Eschatology* (Oxford: Oxford University Press, 1981) 58.

shatters the limitations of our createdness. Christ acts to make us his own body.[15]
Through him we become organic parts of the theanthropic mystery.[16]

The union with life involves a sharing of life. The acts of eating and drinking
become the suitable and appropriate sign of this mystery. Drawing on human
physiology, St. Gregory of Nyssa explains the reason for this with these words:

> Who is not aware that the very nature of our body does not possess life by an
> essential character of its own, but maintains itself and continues in existence
> through the influx of a force from without. . . . Now this force is nourishment
> and is so called. . . . Man finds his chief sustenance in bread. In order to retain
> and preserve moisture he has to drink, not water only, but water often
> sweetened with wine. . . . He who sees these elements, then, sees, in effect, the
> bulk of our body. . . . With good reason, then, do we believe that now also the
> bread which is sanctified by the word of God is changed into the body of God
> the Word. . . . The God who manifested himself mingled himself with our
> perishable nature in order that by communion with his divinity humanity might
> at the same time be divinized, for this reason he plants himself, by the
> economy of his grace, in all believers by means of the flesh which derives its
> subsistence from both wine and bread, mingling himself with the bodies of
> believers, in order that, by union with that which is immortal, man also might
> partake of incorruption.[17]

We have learned to equate food with life because it sustains our earthly
existence. Accordingly, food not only maintains life but also symbolizes it. Hence,
as St. Nicholas Kavasilas observes "it is natural to consider food as the first fruit
of life itself." As such we can agree with Kavasilas's assertion that the "baking of
bread and the making of wine to drink is peculiar to man."[18] In the Eucharist this
distinctively unique human food becomes our gift of life as well as our exchange
of life for life. To quote St. Nicholas Kavasilas,

> For what reason must we offer these oblations to God as first fruits of
> human life?
> The reason is that God gives us life in exchange for these gifts. Now it is
> fitting that the gift should have something in common with the reward, and not
> be utterly removed from it. Since the reward is life, then the offering should
> to some extent be life also; especially since he who prescribes the gift is also
> the giver of life, the just judge who weighs all things. It is he who commands

---

[15]John 5:56; 1 Cor. 10:16-17.

[16]See Archimandrite Vasileios, *Hymn of Entry,* (St. Vladimir's Seminary Press, 1984)
74-77.

[17]St. Gregory of Nyssa, *Catechetical Oration* 37.

[18]St. Nicholas Kavasilas, *A Commentary on the Divine Liturgy* 3.

us to offer bread and wine; it is he who gives us in return the living bread, the chalice of eternal life. Just as he gave the apostles fish for fish, making the fishermen fishers of men; just as he promised to give the young man who asked him about the kingdom the treasures of heaven in exchange for earthly riches; so here he commands those to whom he would give eternal life (that is, his lifegiving body and blood) to offer the food of our fleeting mortal life: so that we may receive life for life, eternity for temporality; so that what is a grace may seem to be an exchange, so that infinite generosity may have the appearance of justice; and thus the word may be fulfilled: "I will set my mercy in the balance."[19]

Although the Eucharist was detached very early[20] from its original setting, its celebration continues to be associated with "table imagery." It is not without significance, then, that the Orthodox still call the mystical center of their churches the holy table (ἁγία τράπεζα).

The Eucharist as Communion

The incarnate Logos himself became the church. To quote Christos Yannaras, Christ is "the temporal beginning and the realization within human nature of the trinitarian mode of existence."[21] He continues, "Christ is the head of the church not because he was her founder, but because he himself constitutes her body. He forms her trinitarian mode of existence, that ethos of the Church which is to be identified with true life."[22]

The church is the great mystery of God and the divine-human encounter. She is a living theanthropic organism: the Body of Christ. She is the extension and fullness of the incarnation or, rather, the incarnate life of the Son of God. Through this incarnate life humanity is continually incorporated into Christ and reunited to God in order to partake of His divine nature (2 Pet 1:4).[23]

In a remarkably insightful passage, St. Symeon of Thessaloniki presents us with a vivid description of the meaning of the Church's theanthropic hypostasis.

---

[19]Ibid., 4.

[20]See Calivas, *The Divine Liturgy: The Time of its Celebration* (in Greek), Analecta Vlatadon 37 (Thessaloniki, 1982) 165ff.

[21]Christos Yannaras, *Freedom of Morality* (St. Vladimir's Seminary Press, 1984) 51.

[22]Ibid.

[23]See George Florovsky, *Bible, Church, Tradition,* vol. 1 (Belmont MA, 1972) 64. It should be noted that, while the beginnings of the church coincide with the incarnation, the church existed in Christ from eternity.

His point is made in a discussion of the service of the Proskomide:[24]

> In the divine figure and action of the holy proskomide we see Jesus Himself and we contemplate the one Church. Through Him, who is the true light, she acquires eternal life, and is illumined and constituted. On the one hand, He is in the center through the Bread; on the other, His Mother is at His right through the particle, while the saints and angels are at the left. And, below Him is the entire devout assemblage (ἄνθροισμα) of those who have believed in Him. There is a great mystery here: God in men and God among the gods, (θεός ἐν ἀνθρώποις καὶ ἐν μέσῳ θεῶν . . .) who have received deification from Him, who is true God by nature, and who was enfleshed for their sake. The future Kingdom is here, too, and the revelation of eternal life: God with us, seen and partaken (θεός μεθ' ἡμῶν ὁρώμενός τε καὶ μεταλαμβανόμενος).[25]

The church, as the body of Christ, is actualized, revealed and expressed within the eucharistic reality. The Eucharist is Christ himself, "who is enthroned on high with the Father and is also invisibly present among us."[26] It is his sacrificed, risen, and deified body, which is given to the faithful "for the forgiveness of sins and life eternal."[27] The church and the Eucharist are united and are synonymous in Christ. The Eucharist exists solely for the church and in the church; for the members of Christ who are the church.[28] The church, however, is not the Eucharist. The church, constituted by Christ, is nourished by the Eucharist and, in it, conceives of herself as the Body of Christ. In the Eucharist the church is always becoming concorporeal

---

[24]The ritual preparation of the eucharistic gifts of the bread and wine is called the *proskomidē*. It is conducted at the *prothesis* (table of preparation). The gifts are brought to the church by the people. The preparation of the bread and wine was once the function of the deacon. By the time of St. Symeon of Thessaloniki (†1429), the function was taken over by a presbyter. The Orthodox used leavened bread for the Eucharist. It is called *prosphoron* or *prosphora* (offering). The ritual preparation of the gifts developed over a period of time. Originally conducted at the start of the "eucharistic" part of the divine liturgy, the Proskomide was transferred after the eighth century to a time before the *enarxis* (beginning) of the Divine Liturgy. The present elaborate rite dates from about the 12th century. It consists of extracting the Lamb from the *prosphoron* and placing it on the *discos*; the filling of the chalice with wine and water; the commemoration of the saints and the placing on the *discos* of a number of particles in their honor; and the remembrance of the faithful, both living and dead by name and the placing of the particles on the *discos* for their salvation.

[25]St. Symeon of Thessaloniki, *Dialogos* 94, PG 155, 285. Cf. his *Apokriseis* 155, 877.

[26]A prayer before Communion from the Divine Liturgy of St. John Chrysostom.

[27]The liturgical formula used at the distribution of Holy Communion.

[28]See Athanasios Yevtic, *The Ecclesiology of St. Paul* (in Greek) (Athens, 1984) 126-42.

(σύσσωμος) with Christ. "We have become concorporeal with Him and with one another. This is why the Church is called the Body of Christ, and each of us His members," says St. Cyril of Alexandria.[29]

The mystery of the concorporality of Christians with Christ is intimately connected with the sacraments of baptism and the Eucharist. Concorporality begins with baptism and is fully revealed and continuously realized in the Eucharist. Georgios Mantzarides thus says, "Baptism is given to man in order to regenerate him and qualify him for communion in the body and blood of Christ. Through baptism the image in man is purified and the imitation of Christ commences, while the holy Eucharist brings about his advance towards the likeness and his full union with Christ."[30]

Christians are grafted by the new birth of baptism into the deified human nature of Christ in order that they may "grow up in every way into him who is the head, into Christ" (Eph 4:15). Thus, the life of God continually becomes their life. This life is constantly present in the church, especially through the Eucharist (Matt 18:20; 1 Cor 10:16-17). Christ abides with his church (Matt 28:20), in order to communicate His divine perfections to the world.[31]

St. Gregory Palamas, in an insightful passage, explains concorporality by using familial imagery. He refers to Christ as the brother, husband, father, and mother of the faithful:

> Christ has become our brother, by sharing our flesh and blood and so becoming assimilated to us. . . . He has joined and bound us to himself, as a husband his wife, by becoming one single flesh with us through the communion of his blood; he has also become our father by divine baptism which renders us like unto him, and he nourishes us at his own breast as a tender mother nourishes her babies. . . .

---

[29]St. Cyril of Alexandria, *Commentary on the Gospel of John 11*, PG 74, 560. See also St. John Chrysostom, *Homily on Matthew* 58.744: "We become a single mass with him, a single body of Christ, and a single flesh."

[30]*The Deification of Man* (Crestwood NY, 1984) 51. Mantzarides correctly makes a distinction between the image and likeness, in keeping with the Greek patristic tradition. In the same work he notes the following about the benefits of baptism: "God confers two benefits on man through baptism, one of these being regeneration of that which is 'in the image' and the other the possibility of realizing that which is 'after the likeness.' The regeneration of the image occurs immediately . . . while the possibility of realizing the 'likeness' is preferred initially in germinal form only, so that it may then be cultivated, not just of itself, but by man in his desire to attain God's likeness" (46).

[31]See Dumitru Staniloe, "The Mystery of the Church," in *Church, Kingdom, World*, Faith and Order paper no. 130, ed. Gennadios Limouris (WCC, 1986) 53, who said, "All who enter into communion with Christ as divine-human Person become in an enlarged sense his body, or his members, drawing even the world of things into this relationship with Him."

> Come, he says, eat my body, drink my blood . . . so that you be not only made after God's image, but become gods and kings, eternal and heavenly, clothing yourselves with me, King and God.[32]

Of special interest in the passage just quoted is the image of conjugal love in relation to the Eucharist. Palamas's imagery echoes the well-known passage of St. Paul in Ephesians (5:21-33). In both passages, we have a strong emphasis on the body. The emphasis, I believe, seeks to underscore the fact that our union with Christ is not one of a moral or an emotional kind. "Christ does not say that He is in us by a relation of an affective kind, but by physical participation (κατὰ μέθεξιν φυσικήν)," notes St. Cyril of Alexandria.[33] In the Eucharist Christ becomes the bridegroom (νυμφίος) of the church, the husband of humankind. Through our union with the deified flesh of Christ we are members of his body (Eph 5:30). St. John Chrysostom explains this understanding thus:

> We must learn the wonder of the mysteries, what they are, and why they were given, and what is their benefit. "We are one body," scripture says, "and members made from His flesh and from his bones. . . . "
> In order, then, that we may become of His flesh, not by charity only, but also in very fact, let us become commingled with that flesh. This, in truth, takes place by means of the food which He has given us as a gift, because He desired to prove the love which He has for us. It is for this reason that He joined himself to us, and has brought His own body down to our level, namely that we might be one, just as a body is joined with the head. . . . And to show the love He has for us, He has made it possible for those who desire, not merely to look upon him, but even to touch Him and to eat Him and to fix their teeth in His flesh, and to be commingled with Him, and to satisfy all their longing. . . . He says, "I nourish mine on my own flesh. . . . I shared in flesh and blood for your sake. I have given back again to you the very flesh and blood through which I had become your kinsman."[34]

Christ is present in the Eucharist in the most real and profound way. The eucharistic gifts, according to the Lord's own declaration, are his very body and blood (Luke 22:19-20). To the eye and taste they remain bread and wine, but "Let faith be your stay," claims St. Cyril of Jerusalem. He continues, "Instead of judging the matter by taste, let faith give you an unwavering confidence that you have been

---

[32]Homily 56, quoted in J. Meyendorf, *A Study of Gregory Palamas* (The Faith Press, 1964) 177. See also Mantzarides, *The Deification of Man,* 53.

[33]Cyril of Alexandria, *Commentary on the Gospel of John,* 10:2, PG 74, 342.

[34]Chrysostom, *Homily on the Gospel of John,* 46.2, PG 59, 260. To speak of flesh and blood is to speak of life. We cannot conceive of or know life, except in terms of flesh and blood. According to the biblical notion flesh denotes the entire human being.

privileged to receive the body and blood of Christ."[35]

Orthodoxy has avoided propounding and expounding theories about the manner of change of the eucharistic food.[36] The change is neither comprehensible nor researchable. We hold firmly to the belief that the eucharistic gifts are really changed into Christ's body and blood in such a way that he is hypostatically present in them; though it should be noted, the eucharistic gifts retain their natural properties.[37]

The change is discerned and recognized by faith. Much in the same way many were able to recognize his glory and discern his power when he sojourned on earth ("You are the Christ, the Son of the living God." Matt 16:16), others could not or would not penetrate his outward appearance ("Is this not the carpenter's son?" —Matt 13:55; and "This man is not from God, for he does not keep the sabbath." —John 9:16). While the mystery is indeed discerned by faith, it does not mean that the change is dependent solely on individual faith. By the power of the Holy Spirit, who descends upon the worshipping community and the gifts, the bread and wine are truly transformed into, and are, the very body and blood of the risen Christ. The consecrated gifts are no longer ordinary bread and wine, neither are they symbols or icons.[38]

A corporeal relationship between Christ and his people flows from the Eucharist. Despite the use of vivid language by the Fathers to describe this corporality, they were quick, too, to forestall any cannibalistic interpretation of the Eucharist.[39] The descriptive language served to forestall an overspiritualization of the sacrament whereby it becomes simply a symbol devoid of reality. St. Symeon the New Theologian summarizes the Greek patristic tradition on this point, writing,

---

[35]Cyril of Jerusalem, *Mystagogical Catechesis,* 4.6.

[36]The term most usually used to describe the transformation of the eucharistic gifts is simply μεταβολή (change). Other terms used by by the Greek Fathers include μεταποίησις (alteration), μετασκευή (transformation), μεταρρύθμισις (change), μεταστοιχείωσις (change). The preposition μετά in composite form implies change.

[37]It has been suggested that the full narrative surrounding the meal at Emmaus (Luke 24:13-35) is a description of the twofold pattern of word and meal, which characterized the eucharistic assembly from primitive times. Of special interest here is that the risen Lord in all his fulness "was known to them at the breaking of the bread" (24:35).

[38]See, e.g., Theophilos of Alexandria, *Sermon on the Mystical Supper,* PG 77, 1018: "The hypostatic wisdom of the Father has built for himself a temple not made by hands. He distributes his body like bread and bestows his life-giving blood like wine. O awesome mystery! O inexpressible economy! O incomprehensible condescension! O unsearchable kindness! Life itself bestows himself on mortals for their food and drink." Cf. St. John of Damascus, *Exposition of Faith* 4.13.94.

[39]See, e.g., Cyril of Jerusalem, *Mystagogical Catechesis* 4.4.

All those who believe in Christ become akin to Him in the spirit of God and form a single body . . . (and) united to Him spiritually in this manner, each of us will form one single spirit with Him and likewise one body, since we corporeally eat His body and drink His blood.[40]

The corporeal relationship with Christ is to be understood in the context of the new life: "that which is born of the flesh is flesh, and that which is born of the Spirit is spirit" (John 3:6).

Partaking of the Eucharist in faith, we are continually enlivened by the Spirit and are united with the glorified body of Christ, in order to become one body with him. His deified human nature, hypostatically united to the second person of the holy Trinity, is the source of our deification.[41]

This union, however, defies all description and explanation. "It is no longer according to the flesh that we know him to be in us, like a newborn child, but he is incorporeally in the body, conjoined to our substance and our nature in a manner beyond description. He deifies us because we are embodied in him: flesh of his flesh and bone of his bones," in the words of St. Symeon the New Theologian.[42]

For the Greek Fathers, the purpose of salvation is to bestow *theōsis* upon humankind.[43] *Theōsis* (deification) means union with God and participation in His personal existence. For this to happen, it is necessary for man to overcome his createdness and to acquire a new mode of existence, that is, to become an authentic person. "Salvation is identified with the realization of personhood," says John Zizioulas.[44] This requires a radical change, which is neither the product of biological or historical evolution, nor the result of some ethical codes of behavior. The change is an ontological change, described in scripture as new birth, the death of the old man, the putting off of the old nature and the putting on of the new.[45] This newness, this radical change, is not accomplished by human effort. It is a gift from God, freely given to all those who would accept it freely. It is made accessible to all through the sacrament of baptism. To quote Zizioulas, "as the conception and birth of man constitute his biological hypostasis, so baptism leads to a new mode

---

[40]St. Symeon, *Ethical Orations* 2.7, *Sources Chrétiennes,* cited in Basil Krivocheine, *In the Light of Christ. St. Symeon the New Theologian* (Crestwood, 1986).

[41]See Mantzarides, *The Deification of Man,* 53-54.

[42]*Ethical Orations* 1.10.55-72.

[43]This idea is succinctly summarized by St. Athanasios the Great in the well-known phrase "God became man so that we might become gods." *On the Incarnation,* 54, PG 25, 192. See also St. Nicholas Kavasilas, *The Life of Christ,* 6, PG 150, 680.

[44]Zizioulas, *Being as Communion* (Crestwood NY, 1985) 50.

[45]John 3:3-6; Rom 6:3-12; Eph 4:22-24; Col 3:1-10.

of existence, to a regeneration, and consequently to a new hypostasis."[46] He calls this new mode of being "the hypostasis of ecclesial existence."[47]

This mode of existence is one of constant becoming. Rooted in the age to come, it is maintained and nourished by the Eucharist, which is "the historical realization and manifestation of the eschatological existence of man . . . (and) at the same time also movement, a progress towards its realization."[48] The eucharistic assembly constitutes the eschatological transcendence of the biological hypostasis. Here the tragic elements of our fallen existence—egocentricity, pride, individualism, envy, anger, division, fear, despair, pain, deceit, untruth, malice, greed, gluttony, passions, sins, corruption, death—are continuously being defeated, in order to make us capable to be love, freedom, and life.[49]

When we have come to experience the mystery of the Eucharist at its deepest levels, we come to understand that being is life, and that life is communion and that communion is love. This understanding of our human existence results from our knowledge and personal experience in the faith of our Triune God.[50]

We become one body with Christ through the Holy Spirit. He dwells in the church and reveals Christ to us and unites us to him. The Holy Spirit is always being sent upon the church at her eucharistic assemblies to abide with God's people and with the gifts presented; to impart charisms and to create unity; and to make real within us the hidden mysteries of God's kingdom. The Holy Spirit changes the eucharistic gifts into the body and blood of Christ.

In the Eucharist we receive and partake of the resurrected Christ. The permanent, constant gift he pours into us is the Holy Spirit, who bears "witness with our spirit that we are children of God, and if children, then heirs . . . with Christ" (Rom 8:16-17).

---

[46]Zizioulas, *Being as Communion,* 53. "Thanks to Christ man can henceforth himself subsist, can affirm his existence as personal not on the basis of the immutable laws of his nature but on the basis of a relationship with God which is identified with what Christ in freedom and love possesses as Son of God with the Father. This adoption of man by God, the identification of his hypostasis with the hypostasis of the Son of God is the essence of baptism." (56)

[47]Ibid., 53.

[48]Ibid., 61.

[49]"God and Father of our Lord and God and Saviour Jesus Christ. . . . You have accepted the gifts. . . . Sanctify also our souls and bodies and spirits. Touch our understandings and search our consciences. Cast out from us every evil imagination, every impure feeling, every base desire, every unbecoming thought, all envy, vanity, and hypocrisy, all lying, deceit, wordly affection, covetousness, vainglory, indifference, vice, passion, anger, malice, blasphemy, and every motion of the flesh and spirit that is not in accordance with Your holy will." Prayer before the Lord's Prayer, Divine Liturgy of St. James.

[50]See Zizioulas, *Being as Communion,* 36-49.

The central fruit of the Eucharist is the communion of the Holy Spirit. He is the one who gives life to our mortal bodies (Rom 8:11). The other fruits of the Eucharist are related to this central gift. Vigilance of soul, forgiveness of sins, a clear conscience are preparation for, as well as the result of our communion with the Holy Spirit. Sonship, manifestation of love in the unity of faith, and the inheritance of the heavenly kingdom are obtained by the communion of the Holy Spirit, who is the pledge of our future hope.

The Holy Spirit is the giver of life, who prepares us for the resurrection and makes us advance toward it. In the words of St. Paul,

> For the law of the Spirit of life in Christ Jesus has set me free from the law of sin and death. . . .
> But you are not in the flesh, you are in the Spirit, if in fact the Spirit of God dwells in you. Any one who does not have the Spirit of Christ does not belong to him. But if Christ is in you, although your bodies are dead because of sin, your spirits are alive because of righteousness. If the Spirit of him who raised Christ Jesus from the dead dwells in you, he who raised Christ Jesus from the dead will give life to your mortal bodies also through his Spirit which dwells in you. (Rom 8:2, 9-11)

The power of life that flows from the Eucharist sanctifies the whole man; the entire human existence, body and soul.[51] In the sacraments, and especially in the Eucharist, "we discover our body to be a liturgical body."[52] The body of death becomes the body of the Resurrection. The seed of immortality, sown inside the body through baptism, is nurtured by the Eucharist.[53] We are placed within the body of Christ in order to become Christ's. Thus, we, too, become a body of communion.

The body is the fundamental and primal reality of communion. It expresses the person. Moreover, because of our fallen condition, the body also masks the person.[54] It has become the bearer of death and the fortress of separation and self-affirmation.

The Lord's body, unlike our own, says Olivier Clement, "is not a fragment of humanity and of the universe to which the individual jealously and desperately clings; his body is the entire universe, the entire humanity assumed by self-giving

---

[51]Olivier Clement, "Life in the Body," *The Ecumenical Review* 33 (1981): 129, points out that the body is neither thing nor instrument, but oneself vis-à-vis the world and others. The corporeal experience is immediate and coincides with one's presence. Hence, the body involves the whole human existence.

[52]Ibid., 131.

[53]Ibid., 135.

[54]See Zizioulas, *Being as Communion,* 50-53; and Clement, "Life in the Body," 128-46.

love and hence freed from opacity and separation. . . . His body is constantly transformed through his constant adherence to the Father into a eucharistic body."[55]

The body of Christ, the body of the church, and the body of the Eucharist make it possible for man to acquire the eucharistic manner of existence. Then, little by little, man, too, becomes communion and love; the flesh of Resurrection and the body of glory.

To begin to love, as Christ has loved us (John 13:34-35), is among the first signs of the transfigured life of communion. The Eucharist is not only communion with Christ; it is communion of the members of the body with each other. In the Divine Liturgy of St. Basil we pray, "And unite us all to one another who become partakers of the one Bread and the Cup in the communion of the Holy Spirit."[56] St. John Chrysostom explains how this is to be accomplished:

> You, according to human capacity, must do what the only begotten Son of God has done, be an agent of peace, for yourself and for others. . . . Let us always be mindful of these words, and also of the holy kisses and of the awe-inspiring embrace which we give one another. For this joins our minds, and causes us all to become one body, for in fact, we all share one body. Let us blend ourselves into one body, not mingling bodies with one another, but joining our souls to one another with the bond of love. For thus we will be able with confidence to enjoy the table set before us. For if we may have countless good works, but if we still harbor grudges, all is pointless and vain, and we will be unable to derive any profit unto salvation. Conscious, then, of these matters, let us abandon all anger, and cleansing our consciences, let us, with gentleness and all forebearance approach the table of Christ.[57]

It is not accidental that the Orthodox Church has maintained the ancient practice of consecrating one bread, or a single portion of a bread, at the divine liturgy. It is the sign of our communion and unity with one another and, as a body, with Christ: "Because there is one bread, we who are many are one body, for we all partake of the one bread" (1 Cor 10:17).[58]

The Eucharist is offered to the church as a whole and not to particular members. It is not intended for individualistic consumption, egocentric satisfaction and exclusivity. The Eucharist is not offered as a reward, but as a remedy for sin,

---

[55]Clement, "Life in the Body," 132.

[56]The Prayer of the Anaphora. It is clear from the prayer of the divine liturgy that the communion of the faithful involves also those who are on the other side of death (life).

[57]Chrysostom, *Sermon on the Betrayal of Judas,* PG 49, 382.

[58]Cf. the well-known passage "As this broken bread was scattered upon the mountain tops and after being harvested was made one, so let thy Church be gathered together from the ends of the earth into thy kingdom." (Didache 9:4)

a provision for life, the communion of the Holy Spirit, and an opening to others. The goal of the Eucharist is to create in us that liturgical ethos, by which individualism is constantly being transformed into unity and communion. This communion neither blurs nor destroys the unique and unrepeatable personality of each member of the body. Rather, it allows the members to realize, ever more fully, their own human personhood by growing ever more godlike. As such, because it is a return to true human existence and life, this communion is highly personal. Moreover, this life is a life of love and freedom (1 Cor 12:12-13).

The Christian exists between the realm of what is and what is to come. In his ecclesial identity he is always in the process of becoming that which he will be. His ecclesial mode of existence and eucharistic hypostasis require of him spiritual vigilance. The observation of God's commandments constitutes the essential preparation and proper disposition for participation in the sacrament of holy communion.[59]

This need for spiritual discernment was addressed by St. Paul to the Corinthians: "for anyone who eats and drinks without discerning the body eats and drinks judgment upon himself" (1 Cor 11:29). Similar admonitions are found in patristic writings[60] and are embedded in the texts of the divine liturgy itself.[61] One such warning in the text of the liturgy is the exclamation, "The Holy Gifts for the Holy People of God."[62] This warning once served as an invitation to holy communion. Another is that made to the laity for communion, "Approach with the fear of God, with faith and with love."

We must take care, however, not to construe these admonitions as deterents to holy communion. After all, we receive the sacrament "for the forgiveness of sins and life eternal." Sanctification (*hagiasmos*) is a fruit of holy communion and not the precondition for its reception. This idea is clearly stated by Kavasilas:

Those whom the priest calls holy are not only those who have attained perfection, but those also who are striving for it without having yet obtained it. Nothing prevents them from being sanctified by partaking of the holy mys-

---

[59]See Symeon the New Theologican, *Ethical Orations,* 3: "Become a saint by practising the commandments of God and then partake of the holy mysteries."

[60]See, e.g., St. Basil the Great, *The Shorter Rules,* 172, PG 31; and St. John Chrysostom, *Homily on I Cor.*

[61]See, e.g., The prayer for the Bowing of the Head (after the Lord's Prayer), in the Divine Liturgy of St. Basil: "Lord Master, . . . bless . . . those who have bowed their heads to You. Distance them from every evil deed, lead them to every good work and make them worthy to partake without condemnation of these, your most pure and life-giving Mysteries."

[62]Cf. *Didache* 10:6: "If anyone is holy, let him come. If anyone is not, let him repent."

teries, and from this point of view being saints. It is in this sense that the whole Church is called holy. . . . The faithful are called saints because of the holy thing of which they partake, because of Him whose Body and Blood they receive. . . . We live by holiness, drawing to ourselves, through the holy mysteries, the sanctity which comes from that Head. . . .[63]

The Eucharist as Sacrifice

The church has a radically new and different understanding of the meaning of sacrifice.[64] In the first place, the initiative for sacrifice is not with man but with God, the One who continually offers himself to us. In the second place, the sacrifice offered by the church is not an act of appeasement, but of *antiprosphora,* an offering in return. Both of these elements constitute the sacrificial character of the Eucharist.

The Lord himself when establishing the sacrament at the Mystical (Last) Supper, gave to the Eucharist its sacrificial character. The words he spoke over the bread and wine are replete with sacrificial overtones and implications.[65] To borrow a term from Bishop Demetrios Trakatellis, they express "aspects of Passion Christology."[66]

The words of the Lord over the bread and wine, also known as the Words of Institution, have been incorporated, in one form or another, into the entire collection of the classical texts of the holy Eucharist. In the Divine Liturgies of St. Basil the Great and St. John Chrysostom, the Anaphora's Words of Institution are identical.[67]

While the form of these words is entirely scriptural, it does not duplicate, in exactness, any of the forms recounted in the four scripture narratives that describe the institution of the Eucharist. The "words of institution" as they appear in the two Divine Liturgies, are as follows.

---

[63]Kavasilas, *A Commentary on the Divine Liturgy,* 36.

[64]See Calivas, *The Divine Liturgy* (Thessaloniki, 1982) 103-108.

[65]Matt 26:26-29; Mark 14:22-25; Luke 22:14-20; 1 Cor 11:23-26.

[66]Trakatellis, *Authority and Passion* (Holy Cross Orthodox Press, 1987) 92.

[67]The Divine Liturgy is the sacred rite by which the Orthodox Church celebrates the mystery of the holy Eucharist. The two Divine Liturgies of Basil and Chrysostom are part of the liturgical rites of the Church of Constantinople, which have become the common rite of all Orthodox Churches.

Take, eat, this is my Body which is broken for you for the forgiveness of sins. Drink of it all of you; this is my Blood of the New Covenant which is shed for you and for many for the forgiveness of sins.[68]

In both of these Anaphoras the "words of institution" are placed between a passage that recounts the entire divine economy for the salvation of the world and the anamnesis: the command "do this in remembrance of me." This command is explicitly stated in the Anaphora of Basil and implied in the Anaphora of Chrysostom. In both Anaphoras the anamnesis, or remembrance, is broadened to include not only the command but also the entire economy of the Son of God, and especially its essential aspects: the passion, the Resurrection, the enthronement at the right hand of God the Father, and the second, glorious coming. Thus, the liturgical, worshipping community is placed directly into and celebrates the mystery of God's divine plan for the world.

Besides the "words of institution," there are numerous other references in the divine liturgy that highlight the sacrificial character of the Eucharist. For example, the Eucharist is characterized as "the sacrifice without the shedding of blood" (θυσία ἀναίμακτος). The Holy Table is, also, referred to as the "holy, heavenly, and spiritual altar."

The sacrificial character of the Eucharist is especially evident in the ritual preparation of the bread and wine. This service is known as the Proskomide.[69] Its description that follows is part of the service of the Proskomide. The sacrificial aspects are self-evident.

The priest conducts the Proskomide at the Prothesis (Table of Preparation). The service begins with a troparion borrowed from the Orthros of the Great and Holy Friday.

You have redeemed us from the curse of the Law by your precious blood. By being nailed to the Cross and pierced with a lance, You have become a fountain of immortality for all people. Glory to You, our Saviour.[70]

The priest proceeds to prepare the Gifts. The portion of the bread to be offered for consecration is called the Lamb (ἀμνός). The loaf of bread from which it is excised is called the oblation or offering (πρόσφορον, προσφορά). While cutting the bread, in order to remove the Lamb, the celebrant recites the words of the Prophet Isaiah

---

[68]Modern liturgical studies have shown that biblical passages are paraphrased rather than literally assimilated in the older liturgical texts.

[69]See above, n. 24.

[70]*The Order of the Divine and Holy Liturgy* (Holy Cross Orthodox Press, 1987) 12.

concerning the suffering servant (53:7-8).[71] The excised Lamb is then incised crosswise. While making the incision the priest recites, "The Lamb of God who takes away the sin of the world is sacrificed for the life and salvation of the world" (John 1:29). Finally, the Lamb is pierced with an instrument called the lance. While doing this the celebrant recites the words, "One of the soldiers pierced his side with a spear and at once there came out blood and water," after which he pours wine and water into the chalice.

The service of Proskomide, among other things, clearly confirms the church's belief that the Eucharist is a sacrifice. According to Bishop Trakatellis, "The institution of the holy Eucharist enables Christ's sacrifice to have true continuity within the life of the church on a liturgical level."[72]

But how are we to understand this sacrifice? Who offers it? How is it related to the "once and for all" sacrifice of the Cross (Rom. 6-10)? How can the deathless and incorruptible Body of the Risen Lord be slain again?

These questions were posed and addressed by St. Nicholas Kavasilas.[73] His

---

[71]These words are also recorded in Acts 8:32-33. Both accounts influenced the formulation of the liturgical text.

[72]Trakatellis, *Authority and Passion,* 93.

[73]*A Commentary on the Divine Liturgy,* 32, PG 150, 440:

The sacrificing of a sheep consists in a changing of its state; it is changed from an unsacrificed sheep to a sacrificed one. The same is true here: the bread is changed from unsacrificed bread into something sacrificed. In other words, it is changed from ordinary unsacrificed bread into that very body of Christ which was truly sacrificed. Through this transformation the sacrifice is truly accomplished, just as that of the sheep was when it was changed from one state to another. For there has been in the sacrifice a transformation not in symbol but in reality; a transformation into the sacrificed Body of the Lord.

If it were the bread which, remaining bread, was to be sacrificed, it would be the bread which was immolated, and the immolation of the bread would then be the sacrifice.

But the transformation has been a double one; the bread, from being unsacrifice has become a thing sacrificed, and it has also been changed from simple bread into the Body of Christ. It follows therefore that this immolation, regarded not as that of the bread but as that of the Body of Chrst, which is the substance with lies beneath the appearance of bread, is truly the sacrifice not of the bread but of the Lamb of God, and is rightly so called.

Now it is clear that, under these conditions, it is not necessary that there should be numerous oblations of the Lord's body. Since the sacrifice consists, not in the real and bloody immolation of that Lamb, but in the transformation of the bread into the sacrificed Lamb, it is obvious that the transformation takes place without the bloody immolation. Thus, though that which is changed is many, and the transformation takes place many times, yet nothing prevents the reality into which it is transformed from being one and the same thing always—a single Body, and the unique sacrifice of that Body.

succinct answers illuminate the mystery.

In the first place, Kavasilas advises us concerning the sacrifice, to keep clearly in mind three basic teachings of the church. First, the sacrifice is not a mere figure, but a true sacrifice; secondly, it is not the bread which is being sacrificed, but the very Body of Christ; and thirdly, Christ was sacrificed once only and for all time.[74]

The sacrifice of the Eucharist, according to Kavasilas, is accomplished at the moment of the Epiclesis,[75] when the Holy Spirit is invoked to come upon the gifts, in order to change the bread into the body of Christ and the wine (mixed with water) into the blood of Christ.

Kavasilas goes on to say that the bread of the Eucharist undergoes a double change. From ordinary bread it is changed into an offering, into a thing that will become sacrificed. This bread of offering is changed by the ineffable power and action of the Holy Spirit into the very body of Christ, the body which was once sacrificed and now is risen and deified. This final transformation of the bread and wine into the Body and Blood of Christ, constitutes the eucharistic sacrifice. To quote Bishop Trakatellis, "the Passion is actualized essentially and perfectly at every celebration of the sacrament."[76]

This does not suggest that the Eucharist attempts to reclaim a past event. The Eucharist does not repeat what cannot be repeated. Christ is not slain anew and repeatedly at every Eucharist. Though the sacrifice is offered many times and in many places, the reality into which the gifts are changed remains always the same: the body of Christ, which was sacrificed once and for all. In the Eucharist the saving work of Christ continues to be active and operative, as well as present and immediate. In the Eucharist we participate mystically in the reality of Jesus Christ, who "is the same yesterday and today and forever" (Heb 13:8). Through the sacraments in general, and the Eucharist in particular, Christ becomes our contemporary.

The Eucharist is neither a mere representation, nor a simple memorial of the sacrifice of the Cross. The eucharistic food is changed concretely and really into the body and blood of the lamb of God, "who gave himself up for the life of the world."[77] However, the nature of this change and the manner by which it occurs

---

[74]Ibid.

[75]The Orthodox Church holds to the belief that the eucharistic gifts are transformed by the power of the Holy Spirit. The Epiclesis (or Invocation) constitutes the nucleus of the Anaphora and represents the Church's profound supplication for divine intervention to affect the change of the Gifts, by which the members of the Church are continually sanctified.

[76]Trakatellis, *Authority and Passion*, 93.

[77]The Anaphora of the Divine Liturgy of St. John Chrysostom.

remains incomprehensible. In the words of Kavasilas, "the changing of the offering into the body and blood, which is true sacrifice, is beyond human power and is brought about by grace."[78]

The true priest and celebrant of the eucharistic mystery is Christ himself, the unique high priest and mediator of the new covenant. He is the one who offers and is offered, the one who receives and distributes.[79]

In the Eucharist the church experiences the eternal priesthood of Christ, the Theanthropos. As he relates to God, Christ the Theanthropos continues in a state of sacrifice before the Father on our behalf (Heb 7:24; 9:24). As he relates to us, Christ the Theanthropos continually offers himself to the faithful through the consecrated gifts: his very own risen and deified Body which for our sake died once and now lives (Heb 10:12; Rev 1:18).

In the Eucharist we come to realize that the altar of God is constantly becoming the table of communion and life. The Eucharist imparts to its partakers the wondrous benefits of Christ's death and Resurrection:

> So that they (the body and blood of Christ) may be to those who partake of them for vigilance of soul, forgiveness of sins, communion of the Holy Spirit, fulfillment of the Kingdom of heaven, confidence before You and not in judgment or condemnation.[80] Unite us all to one another who become partakers of the one Bread and the Cup in the communion of the Holy Spirit . . . that we may find mercy and grace with all the saints who through the ages have pleased You.[81]

Christ's death is life-giving ($\zeta\omega\pi\omega\iota\acute{o}\varsigma$). By his death he conquered death and became "the first fruits of those who have fallen asleep" (1 Cor 15:20-28, 51-57). Through His sacrifice he penetrated the deepest abysses of hell to lead the captives to the limitless expanses of true life. Thus, the Eucharist as sacrifice celebrates the manifestation of the new creation, wrought by God in Christ (2 Cor 5:17-21).

By the power of His sacrifice Christ draws us into his own sacrificial action. The church also offers sacrifice. However, the sacrifice offered by the church and her members can only be an $\dot{\alpha}\nu\tau\iota\pi\rho\sigma\sphi\sigma\rho\acute{\alpha}$, an offering given in return to God on account of the riches of his goodness, mercy, and love. The $\dot{\alpha}\nu\tau\iota\pi\rho\sigma\sphi\sigma\rho\acute{\alpha}$ is, first

---

[78] *A Commentary on the Divine Liturgy,* 51.

[79] These terms are taken from the prayer of the Cherubic Hymn (also known as the Prayer of the Veil), recited by the celebrant before the Great Entrance at the Divine Liturgy. According to Orthodox theology, the celebrant, bishop or presbyter, acts in the place of Christ in the Divine Liturgy.

[80] The Anaphora of the Divine Liturgy of St. John Chrysostom.

[81] The Anaphora of the Divine Liturgy of St. Basil the Great.

of all, a sacrifice of praise and thanksgiving "for all things that we know and do not know, for blessings seen and unseen that have been bestowed upon us."[82]

The ἀντιπροσφορά has a multiplicity of forms, including commitment to the gospel, loyalty to the true faith, fasting, constant prayer, works of charity, and the struggle against the passions. However, the preeminent expression and the most excellent form of the ἀντιπροσφορά is to be found in the Eucharist.

At its deepest level the ἀντιπροσφορά is an act of kenosis (Luke 9:23-25). The ἀντιπροσφορά is constituted by our willingness to lose our life in order to gain it (Matt 16:28). To "offer in return" means that we are able to recognize and accept the limitations of our createdness as well as our complete dependence on God, "in whom we live and move and have our being" (Acts 18:28). Archimandrite Vasileos speaks of it in this way:

> The more we advance voluntarily towards *diminishing,* finally becoming so small that we vanish, the more the glory that cannot be approached shines, realizing and bringing from nonbeing into existence endless new creations and joys.[83]

The full meaning of the ἀντιπροσφορά is contained in the words of the offering in the divine liturgy: "We offer to you these gifts from your own gifts in all and for all" (cf. 1 Chron 29:14). A brief analysis of these words will help us understand more fully the nature and meaning of the sacrifice offered by the church and each of her members.

First, the gifts of the bread and wine, as we have noted above, represent the totality of our life. These gifts are the appropriate symbols of our life as well as the sign of our kenosis, the exchange of life for life.

Second, the words of the offering remind us that the gifts do not belong to us. All things, and especially our life of which these gifts are signs, come from God, the giver of every good and perfect gift (Jas 1:17).

Third, we realize that we stand before God's altar "not because of our righteousness for we have not done anything good upon the earth, but because of his mercy and compassion, which he richly pours upon us" (Liturgy of St. Basil).

Finally, we come to recognize that what we offer is not something that is ours at all, but that which is his already, the sacrifice of his only-begotten son. In the final analysis, our ἀντιπροσφορά can only be Christ himself. His saving work remains constant and immediate for every generation in every place, until he comes again. To quote Archimandrite Vasileos,

---

[82]The Anaphora of the Divine Liturgy of St. John Chrysostom.

[83]Hymn of Entry, 68.

The liturgy of Christ's sacrifice celebrated on the altar forms the heart of our lives and our consciousness of what we are. It takes hold of each one of us personally, and of the liturgical community that we constitute. It composes and holds together everything in and around us. It embodies the invisible and uncreated and brings it near us and into us, tangible and open to our consciousness. It transfigures and sanctifies what is visible and insignificant. . . . Things that cannot be approached, that are far beyond, dwell among us.[84]

In and through the Eucharist the biological mode of existence—with its limitations, contradictions, inconsistencies, and insufficiencies—is being continuously transformed into a sacramental, eucharistic hypostasis, reflecting ever more clearly the realities of the resurrectional life. Here the words of St. Paul are most appropriate:

But now that you have been set free from sin and have become slaves of God, the return you get is sanctification and its end, eternal life. For the wages of sin is death, but the free gift of God is eternal life in Christ Jesus our Lord. (Rom 6:22-23)

---

[84]Ibid., 68.

Indexes

Index of Modern Names

Index of Biblical Texts

Old Testament

[N.B. Septuagint (LXX) numbering, if variant, is given in parentheses.]

New Testament

New Gospel Studies
A Monograph Series for Gospel Research

Series General Editor
William R. Farmer
Perkins School of Theology
Southern Methodist University

25.00